SEVEN SEAS ENTERTAINMENT PRESENTS

LITTLE DEVILS

story and art by UUUMI   VOLUME 3

TRANSLATION
Jennifer and Wesley O'Donnell

ADAPTATION
Casey Lucas

LETTERING AND RETOUCH
Ochie Caraan

COVER DESIGN
KC Fabellon

PROOFREADER
Janet Houck
B. Lana Guggenheim

EDITOR
Shannon Fay

PRODUCTION MANAGER
Lissa Pattillo

MANAGING EDITOR
Julie Davis

EDITOR-IN-CHIEF
Adam Arnold

PUBLISHER
Jason DeAngelis

MAOU KYOUDAI VOLUME 3
© UUUMI 2019
Originally published in Japan in 2019 by TOKUMA SHOTEN PUBLISHING
CO., LTD., Tokyo. English translation rights arranged with TOKUMA SHOTEN
PUBLISHING CO., LTD., Tokyo, through TOHAN CORPORATION, Tokyo.

Seven Seas press and purchase enquiries can be sent to Marketing Manager
Lianne Sentar at press@gomanga.com. Information regarding the distribution
and purchase of digital editions is available from Digital Manager CK Russell
at digital@gomanga.com.

Seven Seas and the Seven Seas logo are trademarks of
Seven Seas Entertainment. All rights reserved.

ISBN: 978-1-64275-027-0

Printed in Canada

First Printing: Decem

10 9 8 7

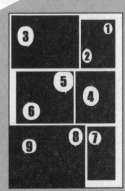

FOLLOW US ONLINE: www.seve_____ment.com

READING DIRECTIONS

This book reads from **right to left**, Japanese style.
If this is your first time reading manga, you start
reading from the top right panel on each page and
take it from there. If you get lost, just follow the
numbered diagram here. It may seem backwards at
first, but you'll get the hang of it! Have fun!!

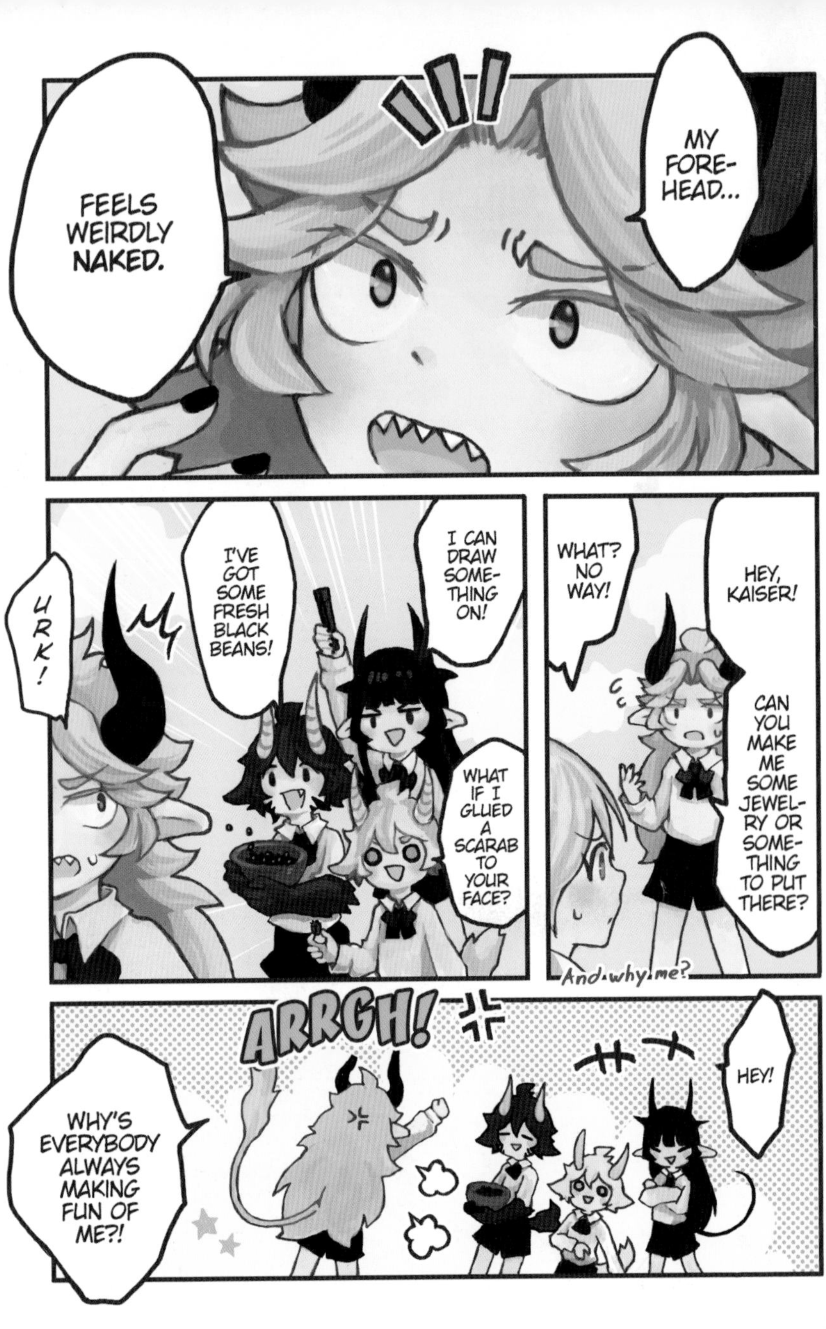
MY FOREHEAD...
FEELS WEIRDLY NAKED.
HEY, KAISER!
CAN YOU MAKE ME SOME JEWELRY OR SOMETHING TO PUT THERE?
WHAT? NO WAY!
And why me?
I CAN DRAW SOMETHING ON!
I'VE GOT SOME FRESH BLACK BEANS!
WHAT IF I GLUED A SCARAB TO YOUR FACE?
URK!
HEY!
ARRGH!
WHY'S EVERYBODY ALWAYS MAKING FUN OF ME?!

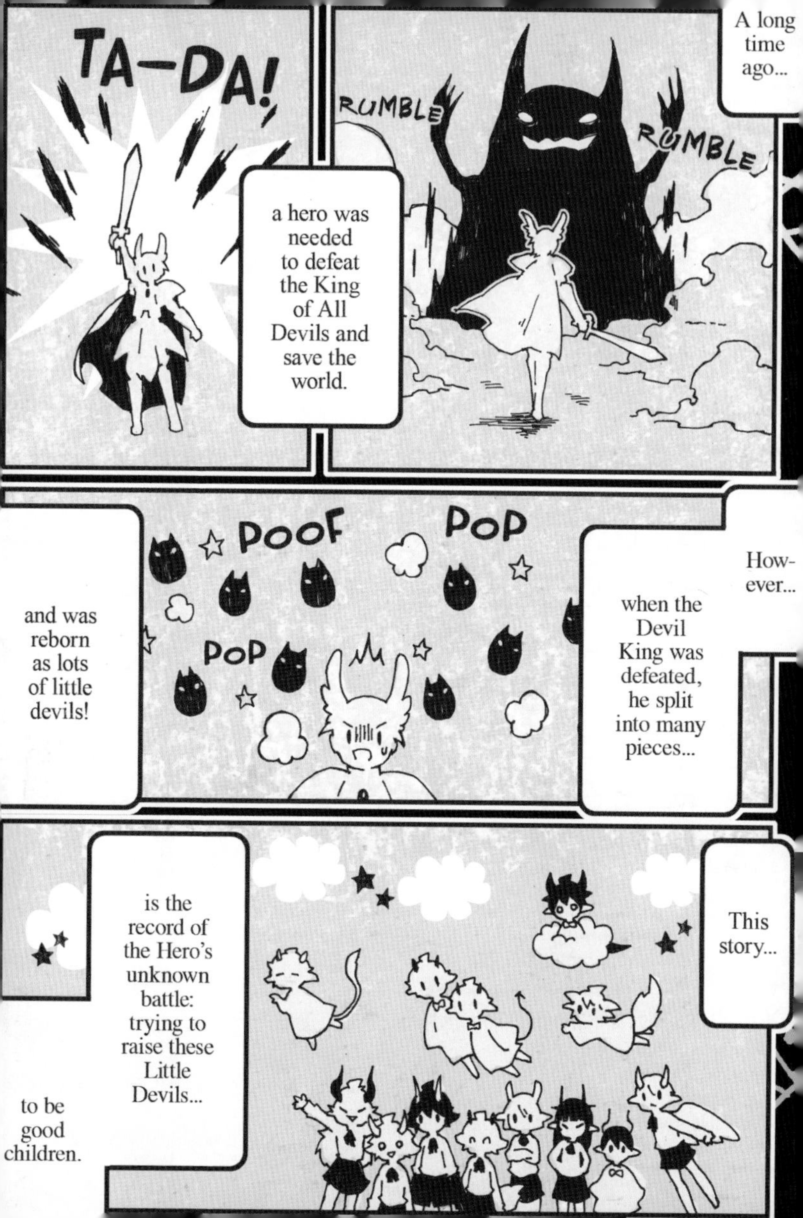
A long time ago...
RUMBLE
RUMBLE
a hero was needed to defeat the King of All Devils and save the world.
TA-DA!
However...
when the Devil King was defeated, he split into many pieces...
POP
POOF
POP
and was reborn as lots of little devils!
This story...
is the record of the Hero's unknown battle: trying to raise these Little Devils...
to be good children.

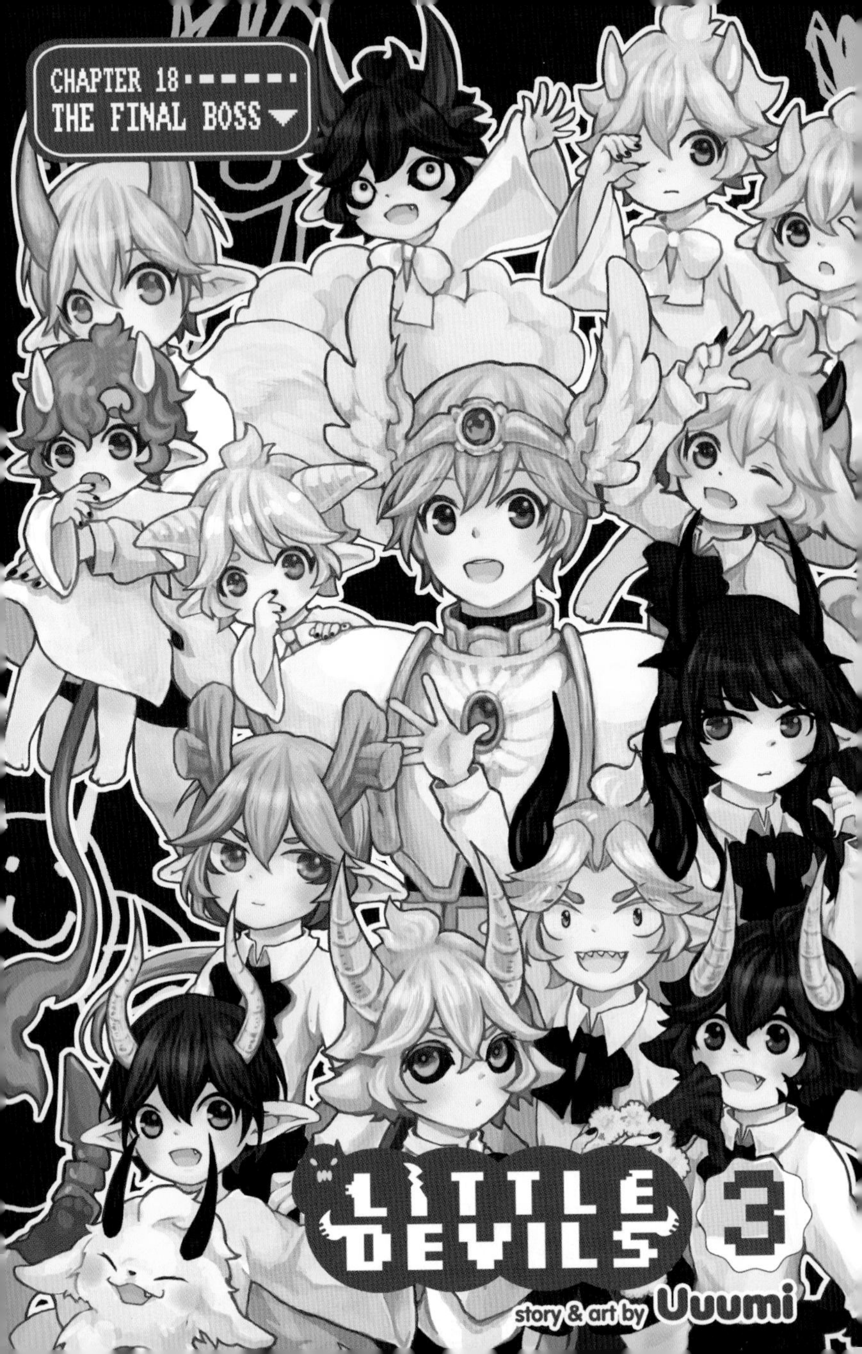
CHAPTER 18
THE FINAL BOSS
LITTLE DEVILS 3
story & art by Uuumi

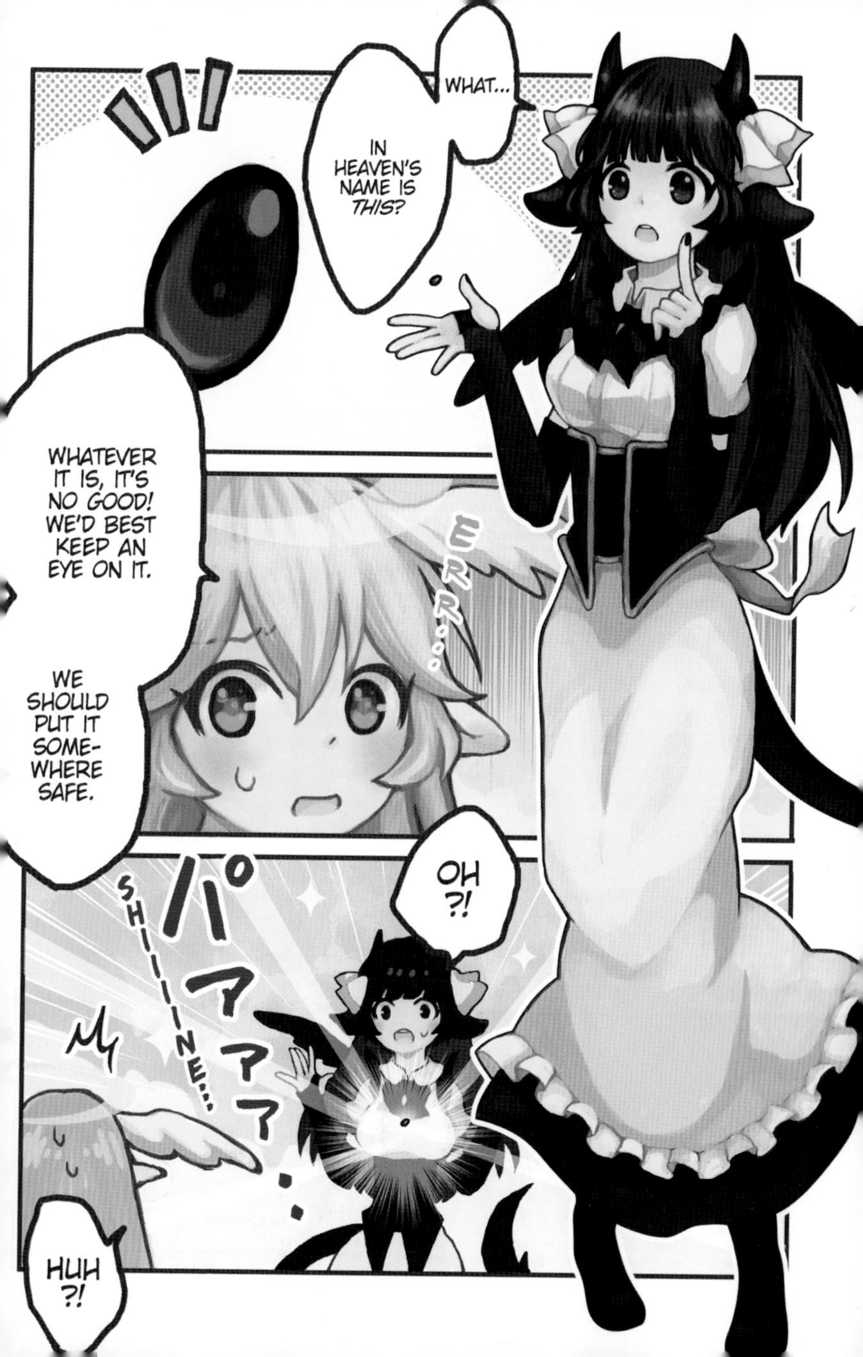
WHAT...
IN HEAVEN'S NAME IS THIS?
WHATEVER IT IS, IT'S NO GOOD! WE'D BEST KEEP AN EYE ON IT.
WE SHOULD PUT IT SOME-WHERE SAFE.
ERR...
OH?!
パァァ
SHIIINE...
HUH?!

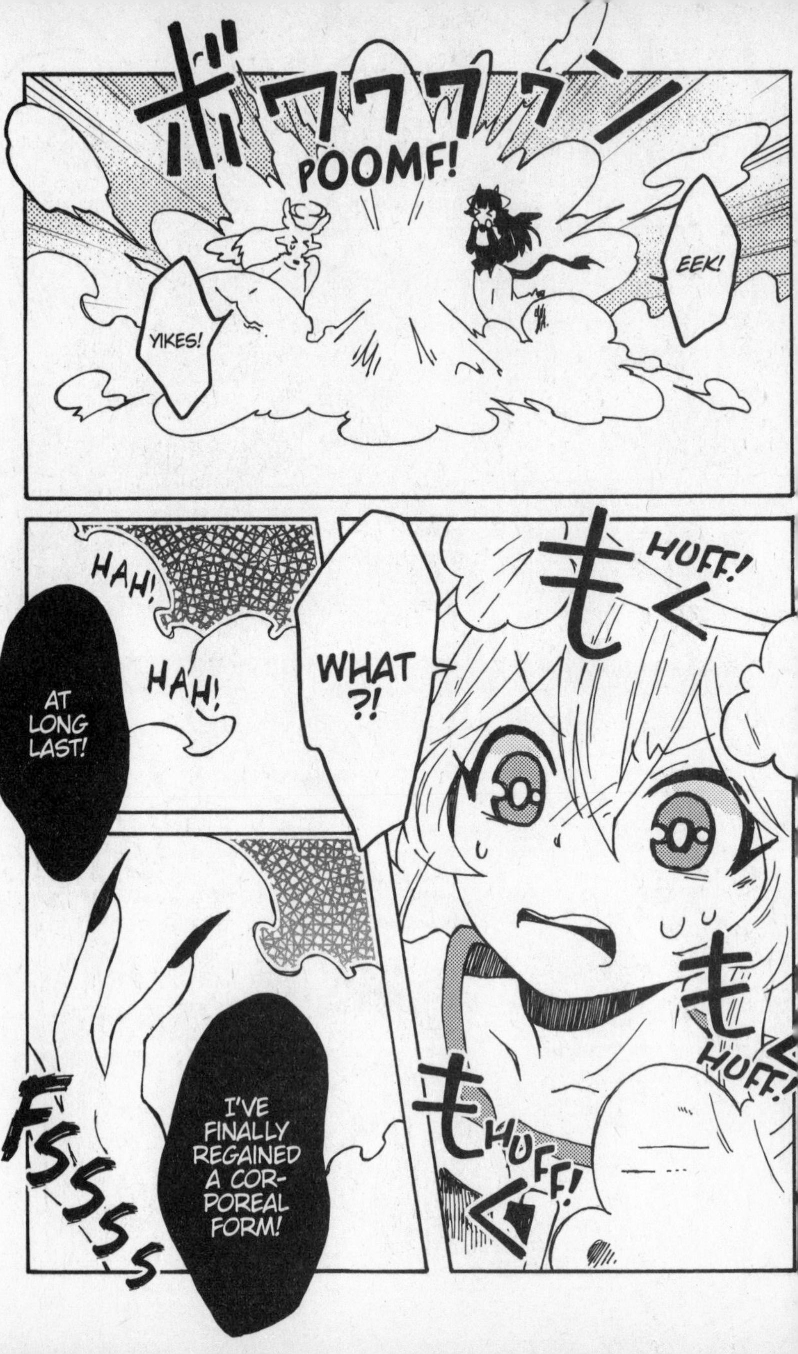
ボワワワン
POOMF!
EEK!
YIKES!
もく
HUFF!
WHAT?!
も
HUFF!
もく
HUFF!
HAH!
HAH!
AT LONG LAST!
FSSSS
I'VE FINALLY REGAINED A CORPOREAL FORM!

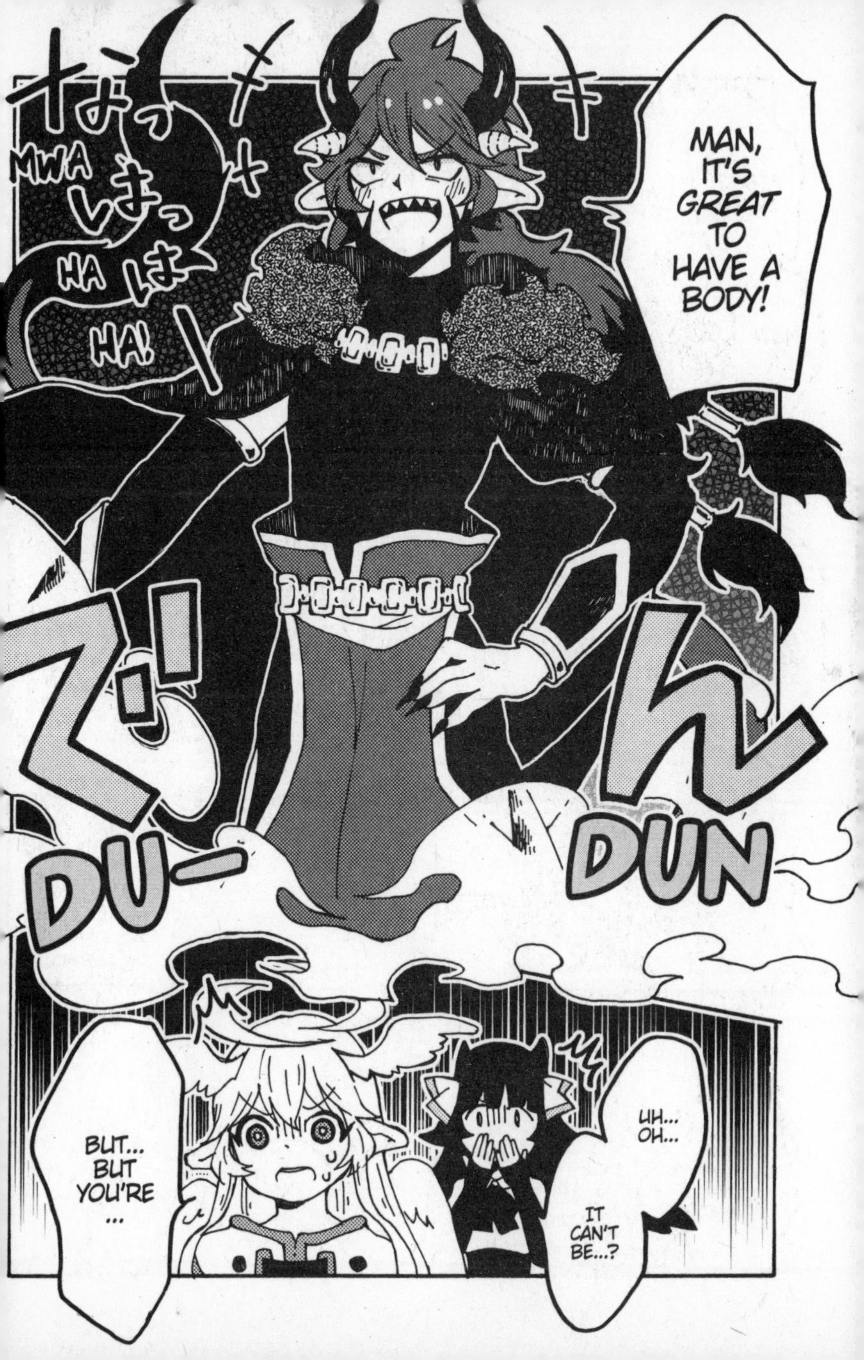
MAN, IT'S GREAT TO HAVE A BODY!
MWA HA HA!
DU- DUN
UH... OH...
IT CAN'T BE...?
BUT... BUT YOU'RE ...

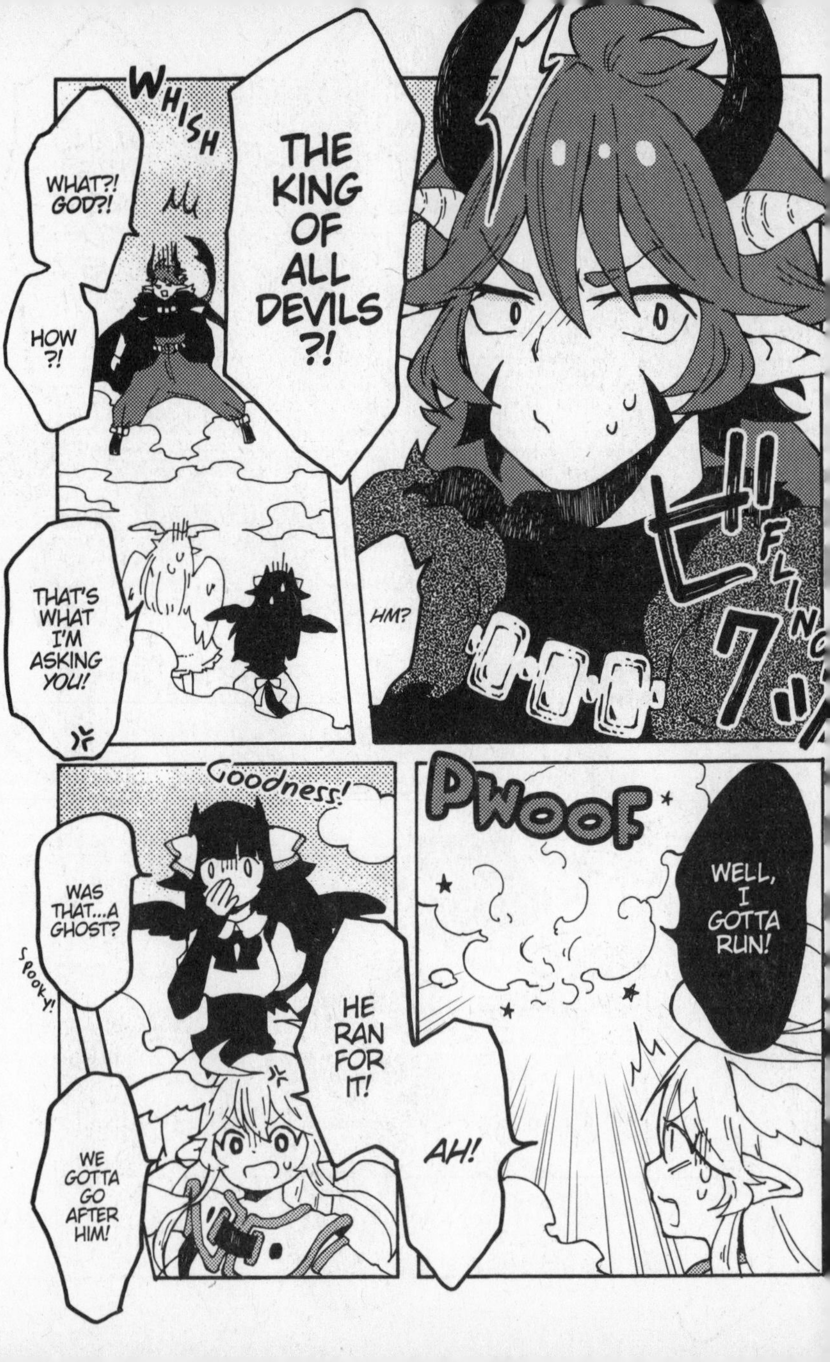
THE KING OF ALL DEVILS?!
HM?
FLING
WHISH
WHAT?! GOD?!
HOW?!
THAT'S WHAT I'M ASKING YOU!
PWOOF
WELL, I GOTTA RUN!
AH!
Goodness!
WAS THAT...A GHOST?
Spooky!
HE RAN FOR IT!
WE GOTTA GO AFTER HIM!

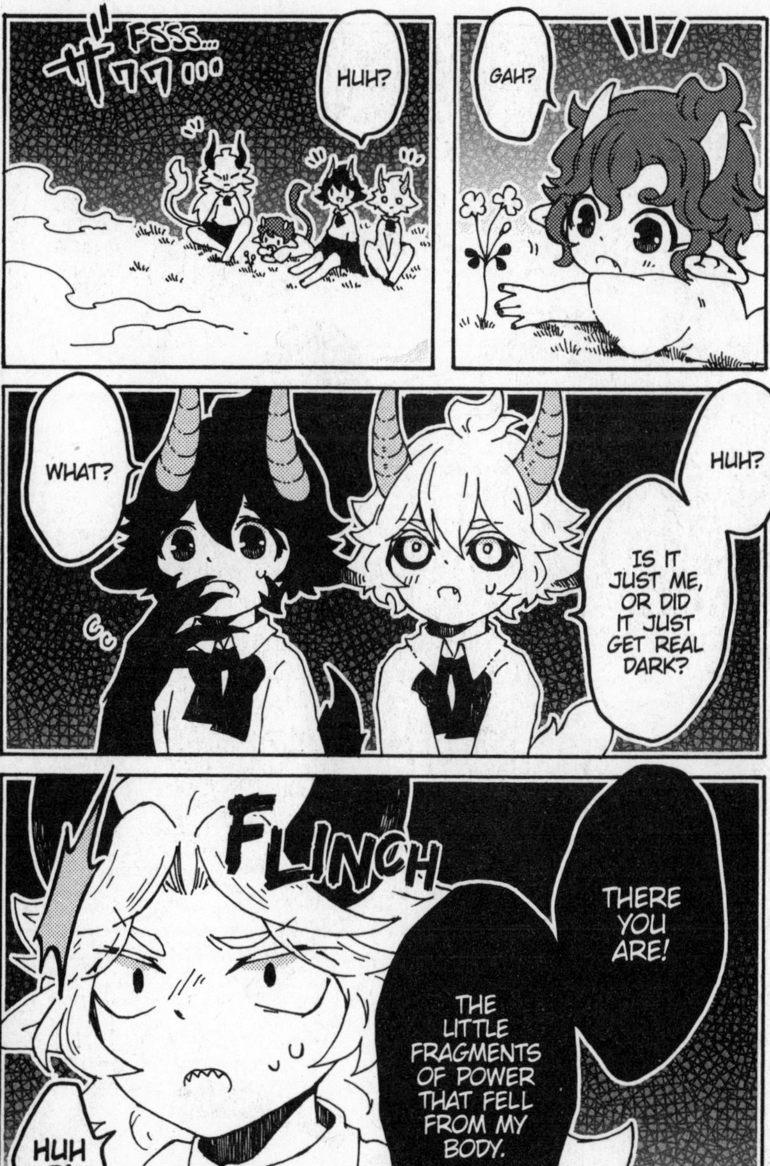
GAH?
HUH?
FSSS...
ザワワ
HUH?
IS IT JUST ME, OR DID IT JUST GET REAL DARK?
WHAT?
THERE YOU ARE!
THE LITTLE FRAGMENTS OF POWER THAT FELL FROM MY BODY.
FLINCH
HUH ?!

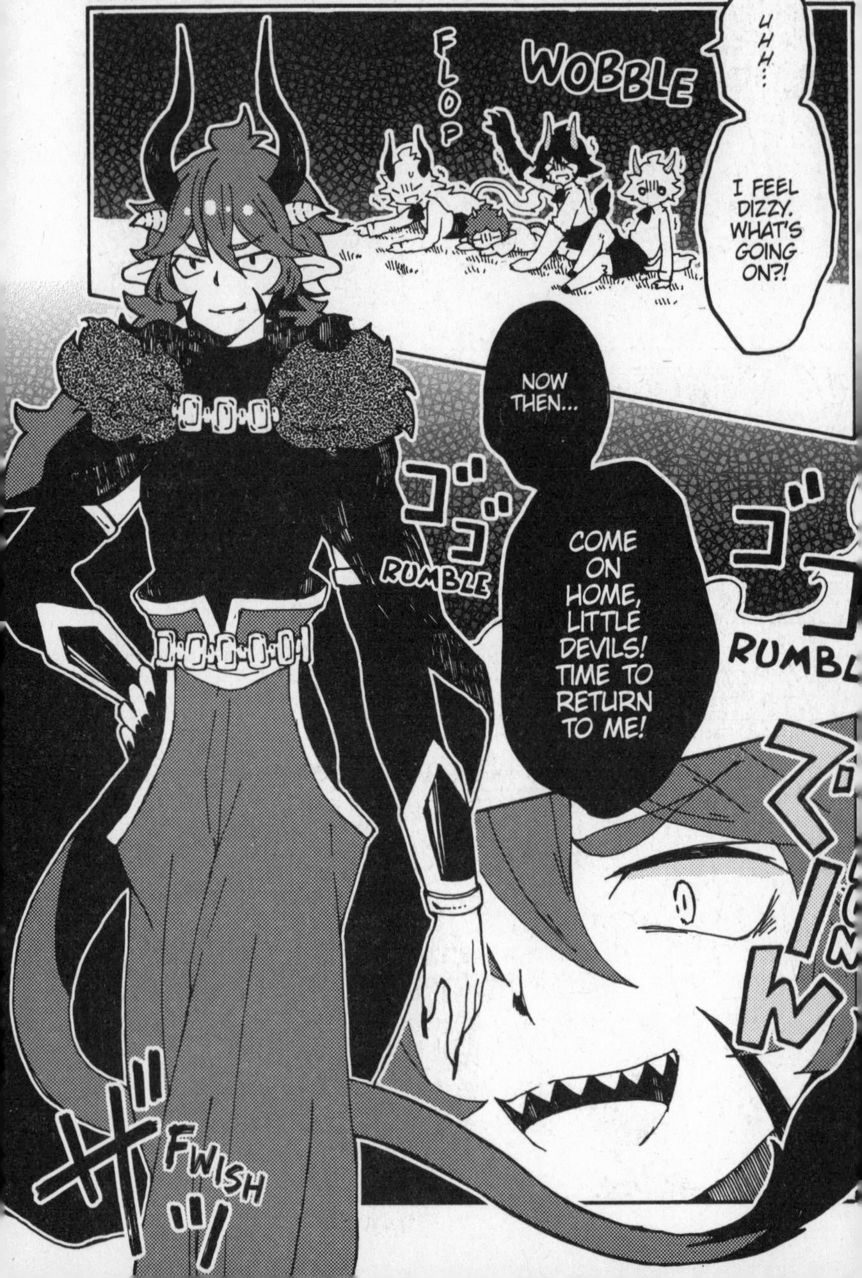

UHH...
I FEEL DIZZY. WHAT'S GOING ON?!
WOBBLE
FLOP
NOW THEN...
COME ON HOME, LITTLE DEVILS! TIME TO RETURN TO ME!
RUMBL
ゴゴ
RUMBLE
FWISH

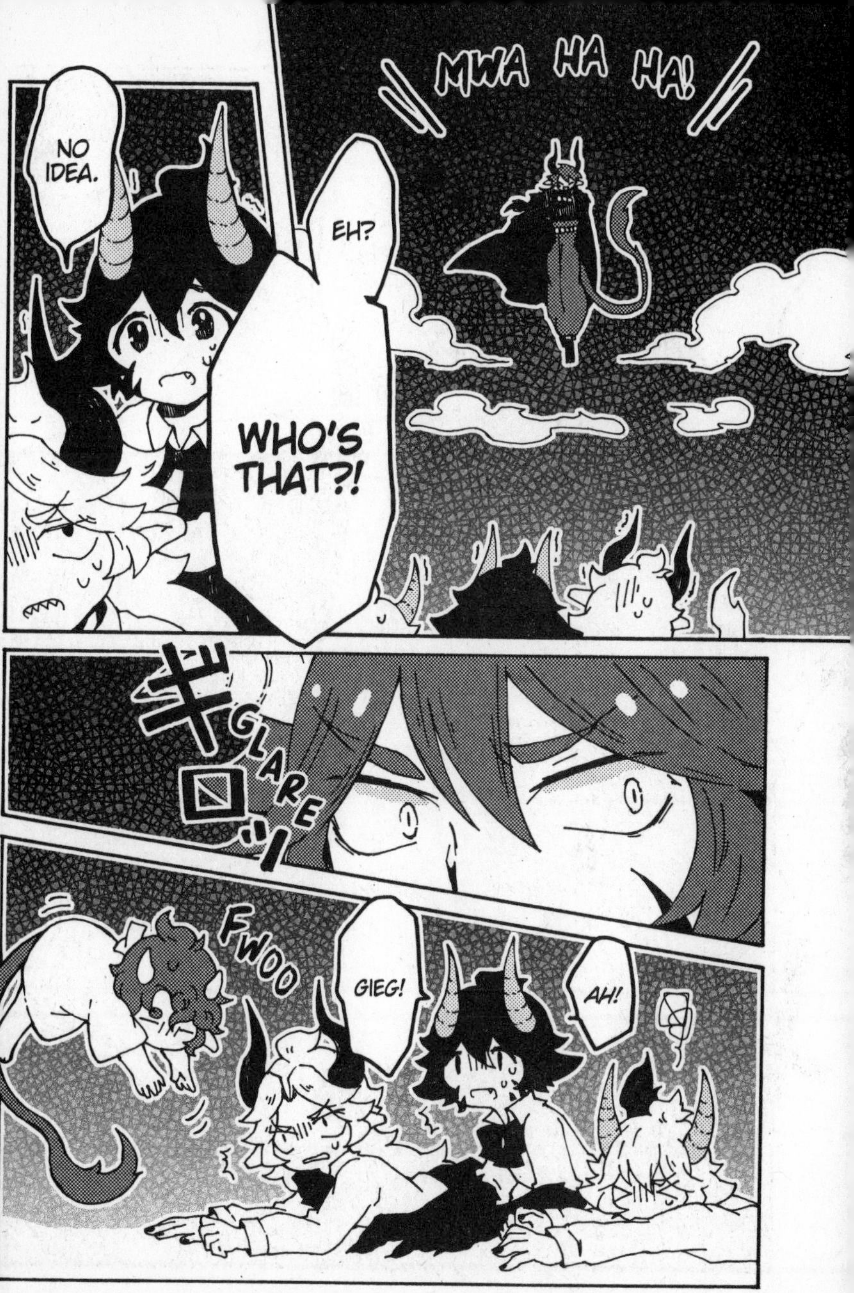
MWA HA HA!
EH?
WHO'S THAT?!
NO IDEA.
GLARE
AH!
GIEG!
FWOO

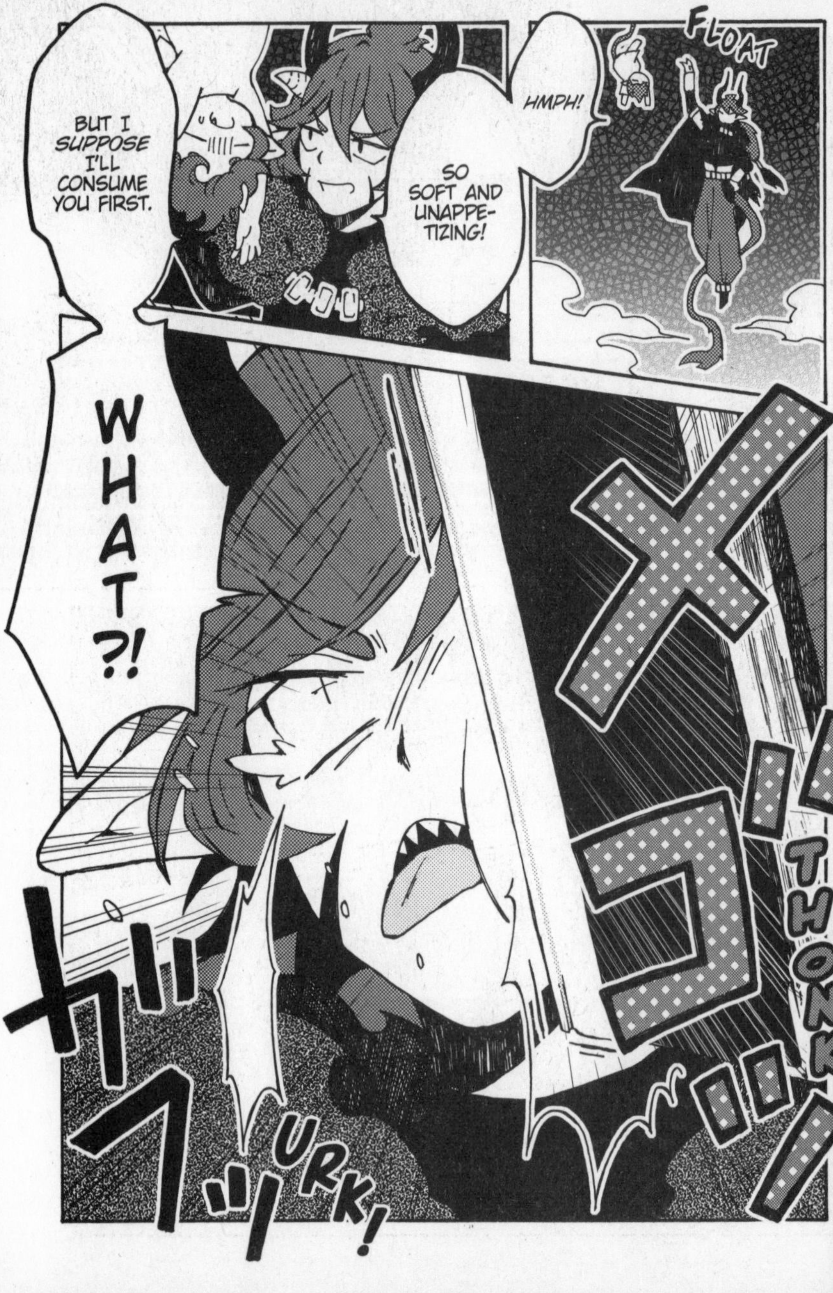
FLOAT
HMPH!
SO SOFT AND UNAPPETIZING!
BUT I SUPPOSE I'LL CONSUME YOU FIRST.
THONK!
WHAT?!
URK!

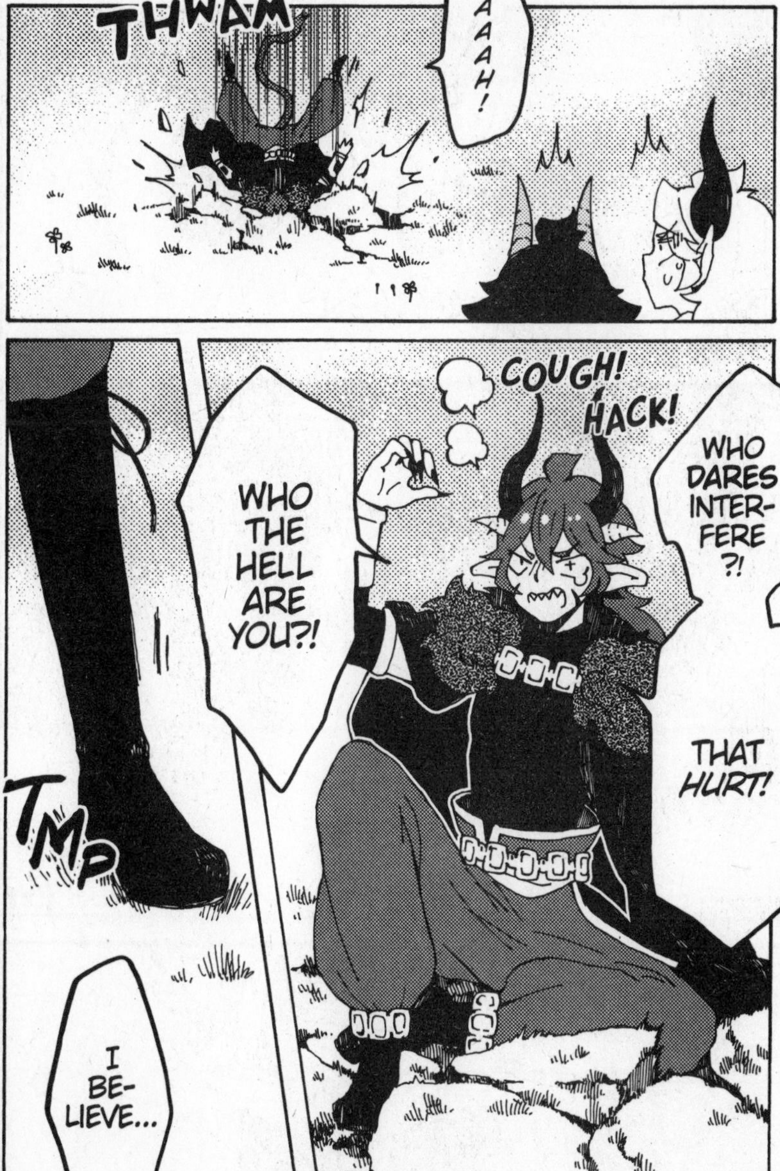
AAAAH!
THWAM
COUGH! HACK!
WHO DARES INTER-FERE ?!
THAT HURT!
WHO THE HELL ARE YOU?!
TMP
I BE-LIEVE...

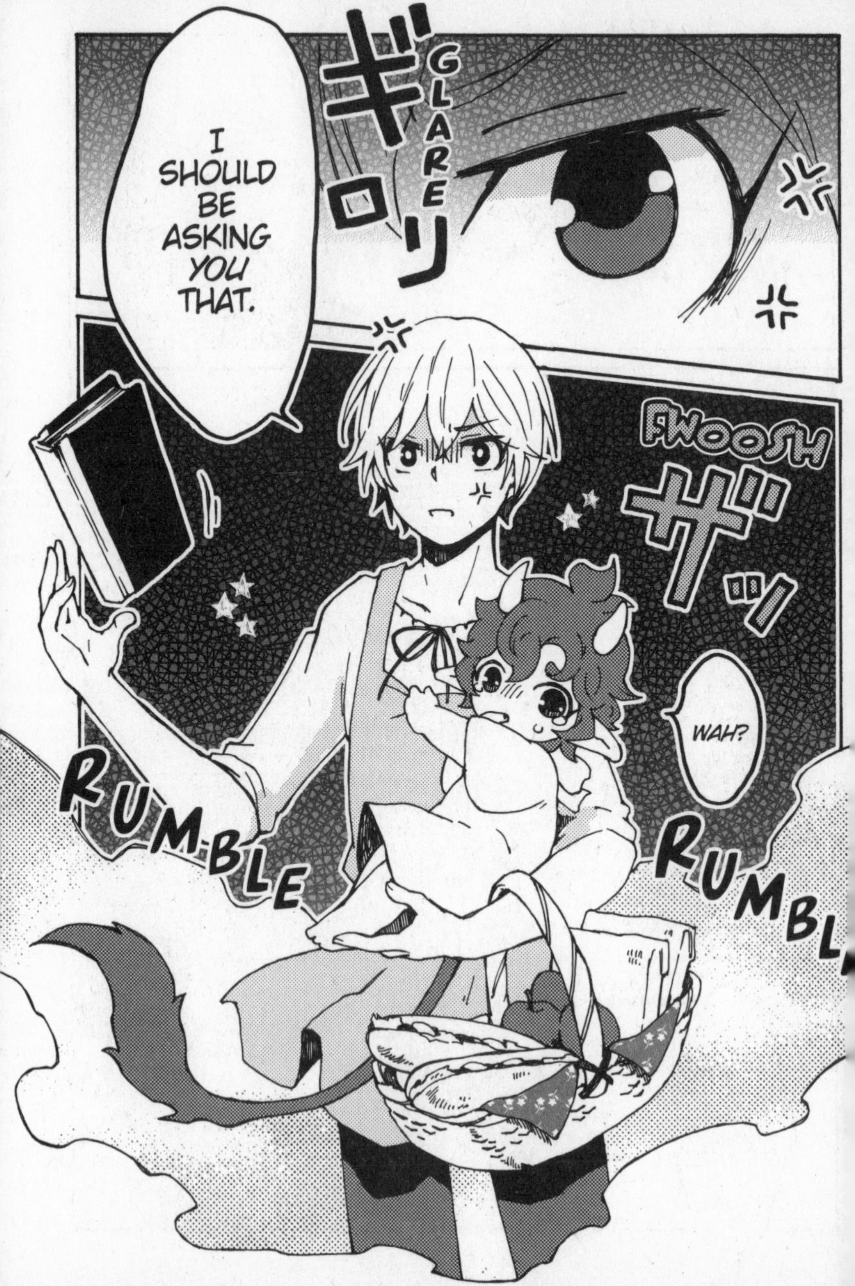
ギロリ
GLARE
I SHOULD BE ASKING YOU THAT.
FWOOSH
ザッ
WAH?
RUMBLE
RUMBLE

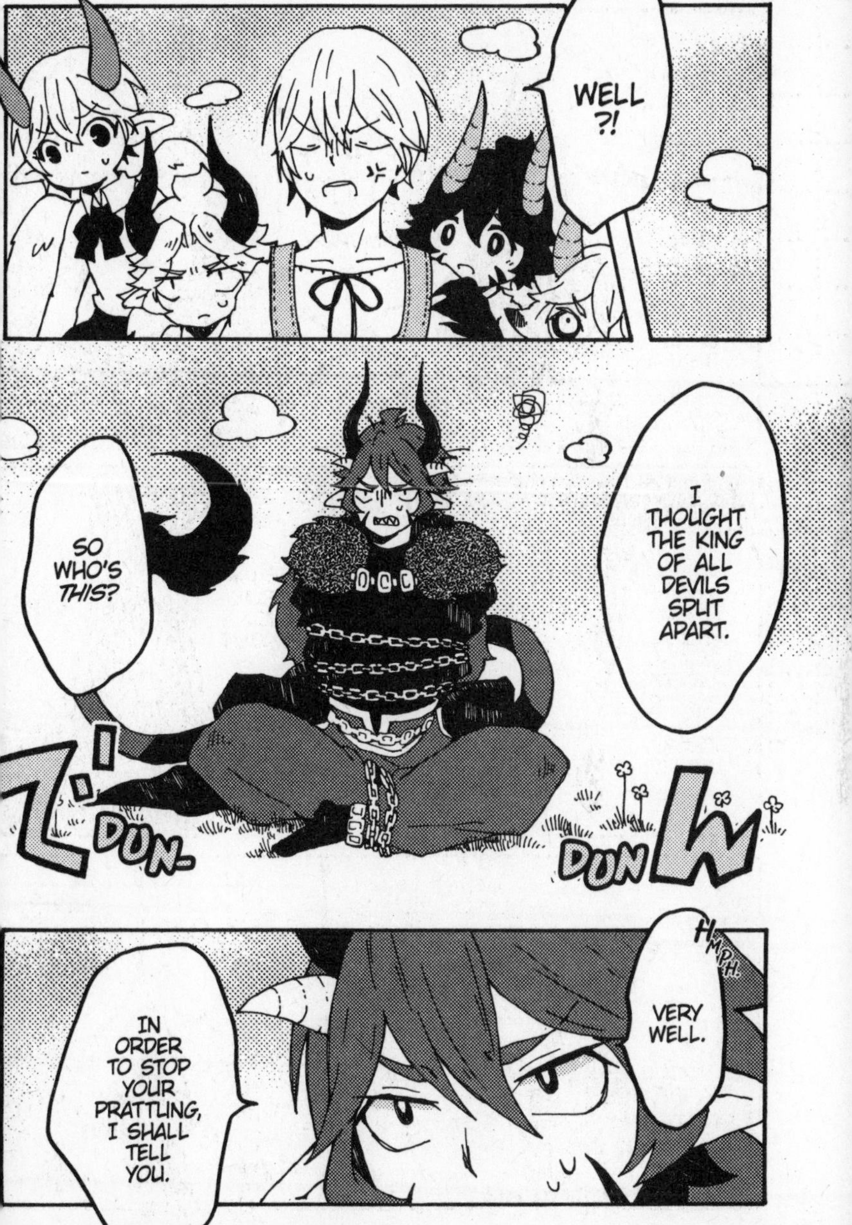
WELL ?!
I THOUGHT THE KING OF ALL DEVILS SPLIT APART.
SO WHO'S *THIS*?
DUN
DUN
HMPH.
VERY WELL.
IN ORDER TO STOP YOUR PRATTLING, I SHALL TELL YOU.

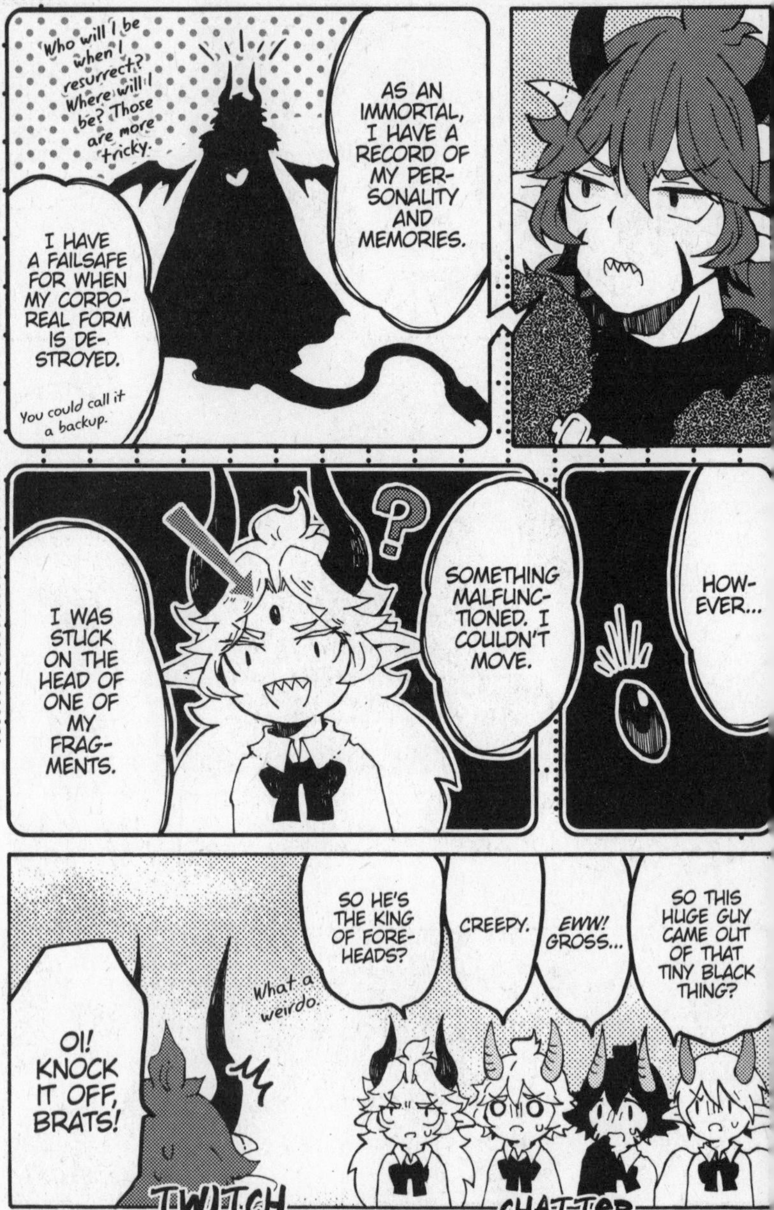
AS AN IMMORTAL, I HAVE A RECORD OF MY PERSONALITY AND MEMORIES.
Who will I be when I resurrect? Where will I be? Those are more tricky.
I HAVE A FAILSAFE FOR WHEN MY CORPOREAL FORM IS DESTROYED.
You could call it a backup.
HOWEVER...
SOMETHING MALFUNCTIONED. I COULDN'T MOVE.
?
I WAS STUCK ON THE HEAD OF ONE OF MY FRAGMENTS.
SO THIS HUGE GUY CAME OUT OF THAT TINY BLACK THING?
EWW! GROSS...
CREEPY.
SO HE'S THE KING OF FOREHEADS?
What a weirdo.
OI! KNOCK IT OFF, BRATS!
CHATTER
TWITCH

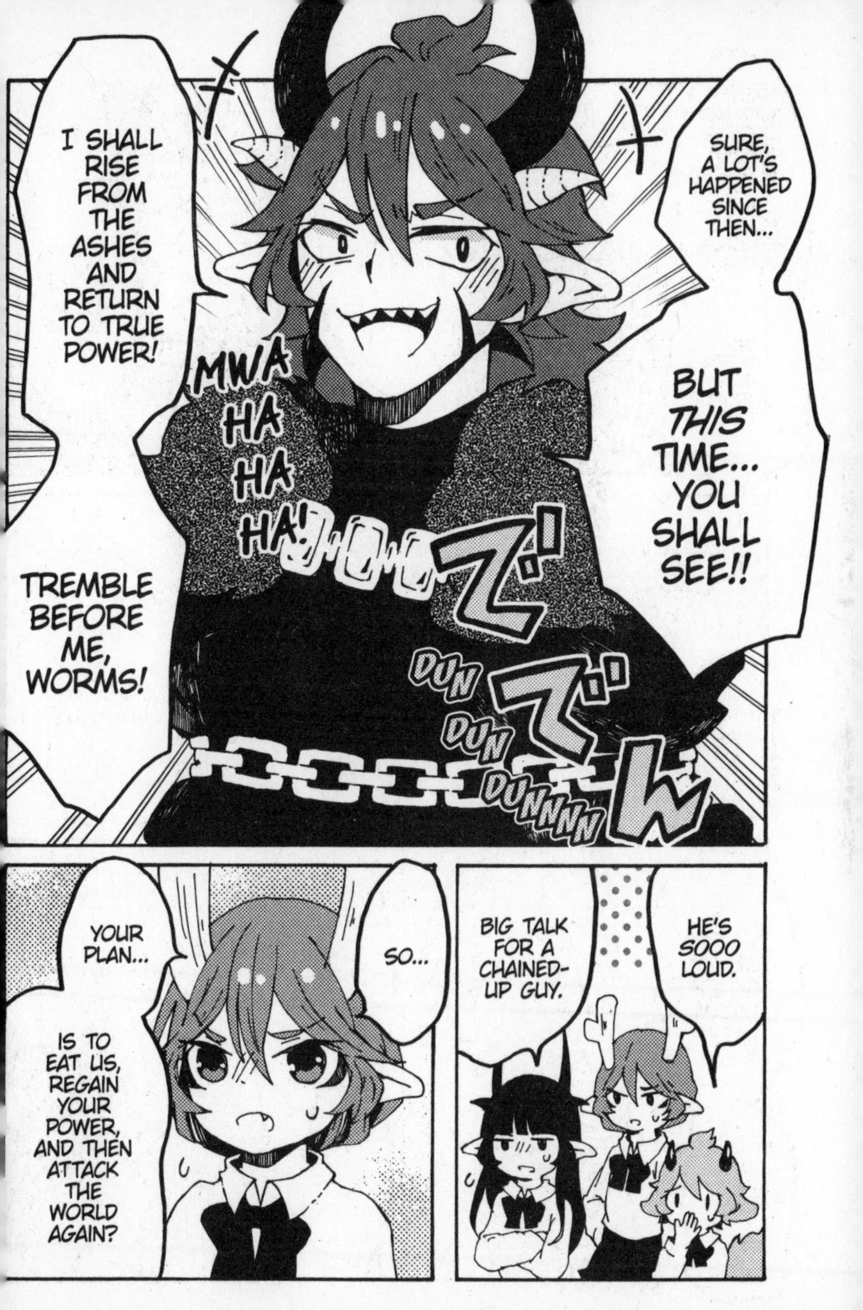
SURE, A LOT'S HAPPENED SINCE THEN...
BUT THIS TIME... YOU SHALL SEE!!
I SHALL RISE FROM THE ASHES AND RETURN TO TRUE POWER!
MWA HA HA HA!
TREMBLE BEFORE ME, WORMS!
ズでん
DUN DUN DUNNNN
HE'S SOOO LOUD.
BIG TALK FOR A CHAINED-UP GUY.
SO...
YOUR PLAN...
IS TO EAT US, REGAIN YOUR POWER, AND THEN ATTACK THE WORLD AGAIN?

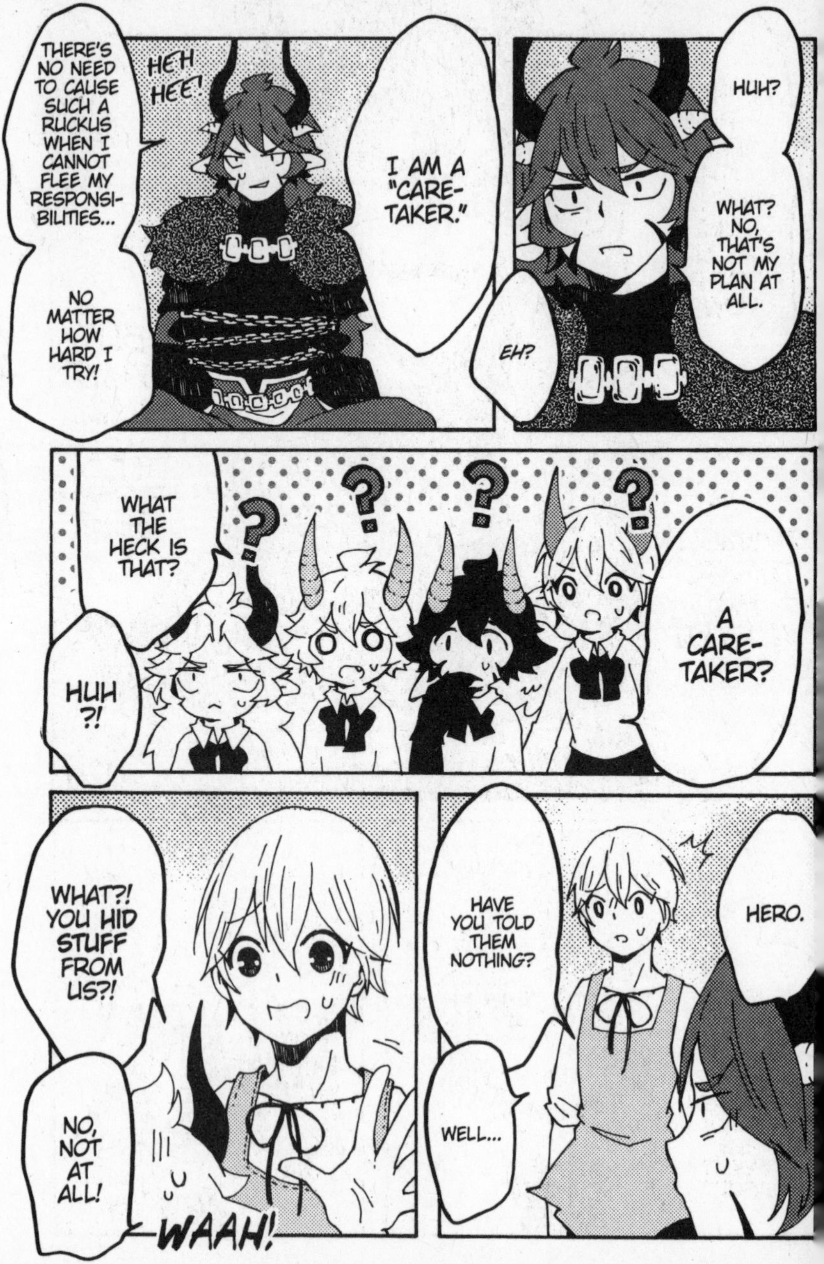
HUH?
WHAT? NO, THAT'S NOT MY PLAN AT ALL.
EH?
I AM A "CARE-TAKER."
HEH HEE!
THERE'S NO NEED TO CAUSE SUCH A RUCKUS WHEN I CANNOT FLEE MY RESPONSI-BILITIES...
NO MATTER HOW HARD I TRY!
?
?
?
?
A CARE-TAKER?
WHAT THE HECK IS THAT?
HUH?!
HERO.
HAVE YOU TOLD THEM NOTHING?
WELL...
WHAT?! YOU HID STUFF FROM US?!
NO, NOT AT ALL!
WAAH!

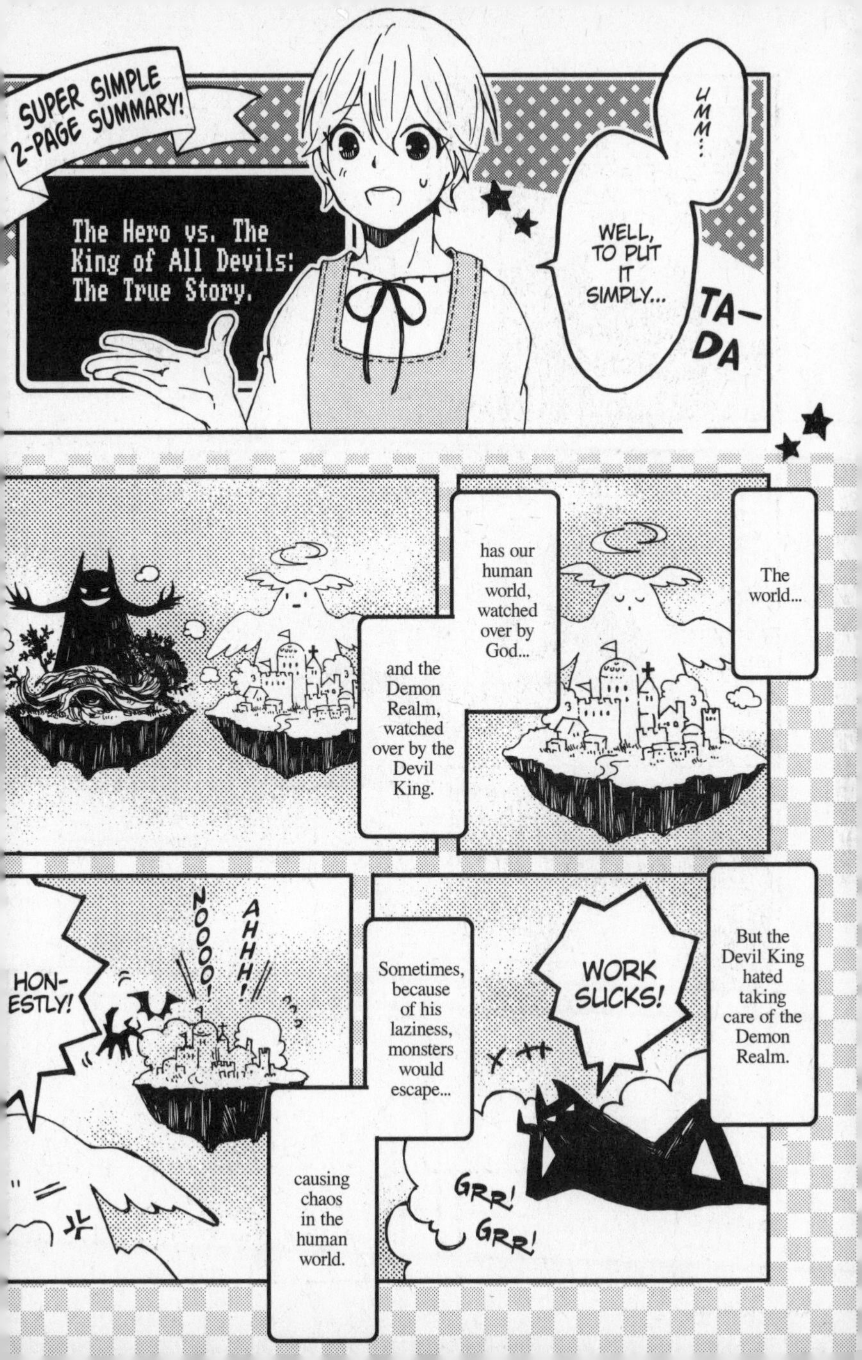
UMMM...
WELL, TO PUT IT SIMPLY...
TA-DA
SUPER SIMPLE 2-PAGE SUMMARY!
The Hero vs. The King of All Devils: The True Story.
The world...
has our human world, watched over by God...
and the Demon Realm, watched over by the Devil King.
But the Devil King hated taking care of the Demon Realm.
WORK SUCKS!
GRR! GRR!
Sometimes, because of his laziness, monsters would escape...
NOOOOO!
AHHHH!
HONESTLY!
causing chaos in the human world.

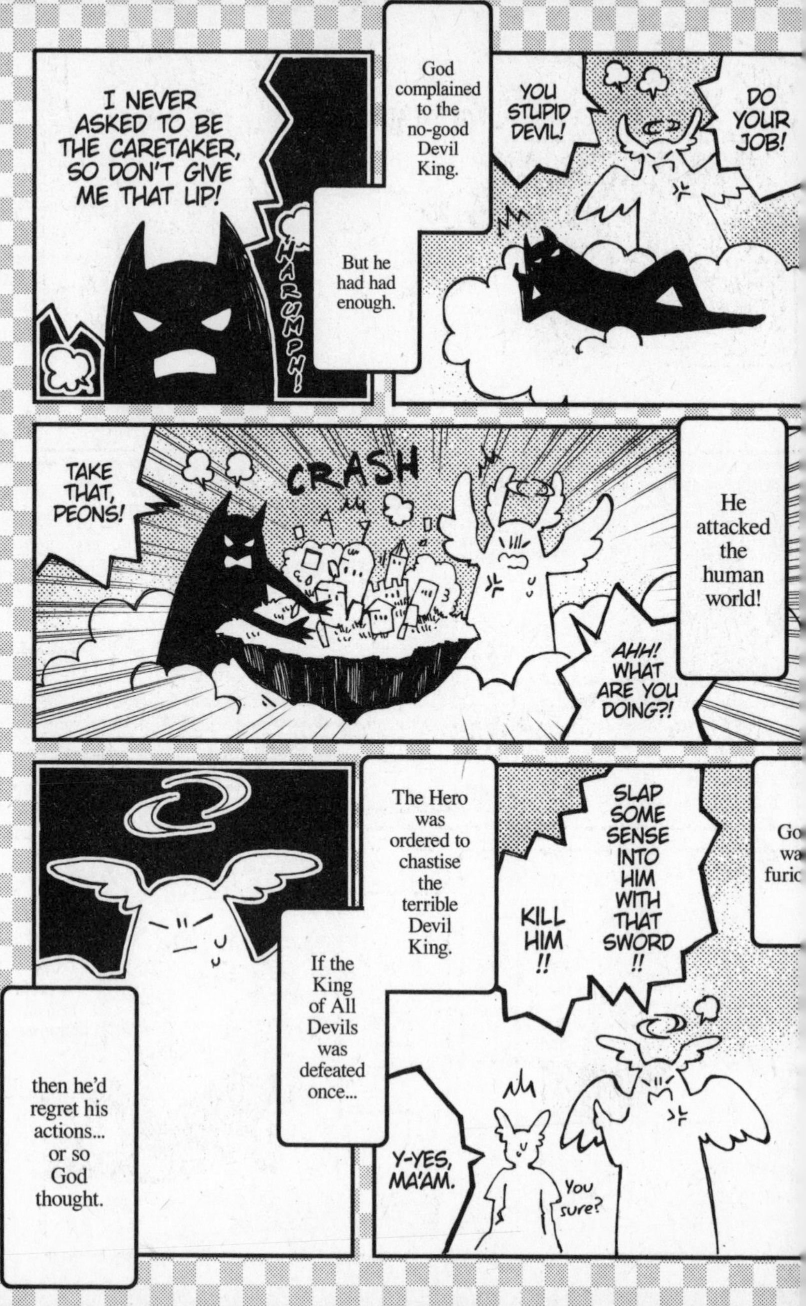
DO YOUR JOB!
YOU STUPID DEVIL!
God complained to the no-good Devil King.
But he had had enough.
HARUMPH!
I NEVER ASKED TO BE THE CARETAKER, SO DON'T GIVE ME THAT LIP!
He attacked the human world!
AHH! WHAT ARE YOU DOING?!
CRASH
TAKE THAT, PEONS!
SLAP SOME SENSE INTO HIM WITH THAT SWORD!!
KILL HIM!!
The Hero was ordered to chastise the terrible Devil King.
Y-YES, MA'AM.
You sure?
If the King of All Devils was defeated once...
then he'd regret his actions... or so God thought.

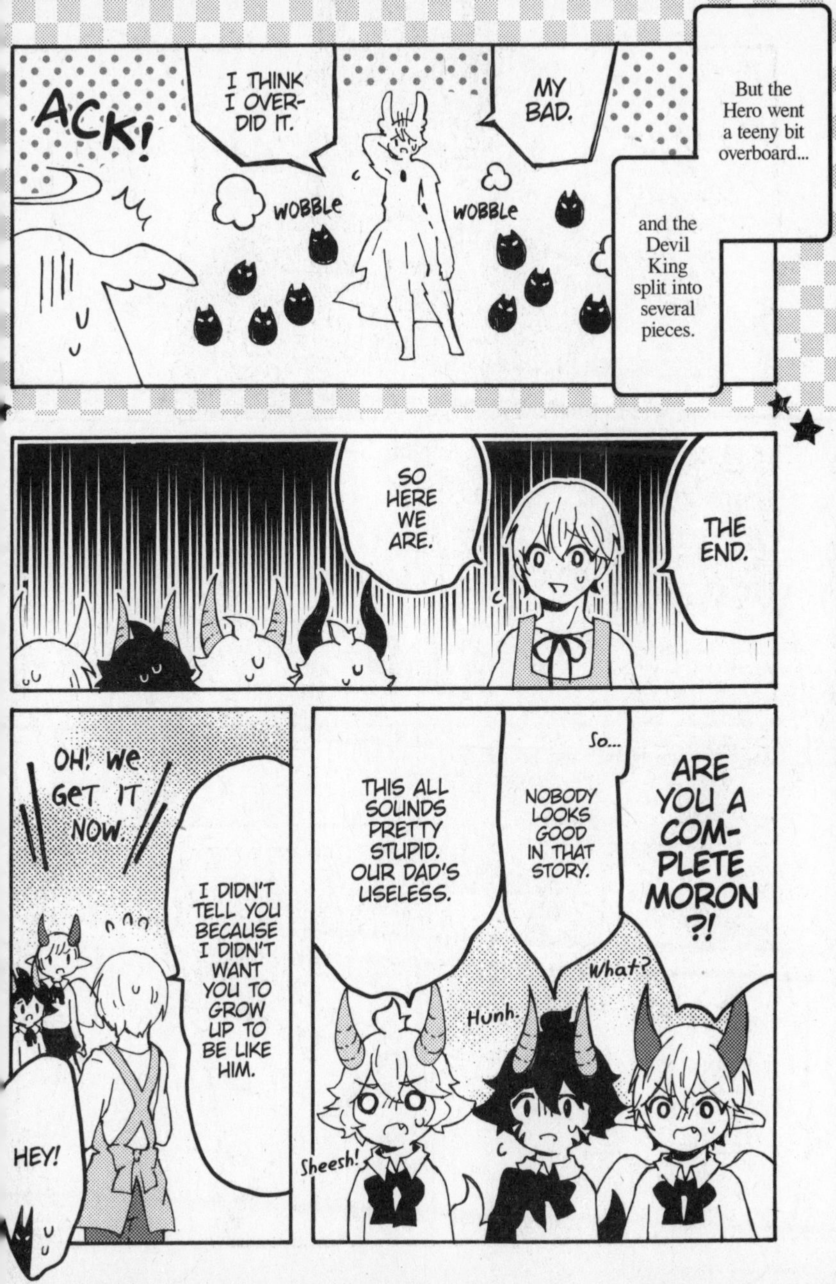
But the Hero went a teeny bit overboard...
and the Devil King split into several pieces.
MY BAD.
I THINK I OVER-DID IT.
WOBBLE
WOBBLE
ACK!
THE END.
SO HERE WE ARE.
So...
ARE YOU A COMPLETE MORON?!
NOBODY LOOKS GOOD IN THAT STORY.
THIS ALL SOUNDS PRETTY STUPID. OUR DAD'S USELESS.
What?
Hunh.
Sheesh!
OH! WE GET IT NOW.
I DIDN'T TELL YOU BECAUSE I DIDN'T WANT YOU TO GROW UP TO BE LIKE HIM.
HEY!

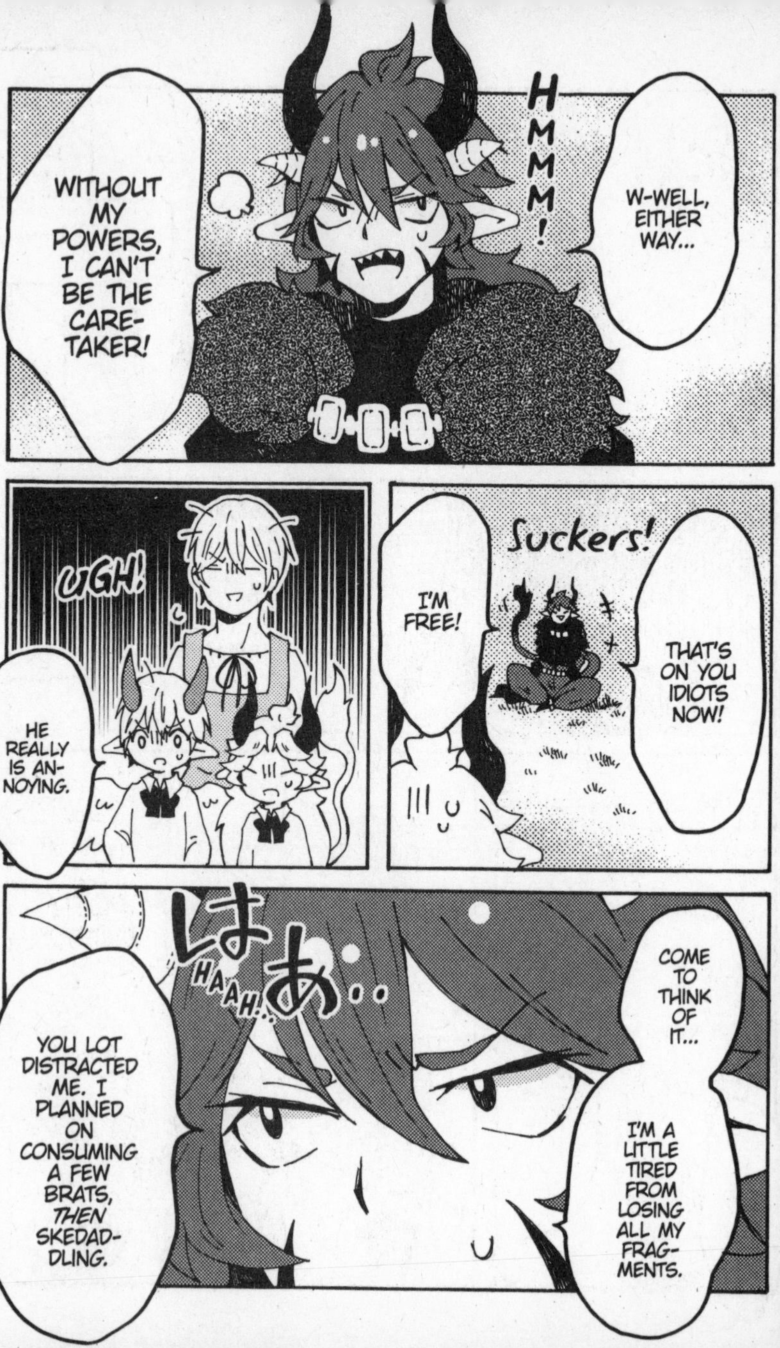
W-WELL, EITHER WAY...
HMMMM!
WITHOUT MY POWERS, I CAN'T BE THE CARE-TAKER!
THAT'S ON YOU IDIOTS NOW!
Suckers!
I'M FREE!
UGH!
HE REALLY IS AN-NOYING.
COME TO THINK OF IT...
I'M A LITTLE TIRED FROM LOSING ALL MY FRAG-MENTS.
はあ・・
HAAAH...
YOU LOT DISTRACTED ME. I PLANNED ON CONSUMING A FEW BRATS, *THEN* SKEDAD-DLING.

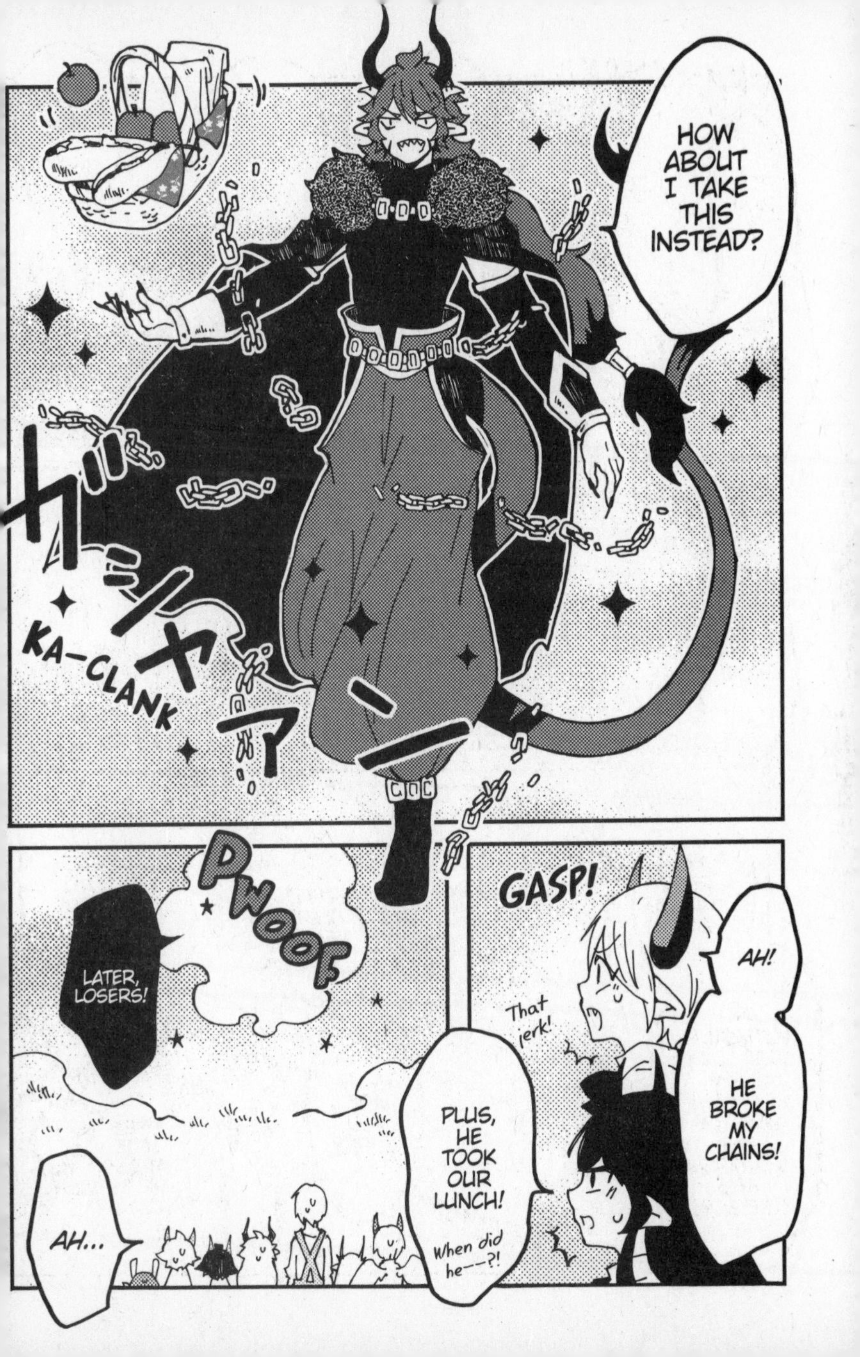
HOW ABOUT I TAKE THIS INSTEAD?
KA-CLANK
GASP!
AH!
HE BROKE MY CHAINS!
That jerk!
PLUS, HE TOOK OUR LUNCH!
When did he--?!
PWOOF
LATER, LOSERS!
AH...

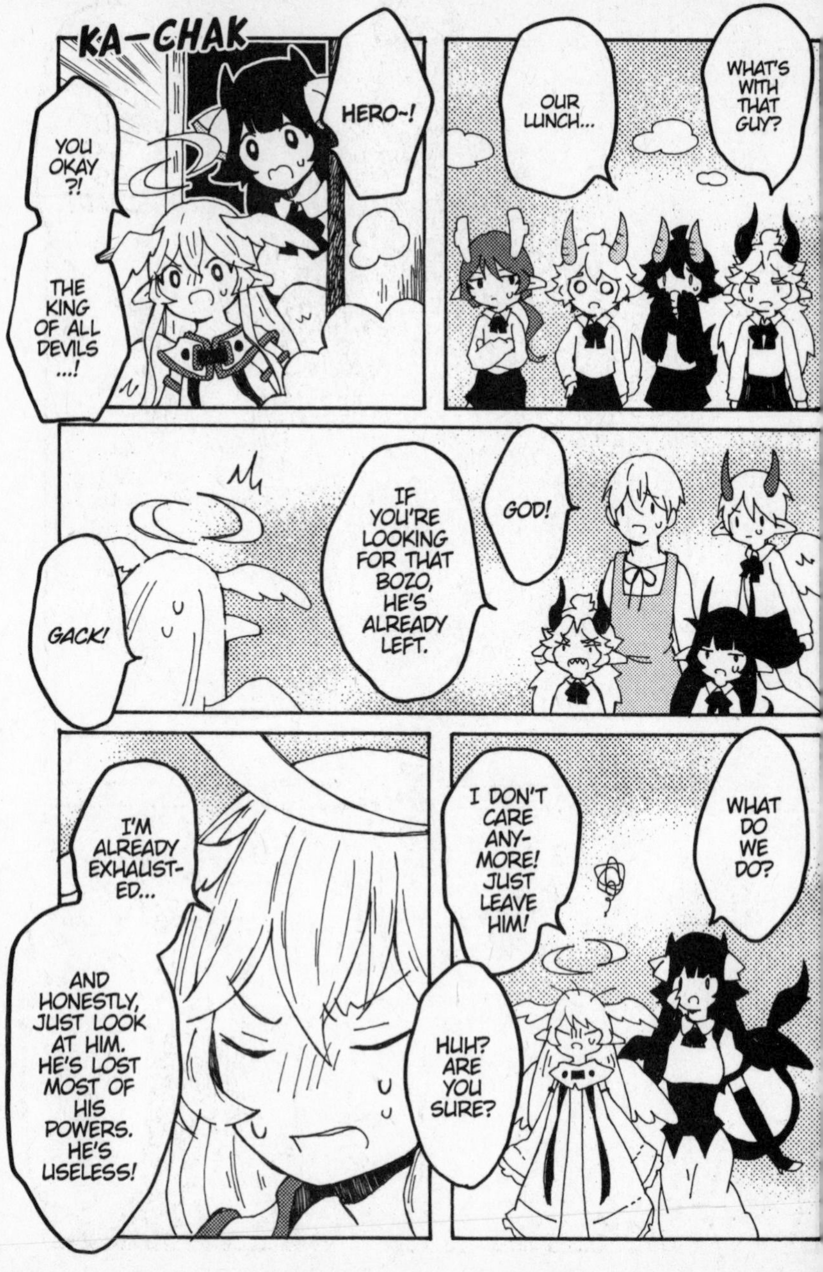
WHAT'S WITH THAT GUY?
OUR LUNCH...
KA-CHAK
HERO~!
YOU OKAY?!
THE KING OF ALL DEVILS...!
GOD!
IF YOU'RE LOOKING FOR THAT BOZO, HE'S ALREADY LEFT.
GACK!
WHAT DO WE DO?
I DON'T CARE ANYMORE! JUST LEAVE HIM!
HUH? ARE YOU SURE?
I'M ALREADY EXHAUSTED...
AND HONESTLY, JUST LOOK AT HIM. HE'S LOST MOST OF HIS POWERS. HE'S USELESS!

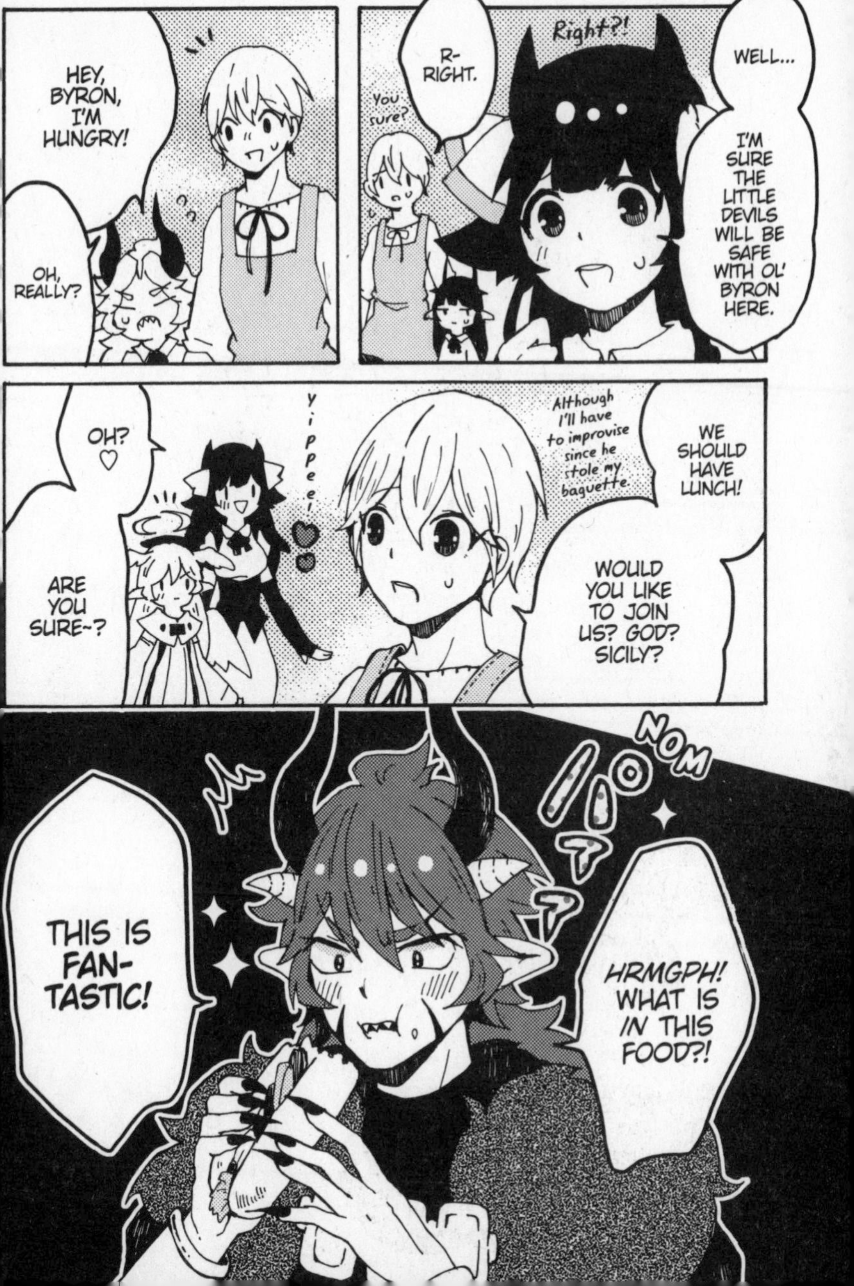
WELL...
I'M SURE THE LITTLE DEVILS WILL BE SAFE WITH OL' BYRON HERE.
Right?!
R-RIGHT.
You sure?
HEY, BYRON, I'M HUNGRY!
OH, REALLY?
WE SHOULD HAVE LUNCH!
Although I'll have to improvise since he stole my baguette.
WOULD YOU LIKE TO JOIN US? GOD? SICILY?
Yippee!
OH? ♡
ARE YOU SURE~?
NOM
HRMGPH! WHAT IS IN THIS FOOD?!
THIS IS FAN-TASTIC!

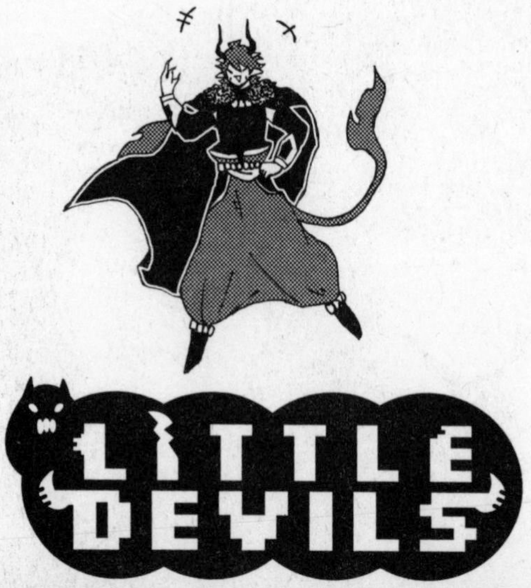

LITTLE DEVILS

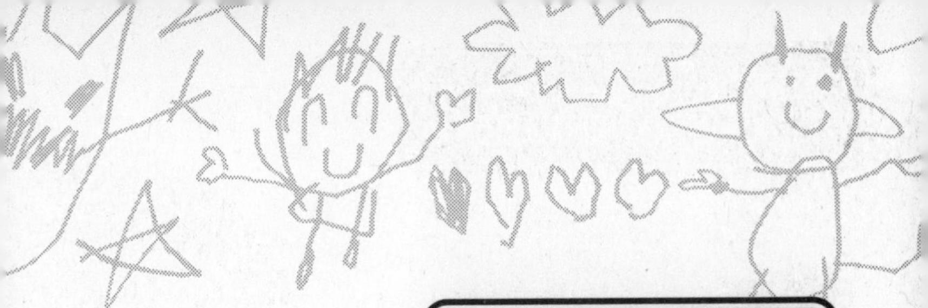

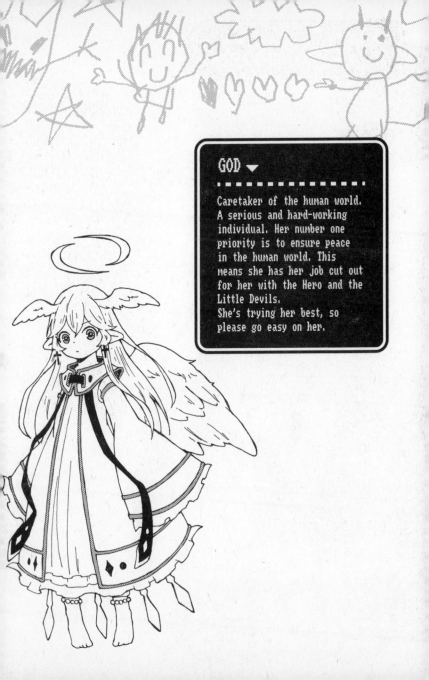

GOD

Caretaker of the human world. A serious and hard-working individual. Her number one priority is to ensure peace in the human world. This means she has her job cut out for her with the Hero and the Little Devils.
She's trying her best, so please go easy on her.

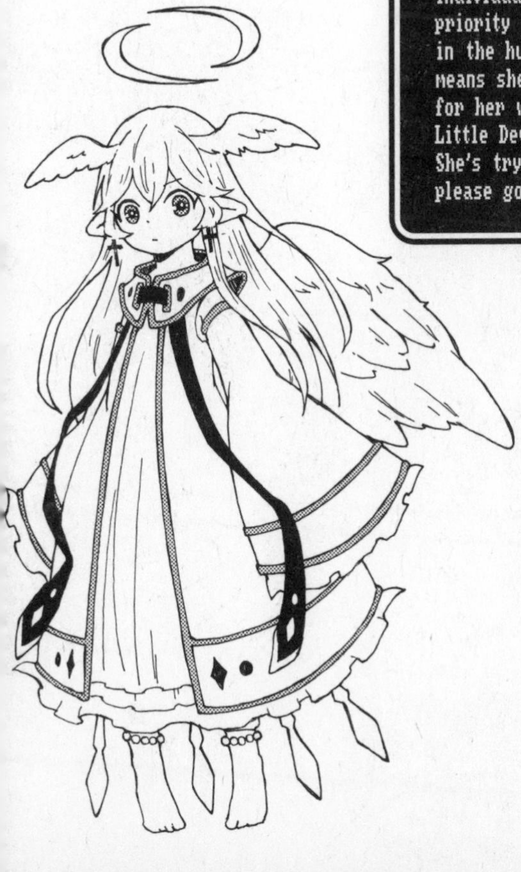

CHAPTER 19
AN ENCHANTING EDUCATION

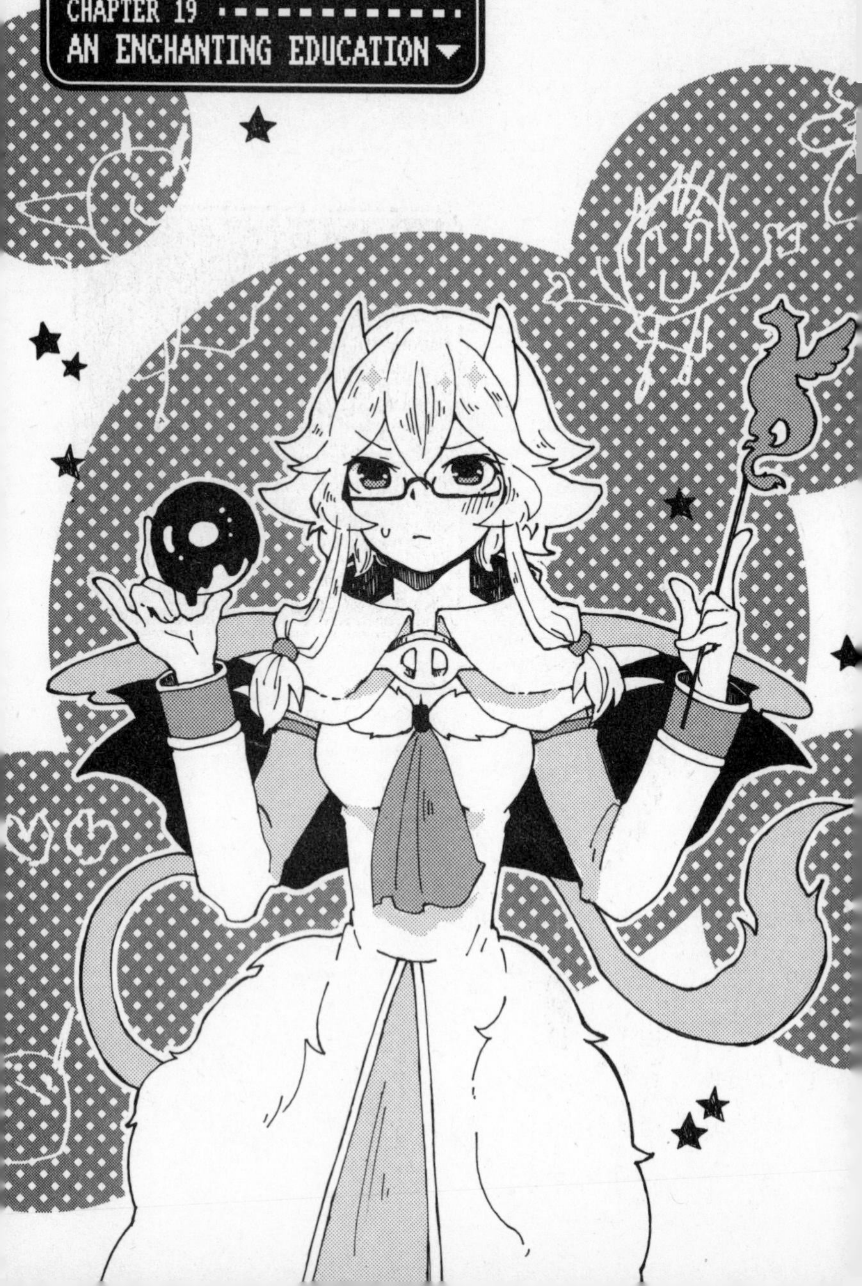

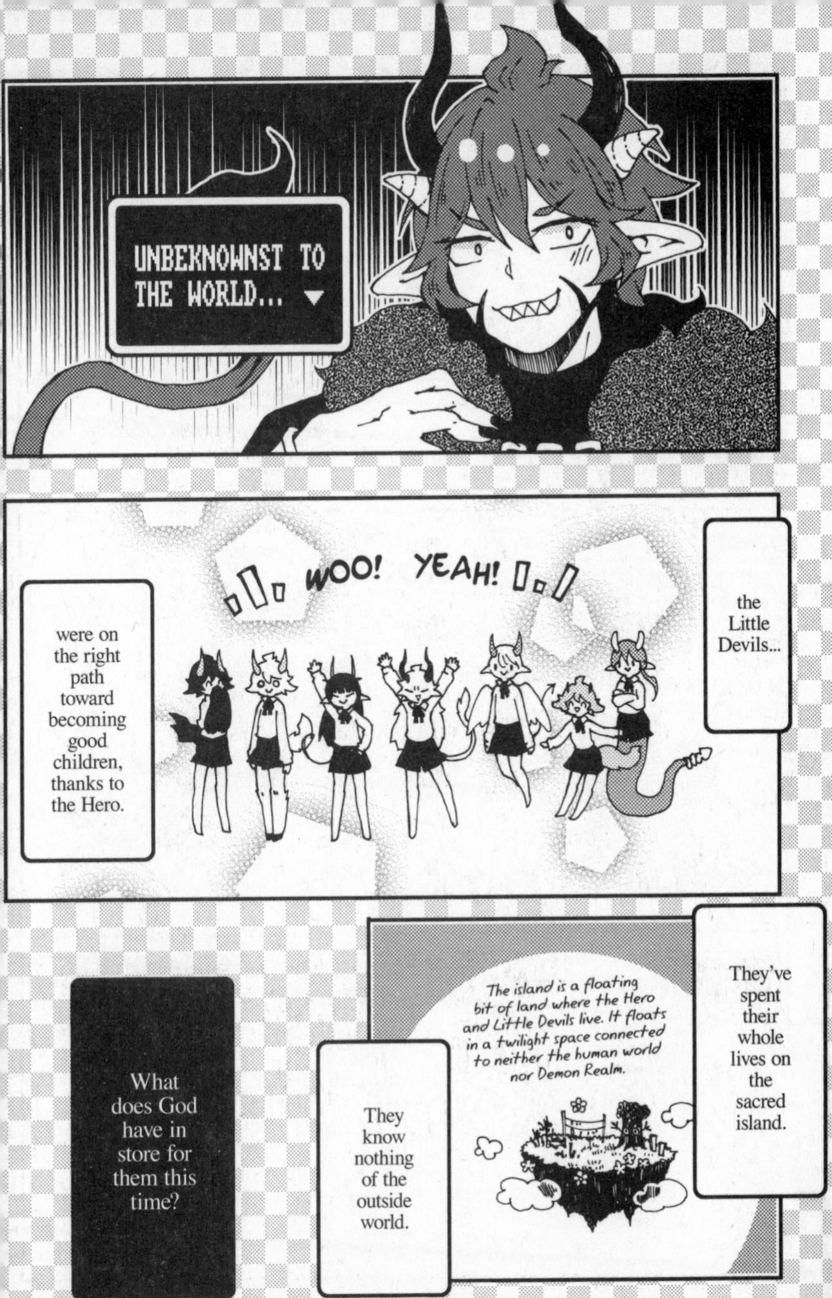
UNBEKNOWNST TO THE WORLD...
the Little Devils...
WOO! YEAH!
were on the right path toward becoming good children, thanks to the Hero.
They've spent their whole lives on the sacred island.
The island is a floating bit of land where the Hero and Little Devils live. It floats in a twilight space connected to neither the human world nor Demon Realm.
They know nothing of the outside world.
What does God have in store for them this time?

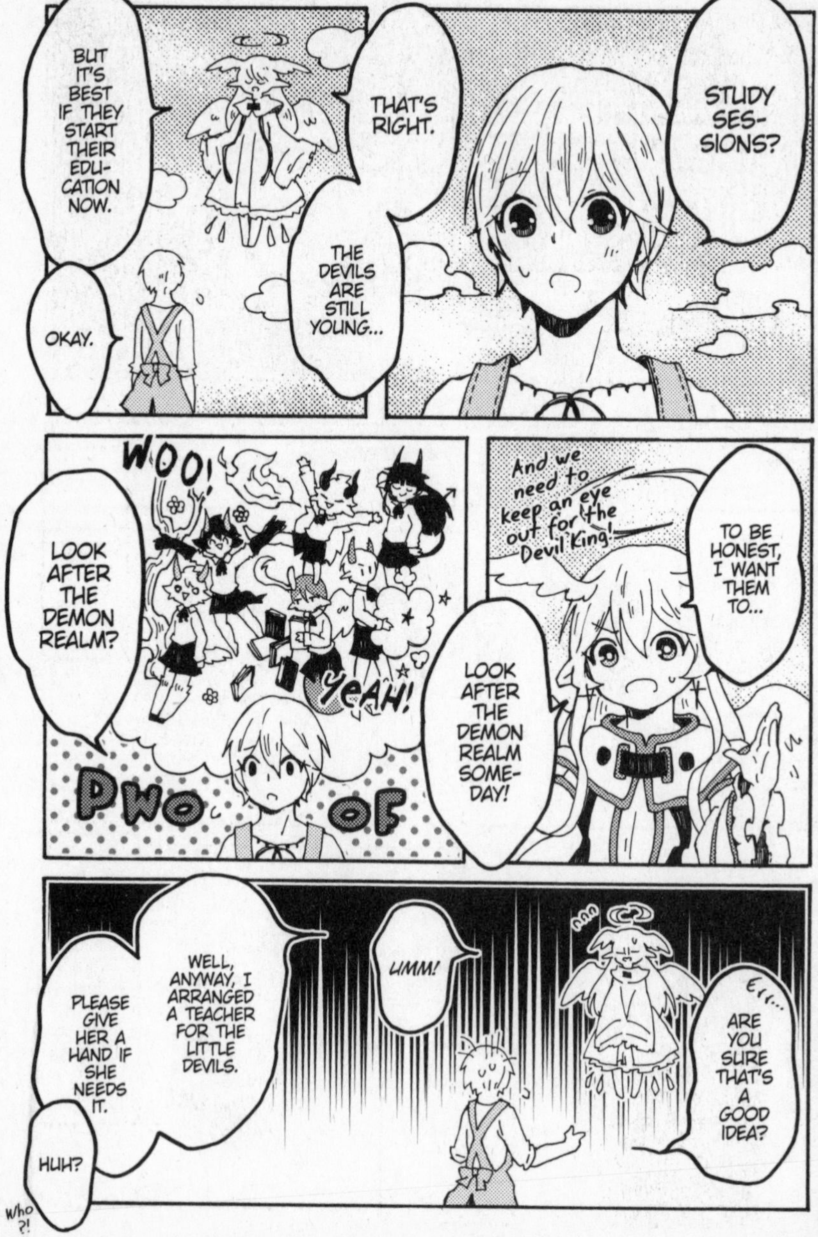
STUDY SESSIONS?
THAT'S RIGHT.
THE DEVILS ARE STILL YOUNG...
BUT IT'S BEST IF THEY START THEIR EDUCATION NOW.
OKAY.
And we need to keep an eye out for the Devil King!
TO BE HONEST, I WANT THEM TO...
LOOK AFTER THE DEMON REALM SOMEDAY!
WOO!
YEAH!
LOOK AFTER THE DEMON REALM?
PWO OF
Err...
ARE YOU SURE THAT'S A GOOD IDEA?
UMM!
WELL, ANYWAY, I ARRANGED A TEACHER FOR THE LITTLE DEVILS.
PLEASE GIVE HER A HAND IF SHE NEEDS IT.
HUH?
Who?!

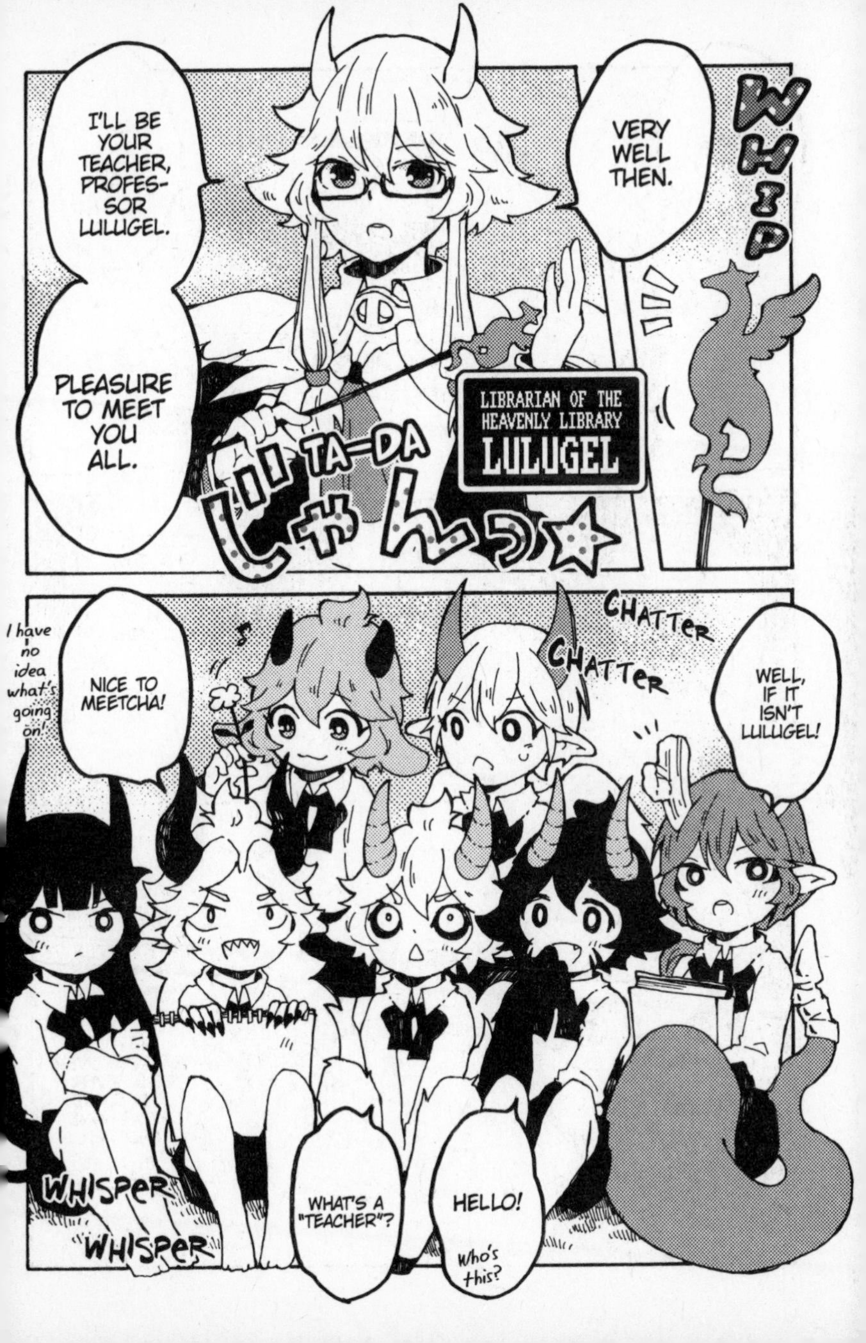
VERY WELL THEN.
WHIP
I'LL BE YOUR TEACHER, PROFES-SOR LULUGEL.
PLEASURE TO MEET YOU ALL.
LIBRARIAN OF THE HEAVENLY LIBRARY
LULUGEL
TA-DA
しゃんっ☆
CHATTER
CHATTER
WELL, IF IT ISN'T LULUGEL!
NICE TO MEETCHA!
I have no idea what's going on!
HELLO!
Who's this?
WHAT'S A "TEACHER"?
WHISPER
WHISPER

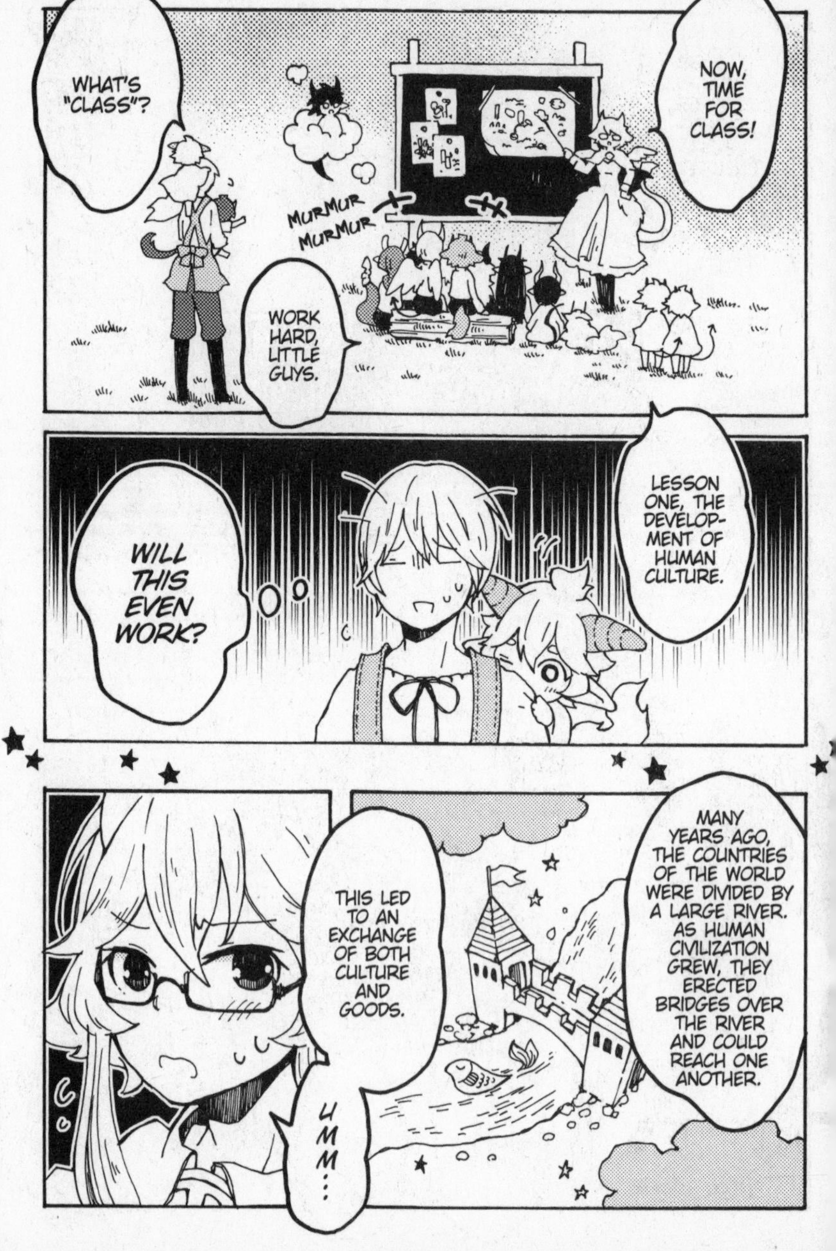
NOW, TIME FOR CLASS!
WHAT'S "CLASS"?
MURMUR MURMUR
WORK HARD, LITTLE GUYS.
LESSON ONE, THE DEVELOPMENT OF HUMAN CULTURE.
WILL THIS EVEN WORK?
MANY YEARS AGO, THE COUNTRIES OF THE WORLD WERE DIVIDED BY A LARGE RIVER. AS HUMAN CIVILIZATION GREW, THEY ERECTED BRIDGES OVER THE RIVER AND COULD REACH ONE ANOTHER.
THIS LED TO AN EXCHANGE OF BOTH CULTURE AND GOODS.
UMM...

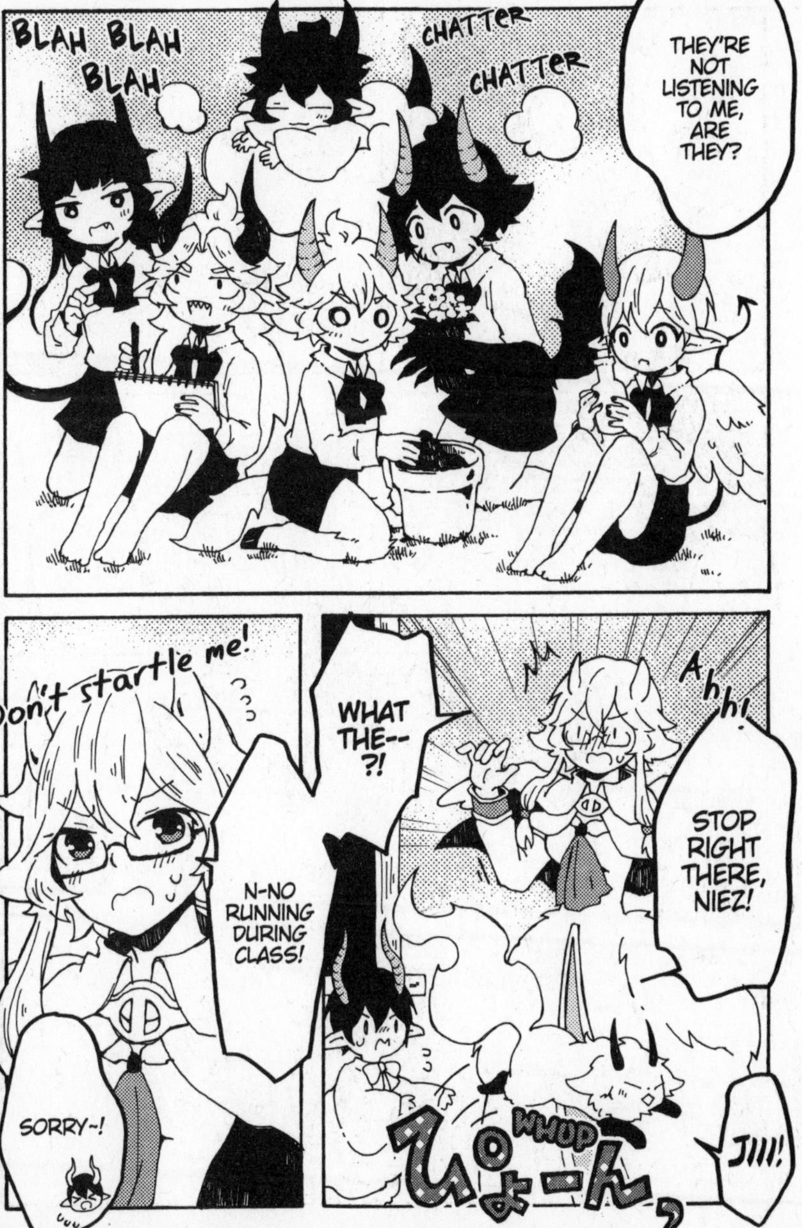
THEY'RE NOT LISTENING TO ME, ARE THEY?
CHATTER
CHATTER
BLAH BLAH BLAH
Ahh!
STOP RIGHT THERE, NIEZ!
WHAT THE--?!
JIII!
ひょーん
WHUP
Don't startle me!
N-NO RUNNING DURING CLASS!
SORRY~!

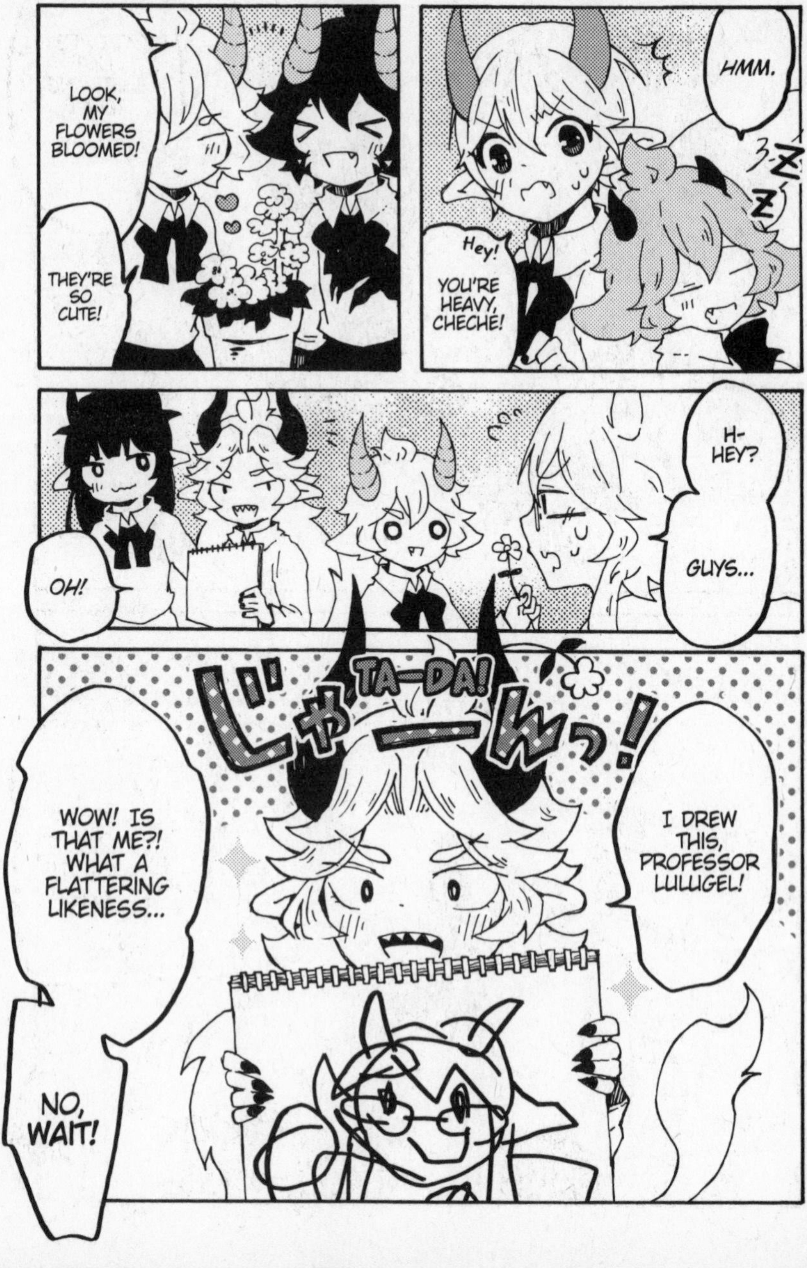
HMM.
Hey!
YOU'RE HEAVY, CHECHE!
LOOK, MY FLOWERS BLOOMED!
THEY'RE SO CUTE!
H-HEY?
GUYS...
OH!
TA-DA!
じゃーんっ!
I DREW THIS, PROFESSOR LULUGEL!
WOW! IS THAT ME?! WHAT A FLATTERING LIKENESS...
NO, WAIT!

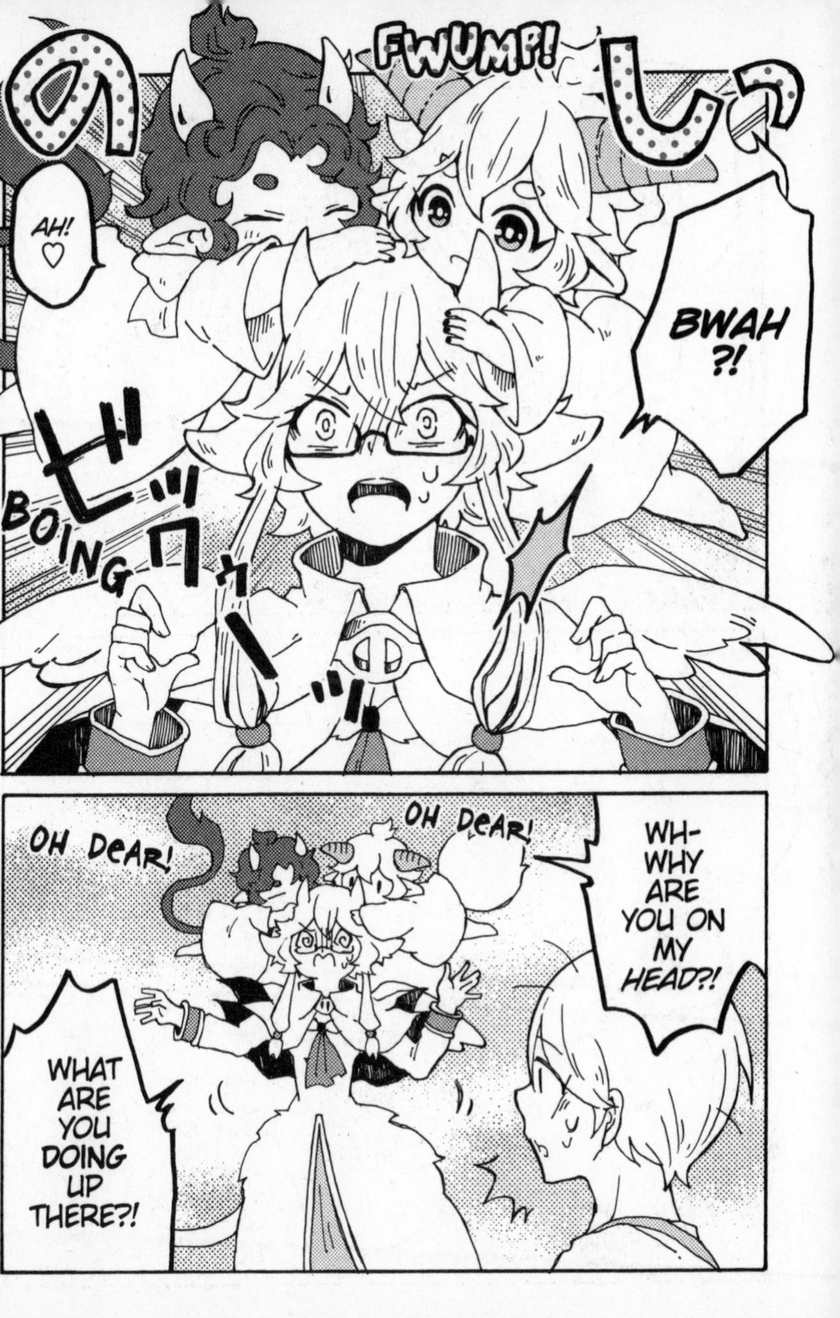
のしっ
FWUMP!
BWAH ?!
AH! ♡
ビクッ
BOING
WH- WHY ARE YOU ON MY HEAD?!
OH DEAR!
OH DEAR!
WHAT ARE YOU DOING UP THERE?!

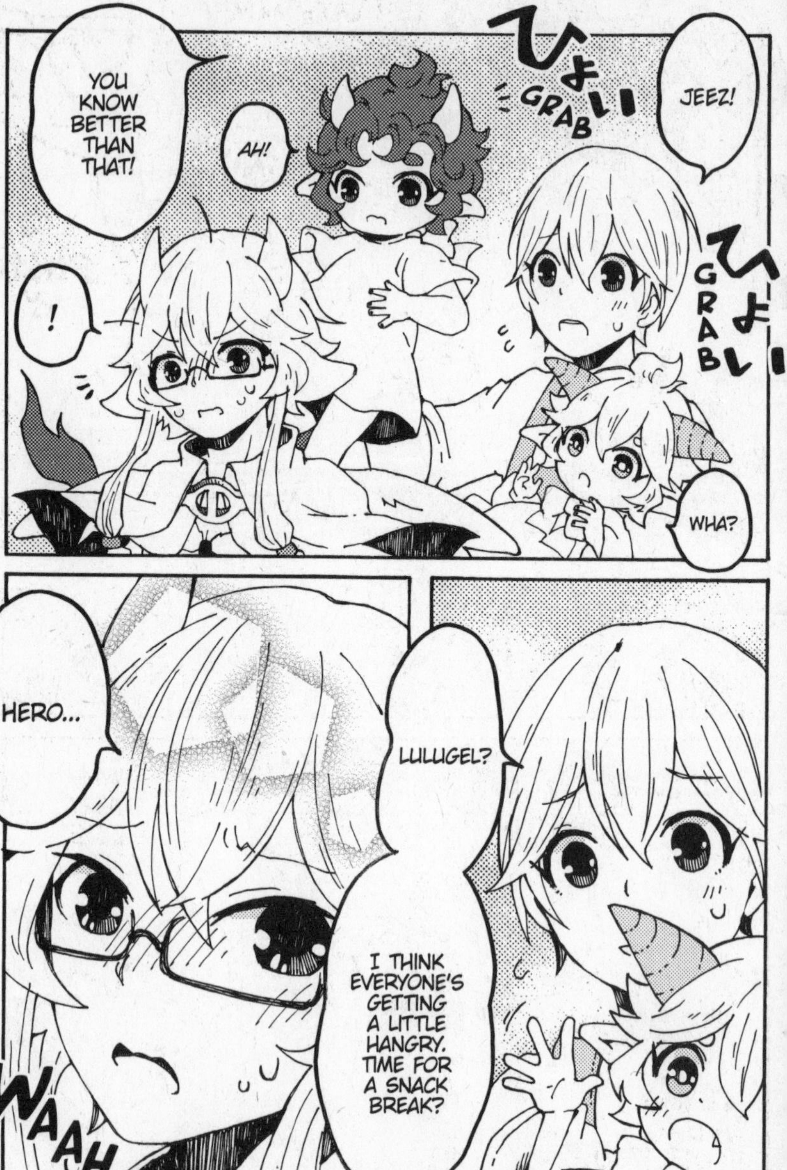

JEEZ!
ひょい GRAB
ひょい GRAB
YOU KNOW BETTER THAN THAT!
AH!
WHA?
!
LULUGEL?
I THINK EVERYONE'S GETTING A LITTLE HANGRY. TIME FOR A SNACK BREAK?
HERO...
WAAAH!

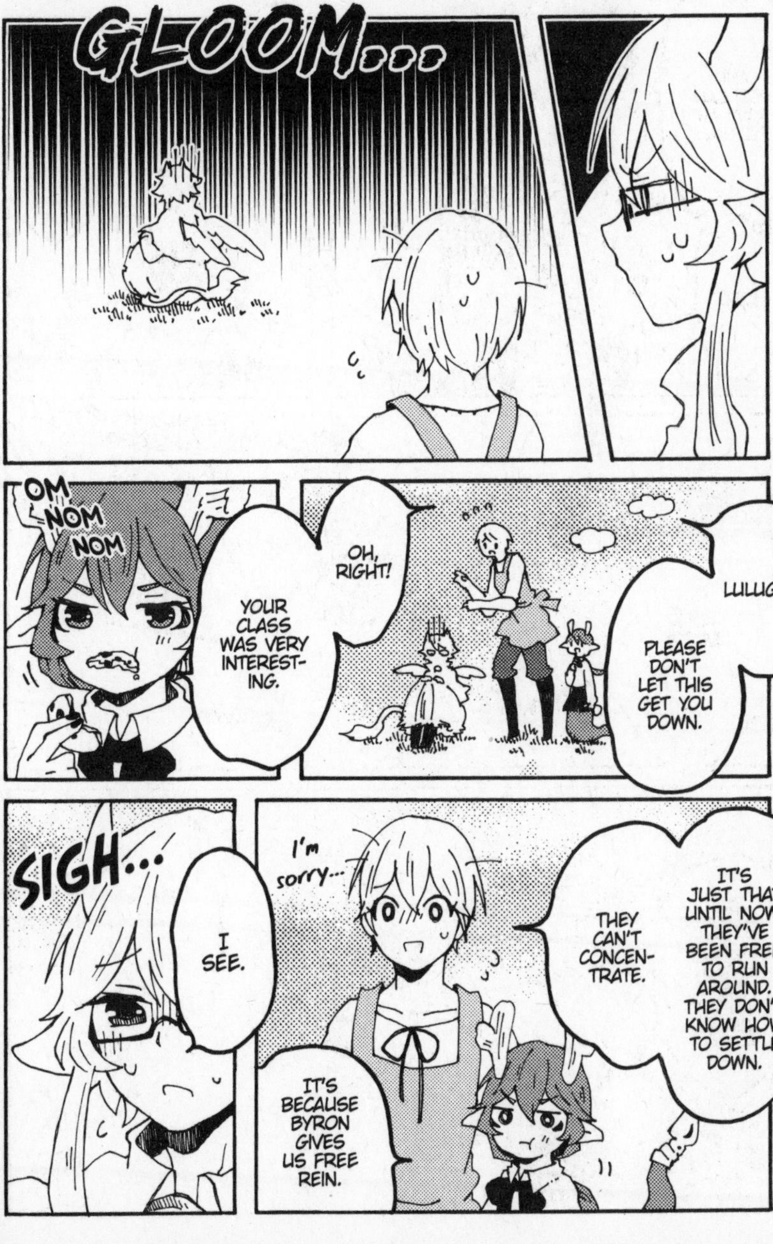
GLOOM...
LULUGEL?
PLEASE DON'T LET THIS GET YOU DOWN.
OH, RIGHT!
YOUR CLASS WAS VERY INTEREST-ING.
OM NOM NOM
IT'S JUST THAT UNTIL NOW, THEY'VE BEEN FREE TO RUN AROUND. THEY DON'T KNOW HOW TO SETTLE DOWN.
THEY CAN'T CONCEN-TRATE.
I'm sorry...
IT'S BECAUSE BYRON GIVES US FREE REIN.
SIGH...
I SEE.

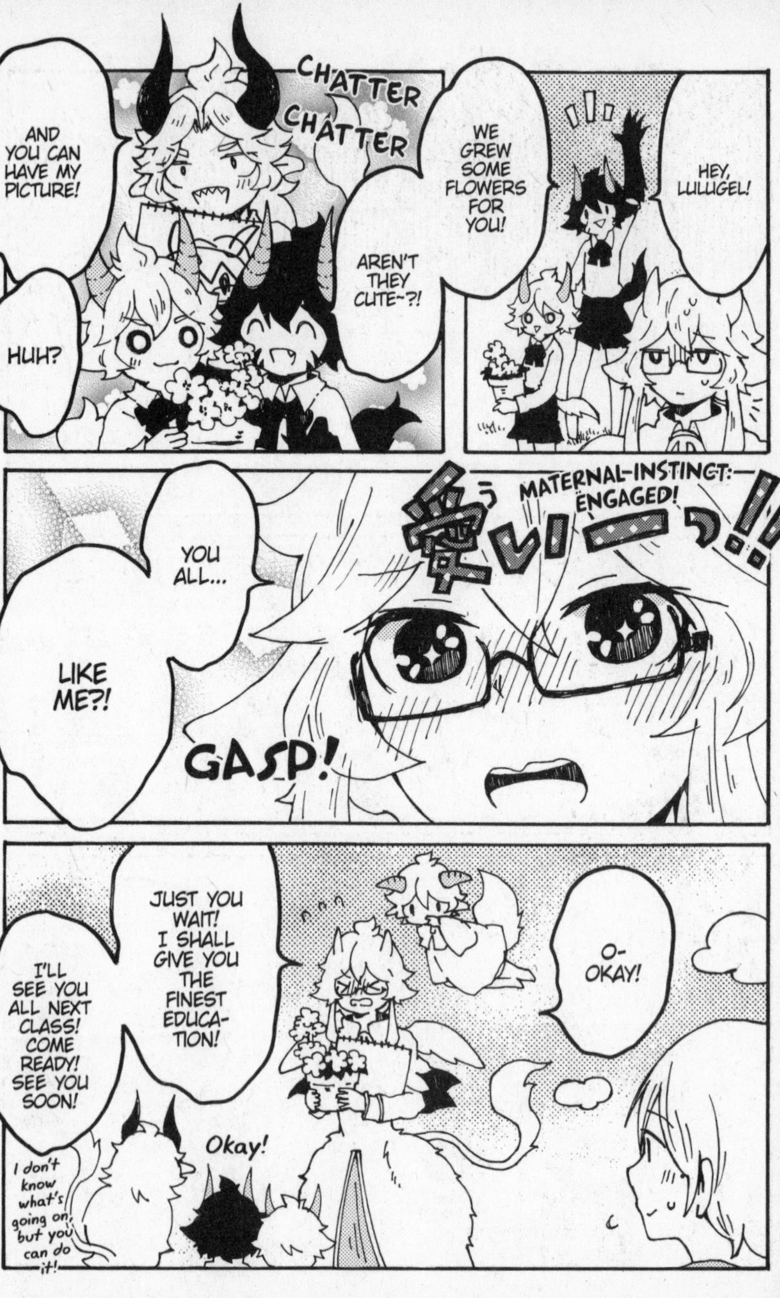
HEY, LULUGEL!
WE GREW SOME FLOWERS FOR YOU!
CHATTER CHATTER
AREN'T THEY CUTE~?!
AND YOU CAN HAVE MY PICTURE!
HUH?
愛い——っ!!!
MATERNAL-INSTINCT: ENGAGED!
YOU ALL...
LIKE ME?!
GASP!
O-OKAY!
JUST YOU WAIT! I SHALL GIVE YOU THE FINEST EDUCATION!
I'LL SEE YOU ALL NEXT CLASS! COME READY! SEE YOU SOON!
Okay!
I don't know what's going on, but you can do it!

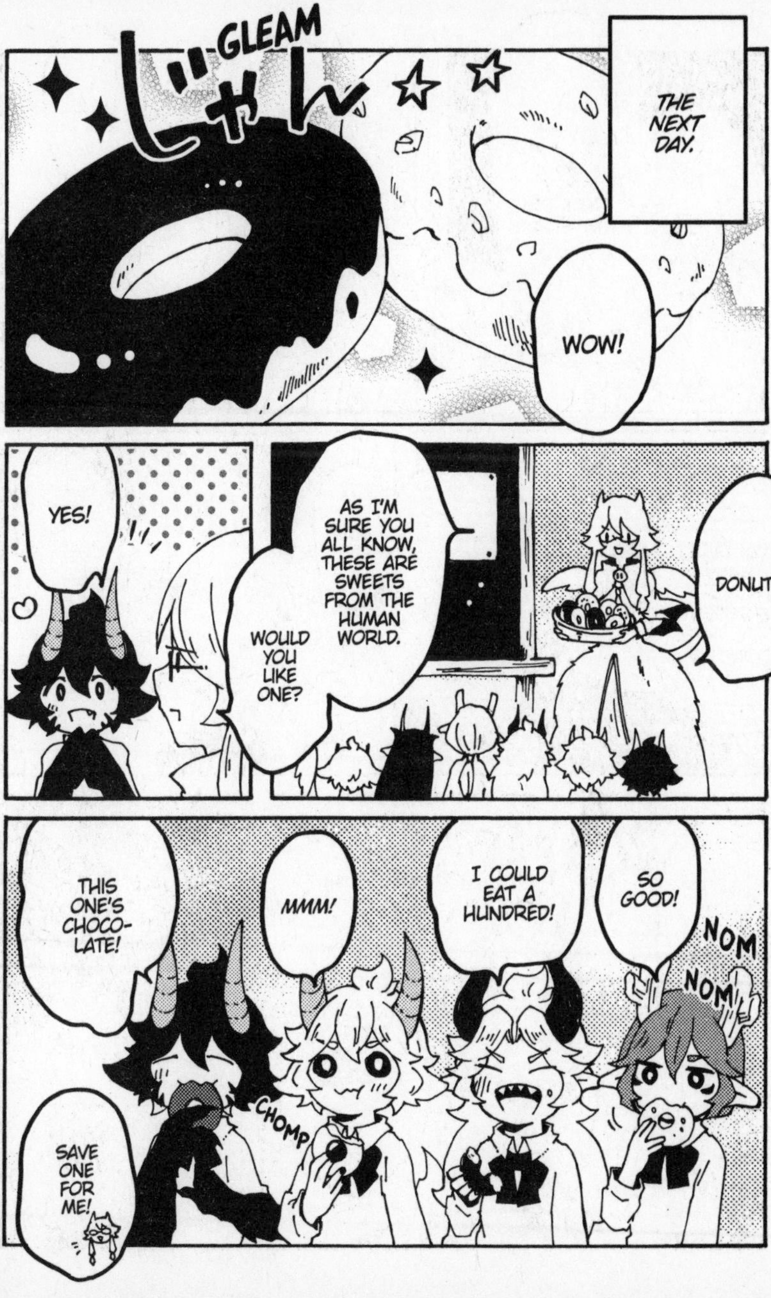
THE NEXT DAY.
WOW!
しゃん GLEAM
DONUTS!
AS I'M SURE YOU ALL KNOW, THESE ARE SWEETS FROM THE HUMAN WORLD.
WOULD YOU LIKE ONE?
YES!
NOM NOM
SO GOOD!
I COULD EAT A HUNDRED!
MMM!
CHOMP
THIS ONE'S CHOCO-LATE!
SAVE ONE FOR ME!

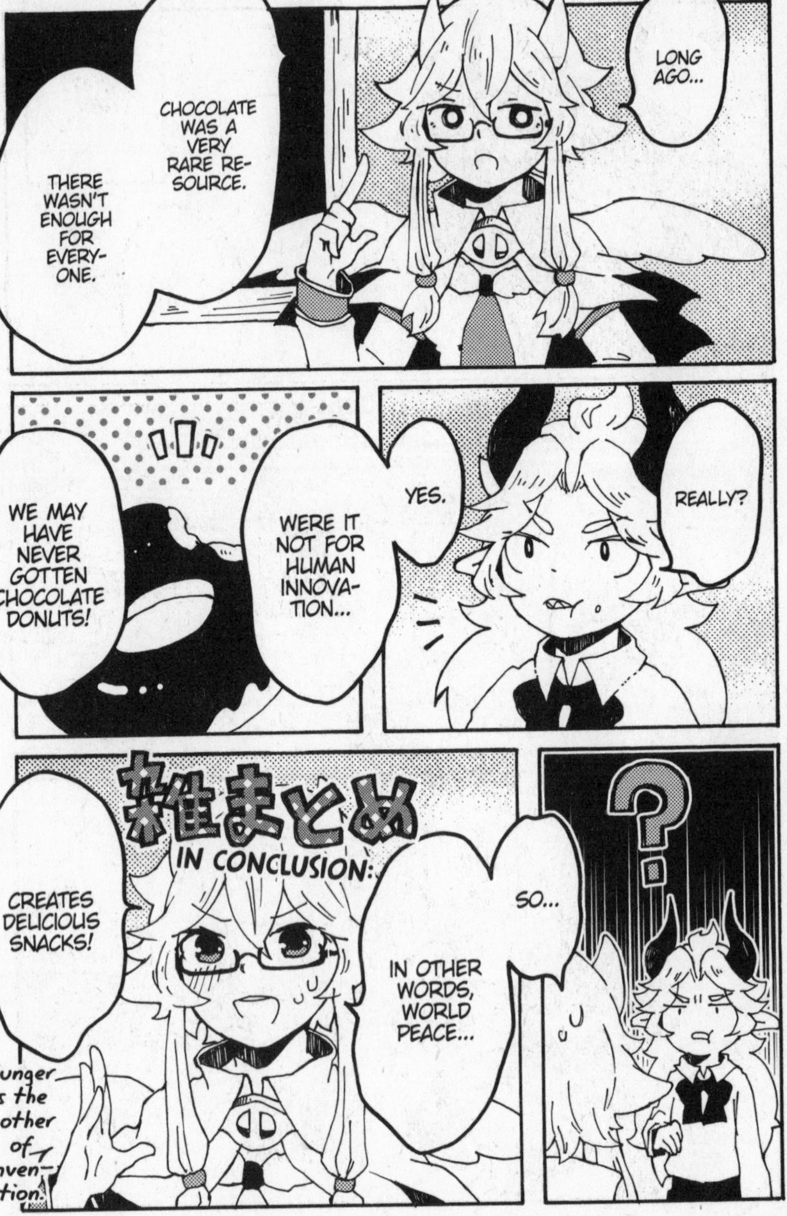
LONG AGO...
CHOCOLATE WAS A VERY RARE RESOURCE.
THERE WASN'T ENOUGH FOR EVERYONE.
REALLY?
YES.
WERE IT NOT FOR HUMAN INNOVATION...
WE MAY HAVE NEVER GOTTEN CHOCOLATE DONUTS!
?
雑まとめ
IN CONCLUSION:
SO...
IN OTHER WORDS, WORLD PEACE...
CREATES DELICIOUS SNACKS!
Hunger is the mother of invention.

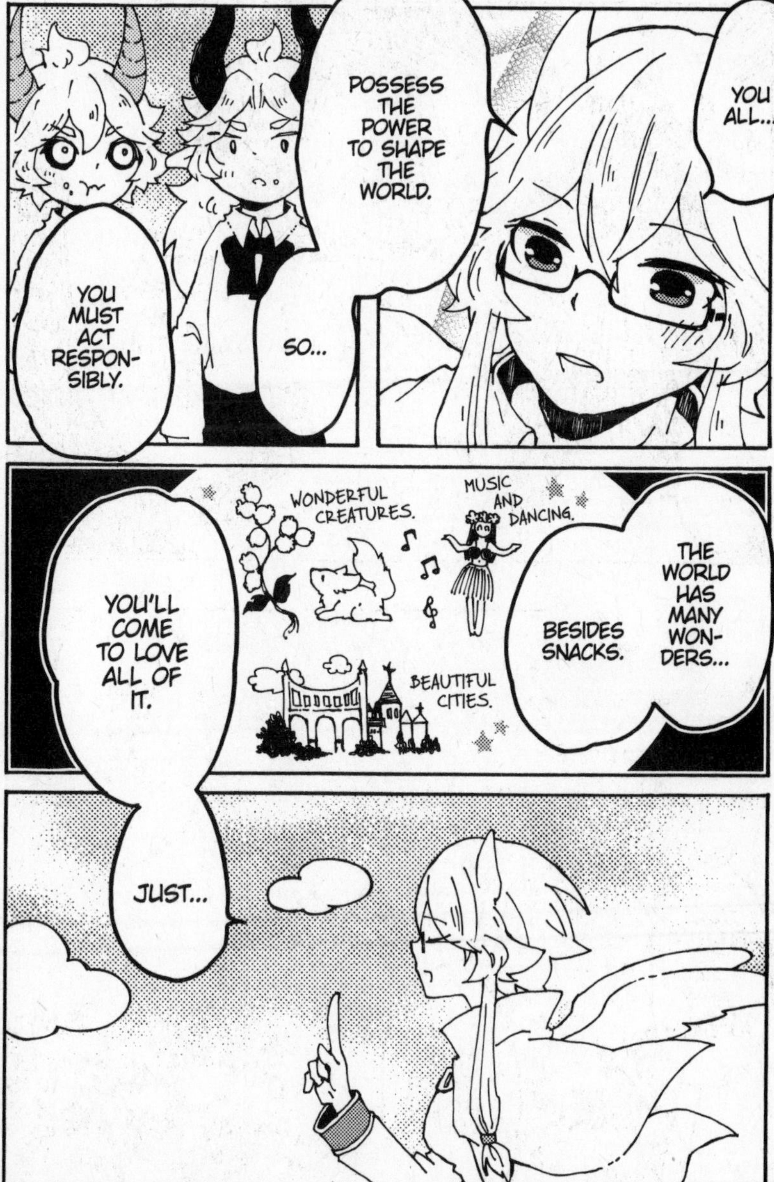
YOU ALL...
POSSESS THE POWER TO SHAPE THE WORLD.
SO...
YOU MUST ACT RESPON-SIBLY.
THE WORLD HAS MANY WON-DERS...
BESIDES SNACKS.
MUSIC AND DANCING.
WONDERFUL CREATURES.
BEAUTIFUL CITIES.
YOU'LL COME TO LOVE ALL OF IT.
JUST...

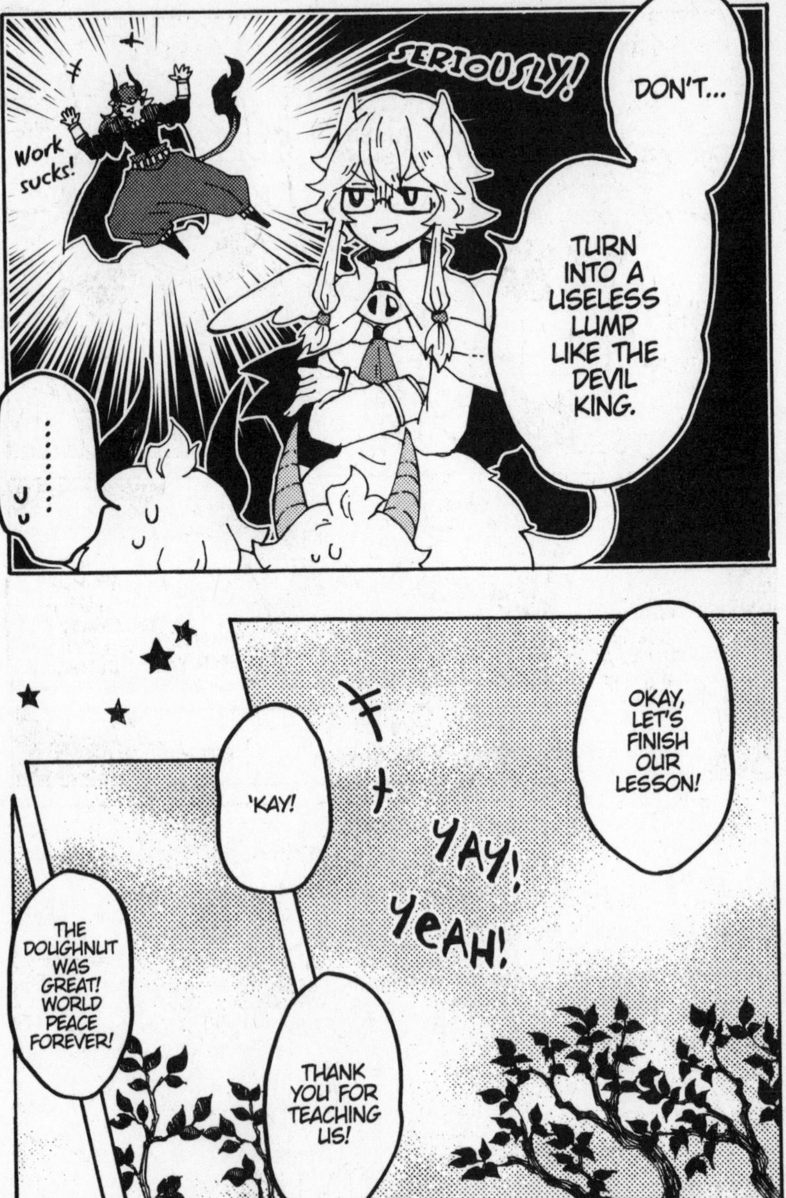
DON'T...
TURN INTO A USELESS LUMP LIKE THE DEVIL KING.
SERIOUSLY!
Work sucks!
......
OKAY, LET'S FINISH OUR LESSON!
YAY!
YEAH!
'KAY!
THANK YOU FOR TEACHING US!
THE DOUGHNUT WAS GREAT! WORLD PEACE FOREVER!

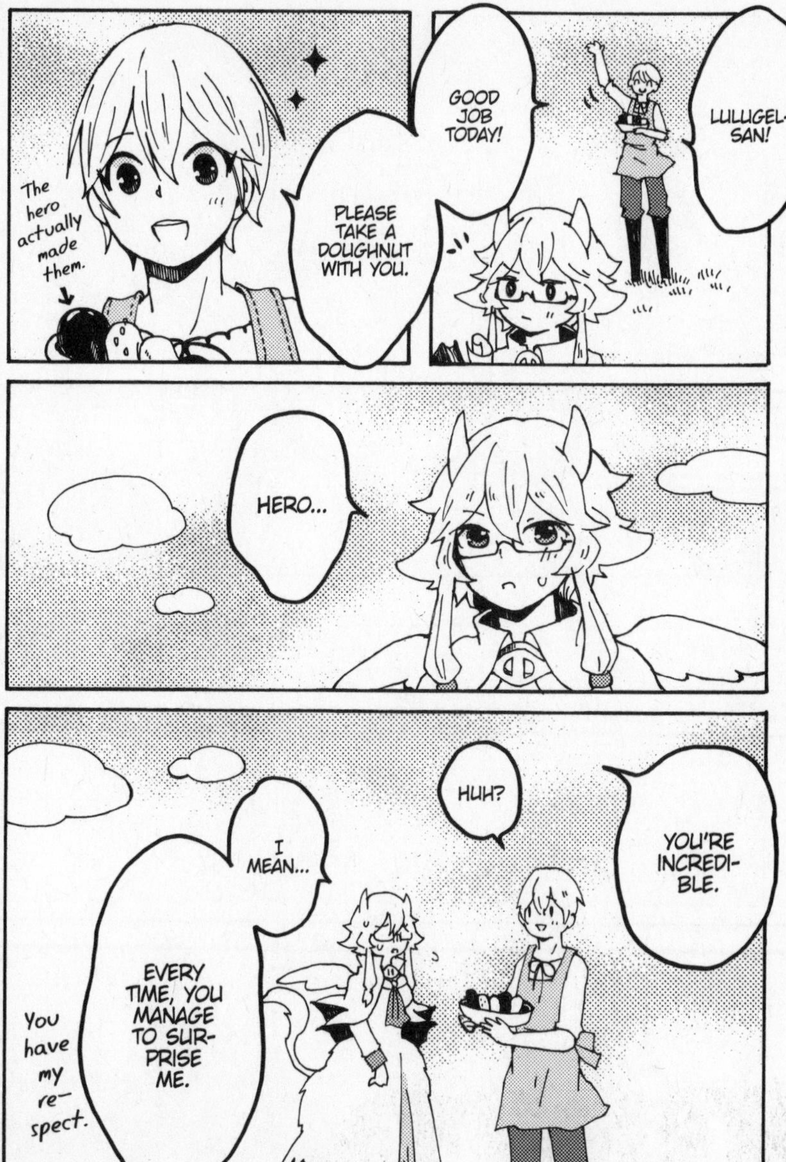
LULUGEL-SAN!
GOOD JOB TODAY!
PLEASE TAKE A DOUGHNUT WITH YOU.
The hero actually made them.
HERO...
YOU'RE INCREDIBLE.
HUH?
I MEAN...
EVERY TIME, YOU MANAGE TO SURPRISE ME.
You have my respect.

LITTLE DEVILS

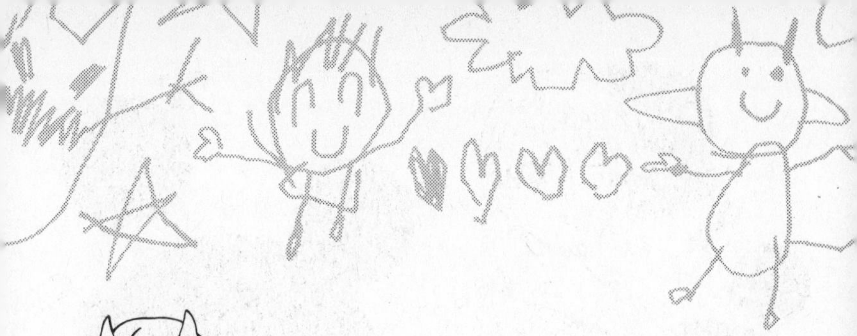

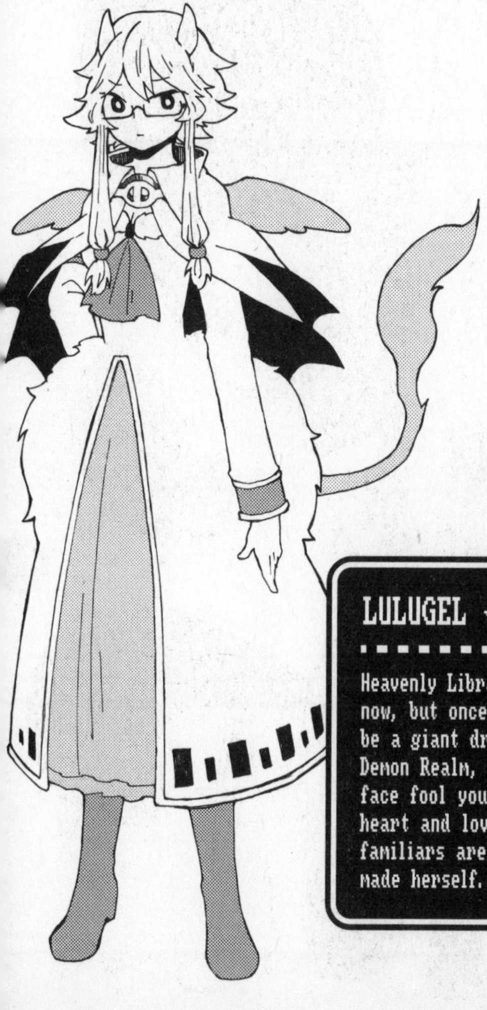

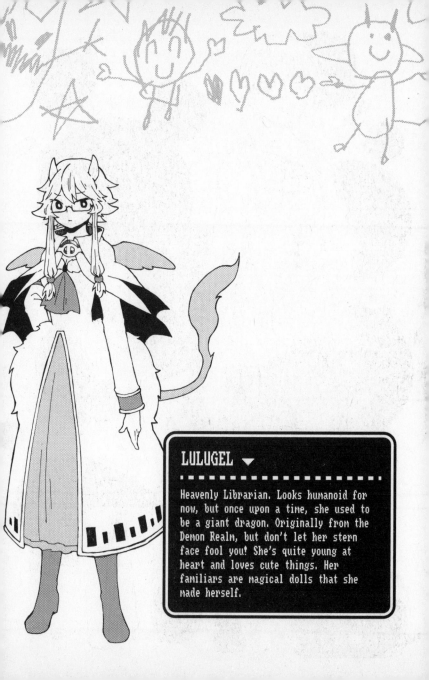

LULUGEL ▼

Heavenly Librarian. Looks humanoid for now, but once upon a time, she used to be a giant dragon. Originally from the Demon Realm, but don't let her stern face fool you! She's quite young at heart and loves cute things. Her familiars are magical dolls that she made herself.

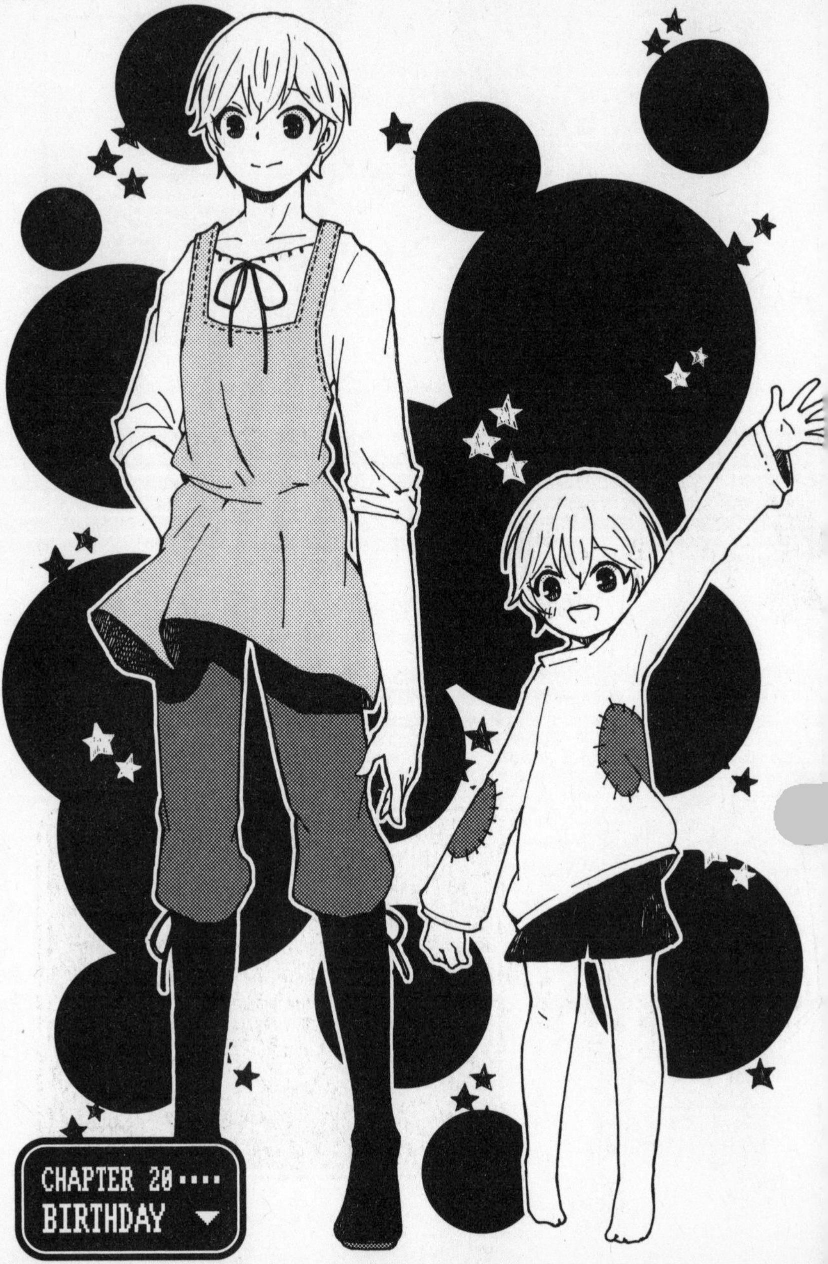
CHAPTER 20 ....
BIRTHDAY

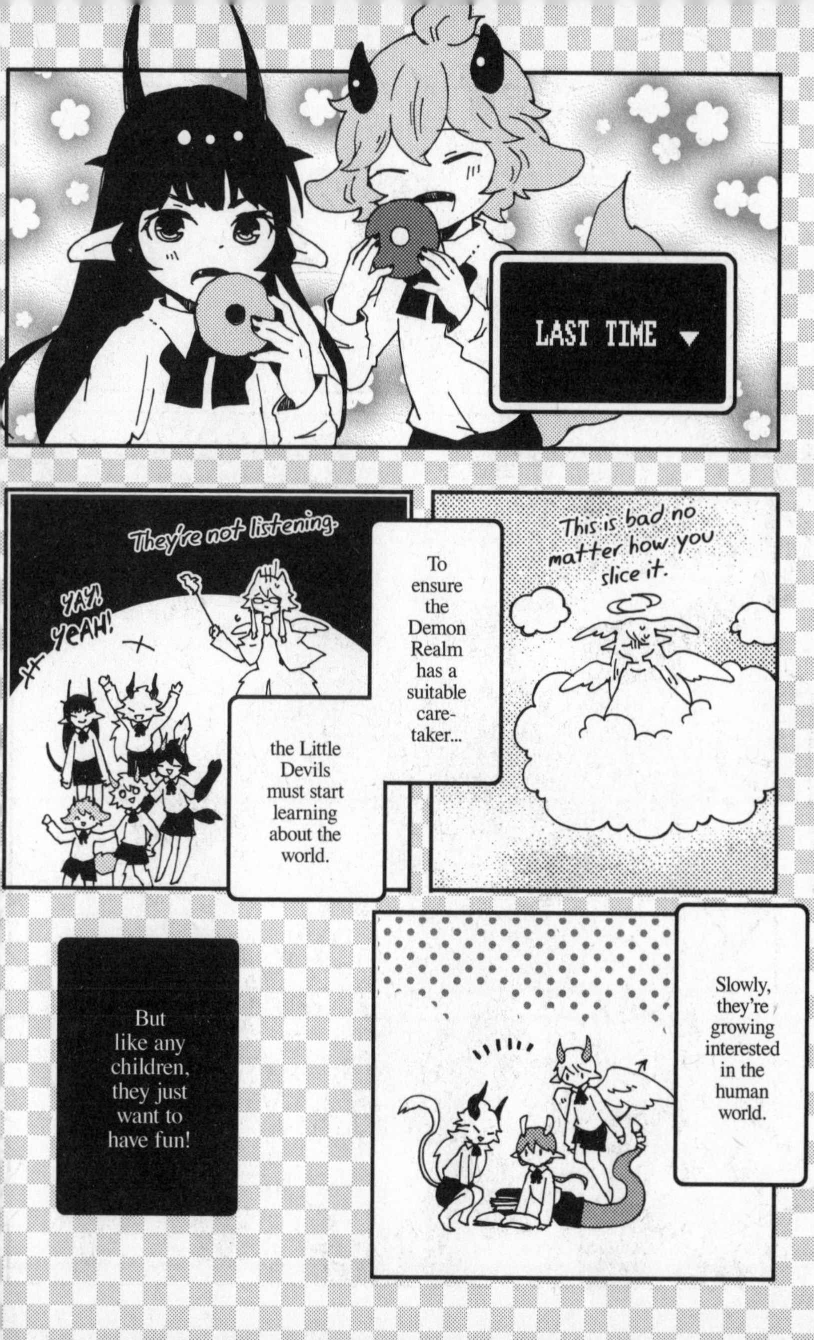
LAST TIME ▼
This is bad no matter how you slice it.
To ensure the Demon Realm has a suitable caretaker...
They're not listening.
YAY! YEAH!
the Little Devils must start learning about the world.
Slowly, they're growing interested in the human world.
But like any children, they just want to have fun!

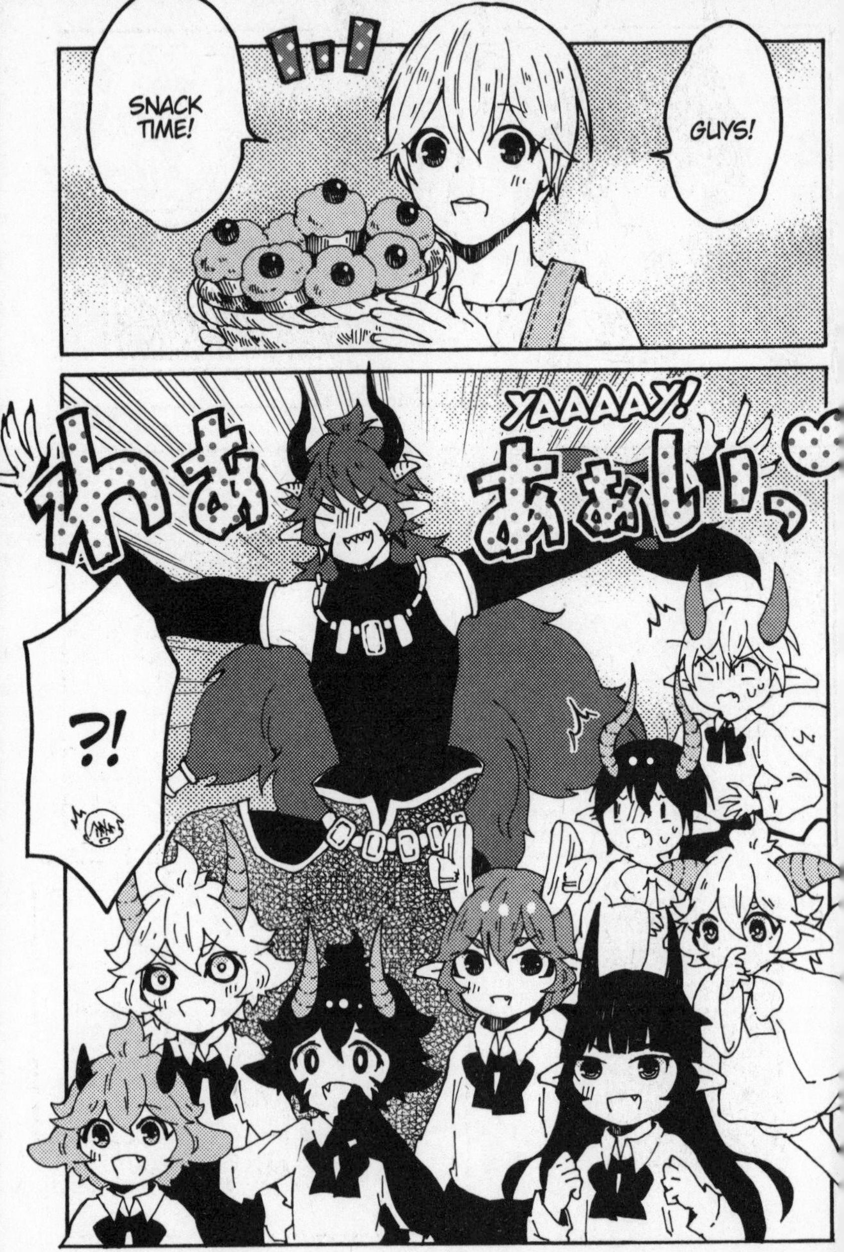
GUYS!
SNACK TIME!
YAAAAY!
?!

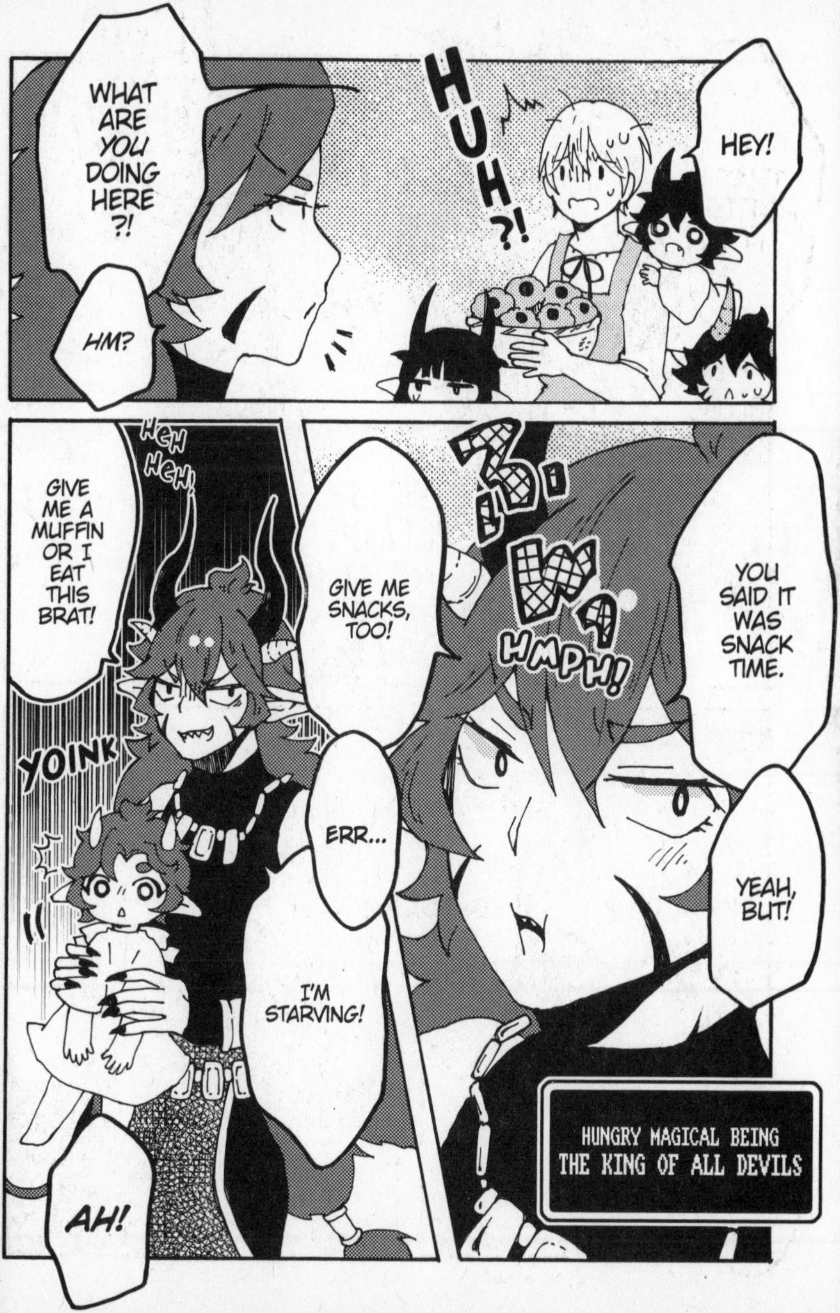
HEY!
HUH?!
WHAT ARE YOU DOING HERE?!
HM?
YOU SAID IT WAS SNACK TIME.
HMPH!
GIVE ME SNACKS, TOO!
YEAH, BUT!
ERR...
I'M STARVING!
HUNGRY MAGICAL BEING THE KING OF ALL DEVILS
HEH HEH!
GIVE ME A MUFFIN OR I EAT THIS BRAT!
YOINK
AH!

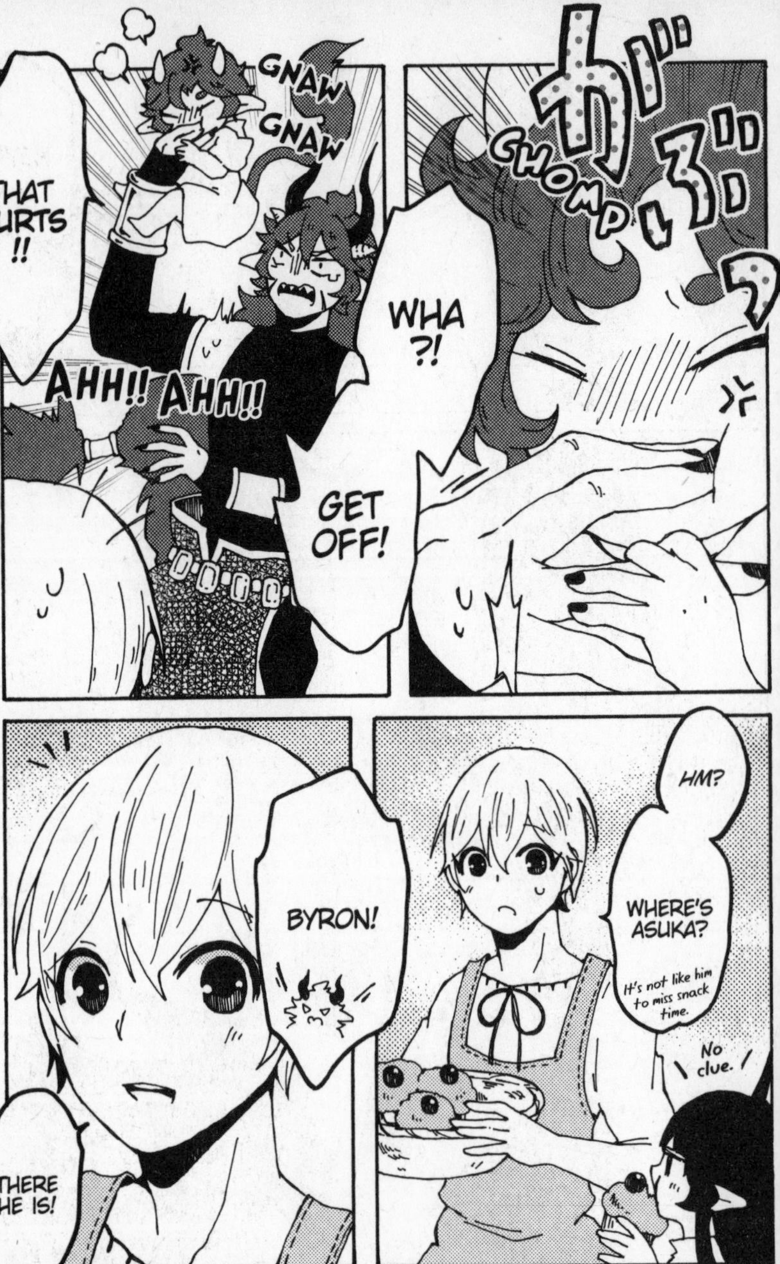
がぶっ
CHOMP
WHA ?!
GET OFF!
GNAW GNAW
THAT HURTS !!
AHH!! AHH!!
HM?
WHERE'S ASUKA?
It's not like him to miss snack time.
No clue.
BYRON!
THERE HE IS!

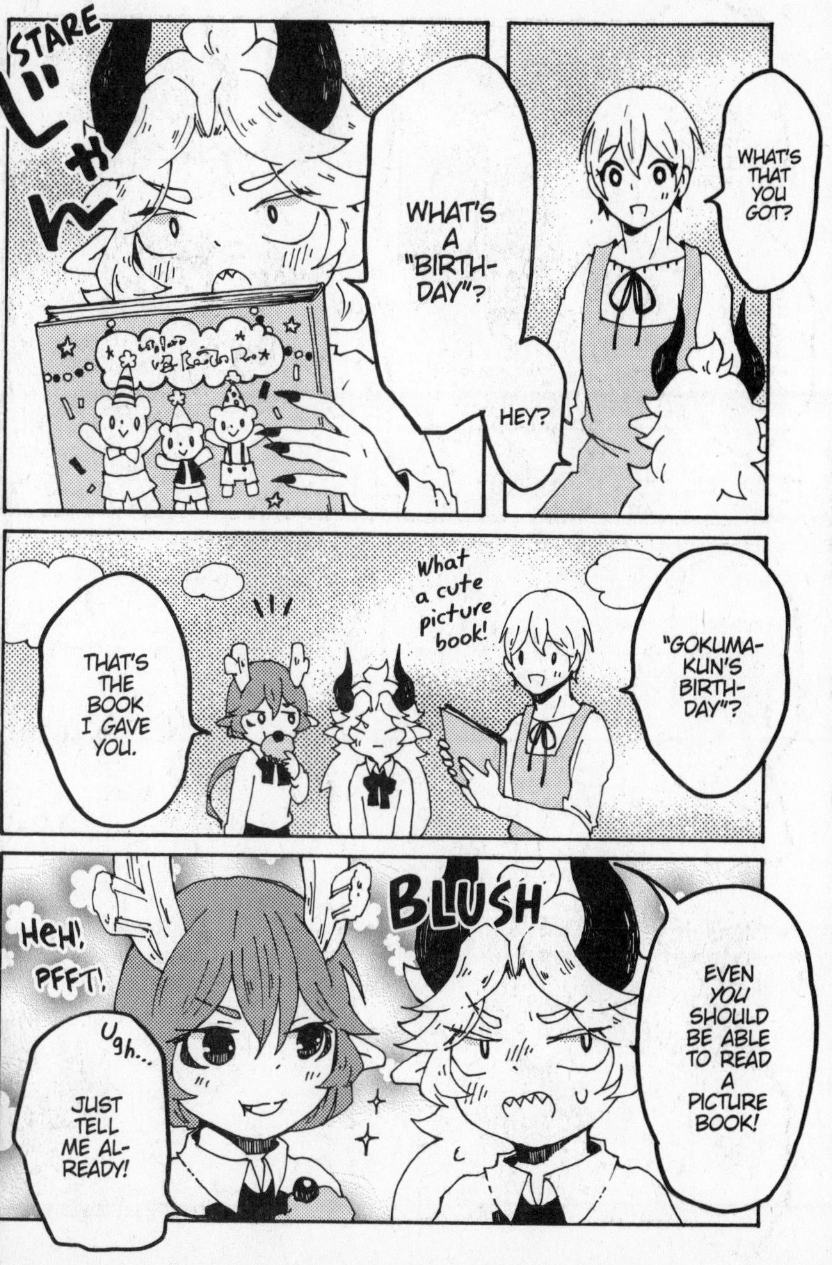
WHAT'S THAT YOU GOT?
STARE
WHAT'S A "BIRTH-DAY"?
HEY?
"GOKUMA-KUN'S BIRTH-DAY"?
What a cute picture book!
THAT'S THE BOOK I GAVE YOU.
EVEN YOU SHOULD BE ABLE TO READ A PICTURE BOOK!
BLUSH
HeH! PFFT!
Ugh...
JUST TELL ME AL-READY!

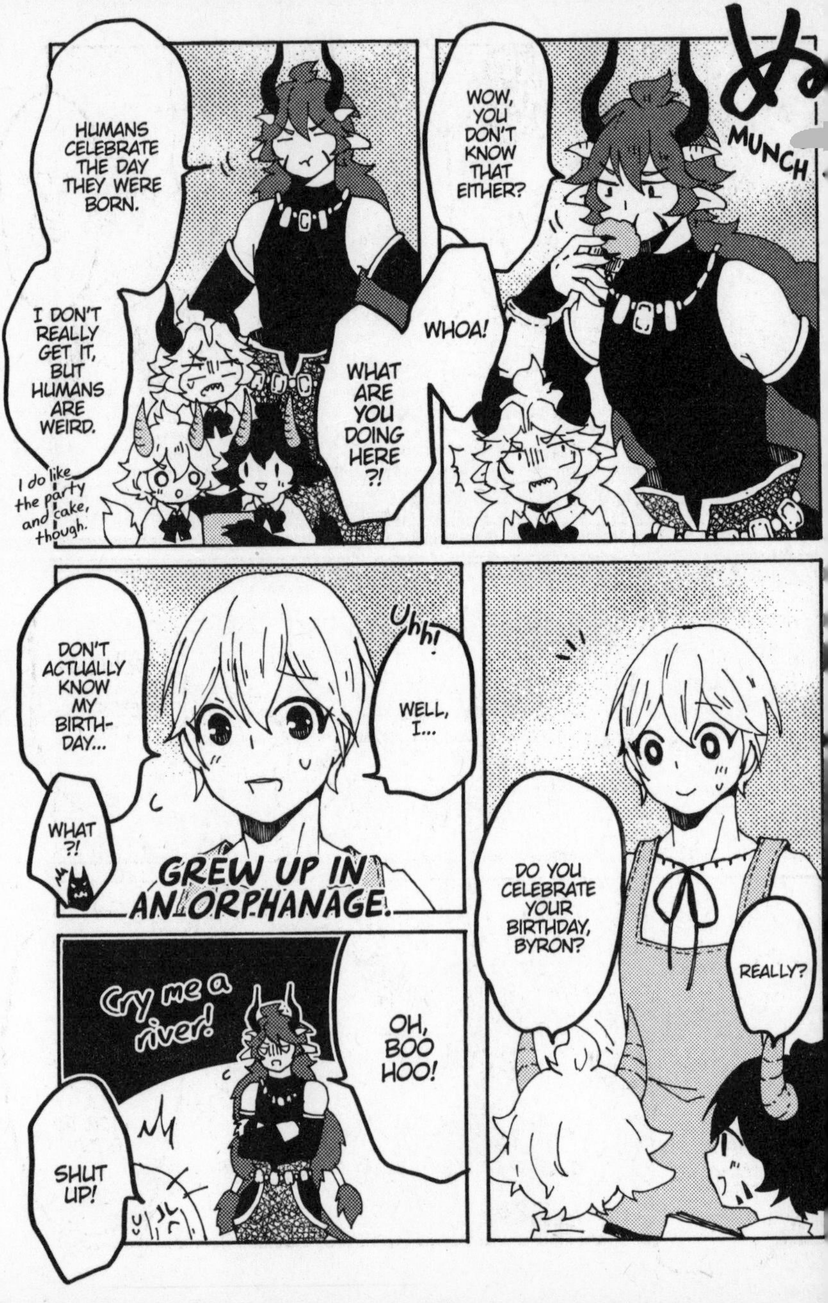
WOW, YOU DON'T KNOW THAT EITHER?
MUNCH
WHOA!
WHAT ARE YOU DOING HERE?!
HUMANS CELEBRATE THE DAY THEY WERE BORN.
I DON'T REALLY GET IT, BUT HUMANS ARE WEIRD.
I do like the party and cake, though.
DO YOU CELEBRATE YOUR BIRTHDAY, BYRON?
REALLY?
Uhh!
WELL, I...
GREW UP IN AN ORPHANAGE.
DON'T ACTUALLY KNOW MY BIRTH-DAY...
WHAT?!
OH, BOO HOO!
Cry me a river!
SHUT UP!

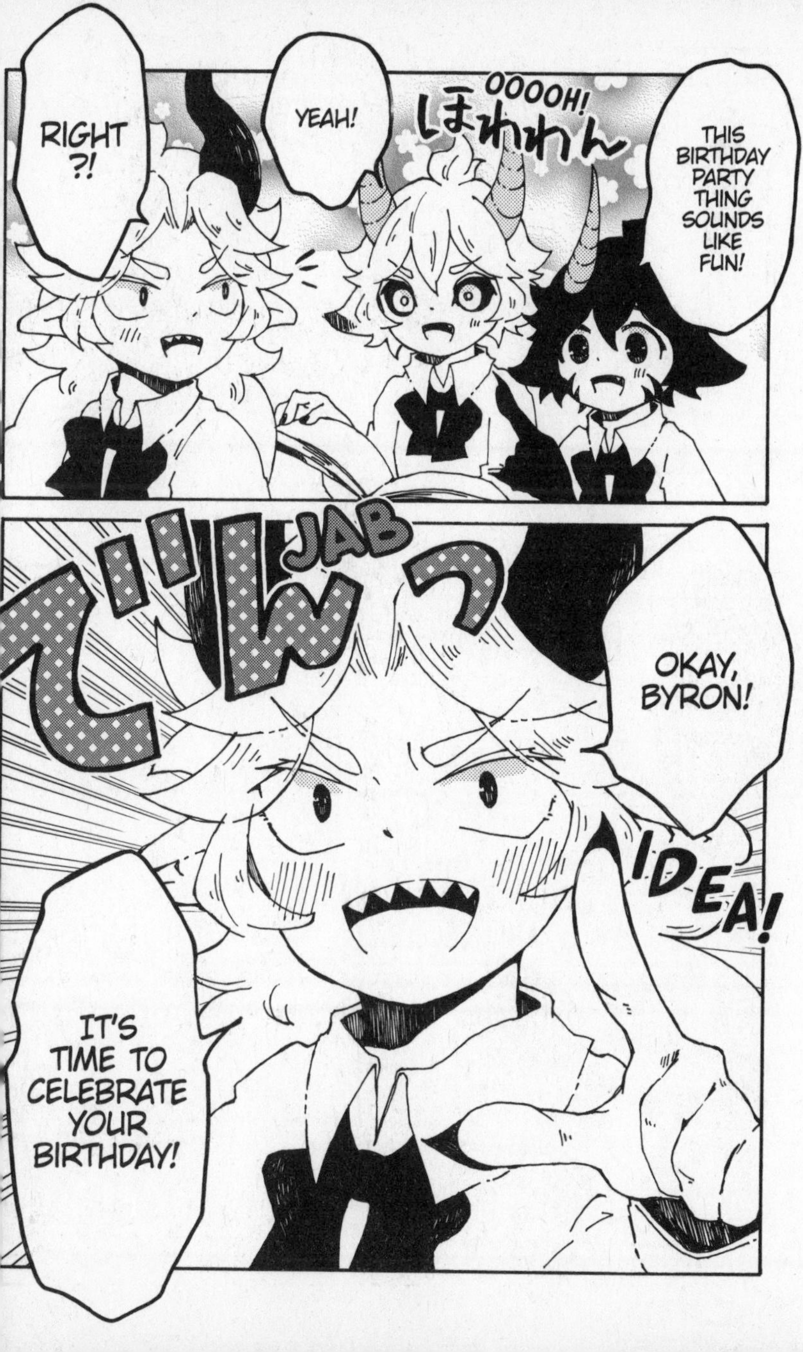
THIS BIRTHDAY PARTY THING SOUNDS LIKE FUN!
OOOOH!
ほわわん
YEAH!
RIGHT ?!
OKAY, BYRON!
JAB
でんっ
IDEA!
IT'S TIME TO CELEBRATE YOUR BIRTHDAY!

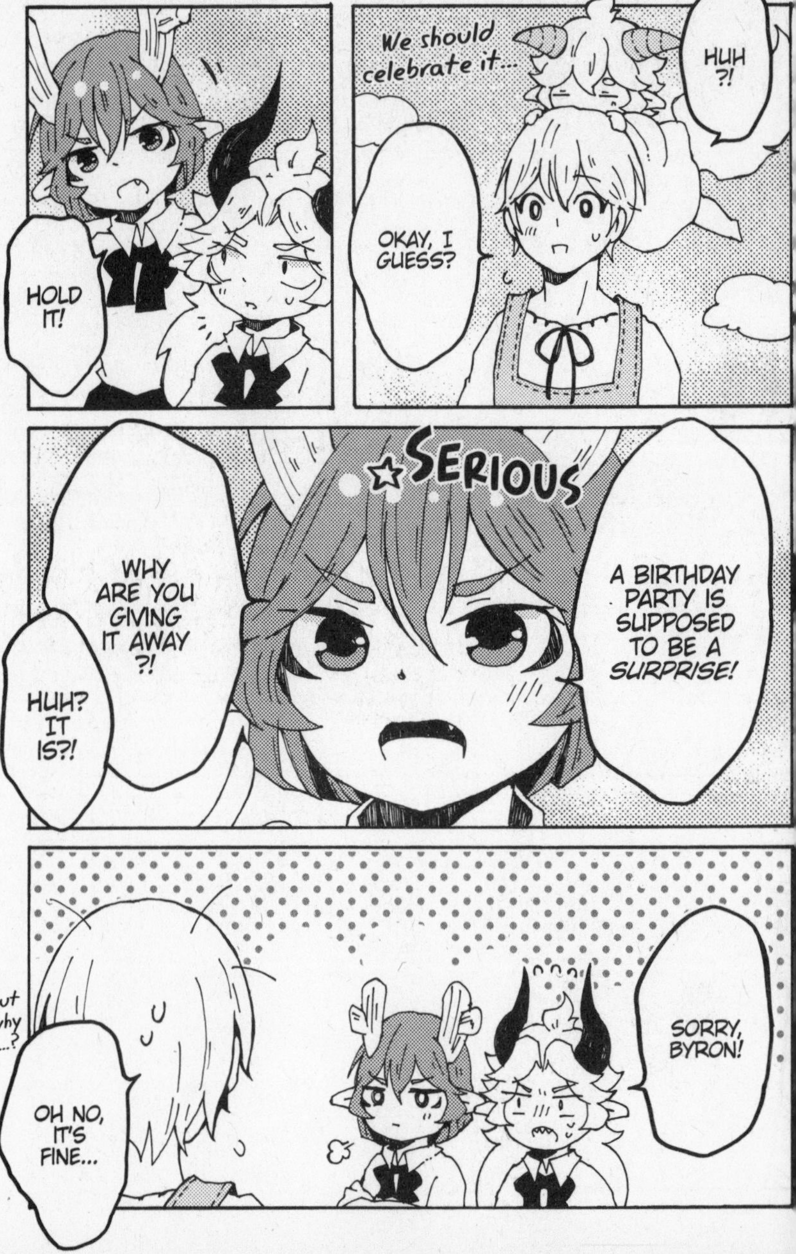
HUH ?!
We should celebrate it...
OKAY, I GUESS?
HOLD IT!
SERIOUS
A BIRTHDAY PARTY IS SUPPOSED TO BE A SURPRISE!
WHY ARE YOU GIVING IT AWAY ?!
HUH? IT IS?!
SORRY, BYRON!
But why...?
OH NO, IT'S FINE...

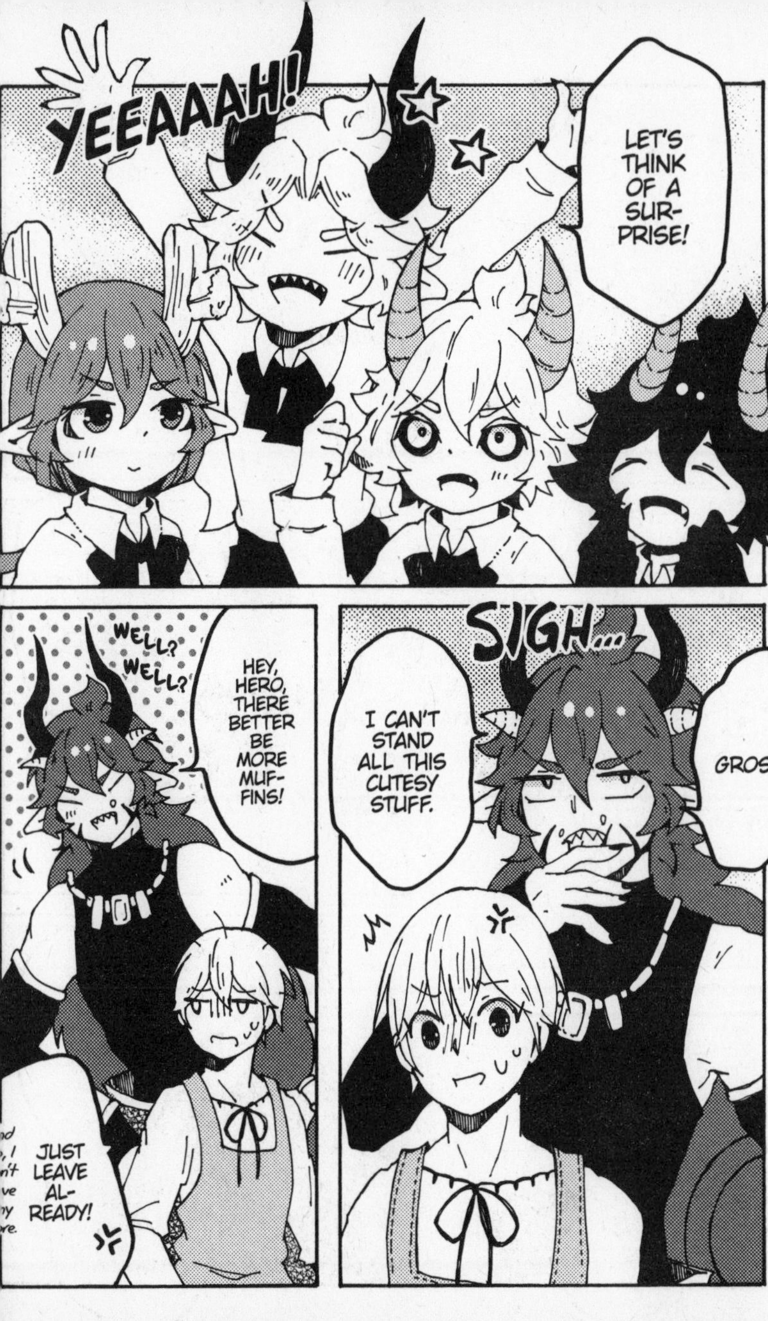
LET'S THINK OF A SUR-PRISE!
YEEAAAH!
SIGH...
GROSS.
I CAN'T STAND ALL THIS CUTESY STUFF.
HEY, HERO, THERE BETTER BE MORE MUF-FINS!
WELL? WELL?
JUST LEAVE AL-READY!

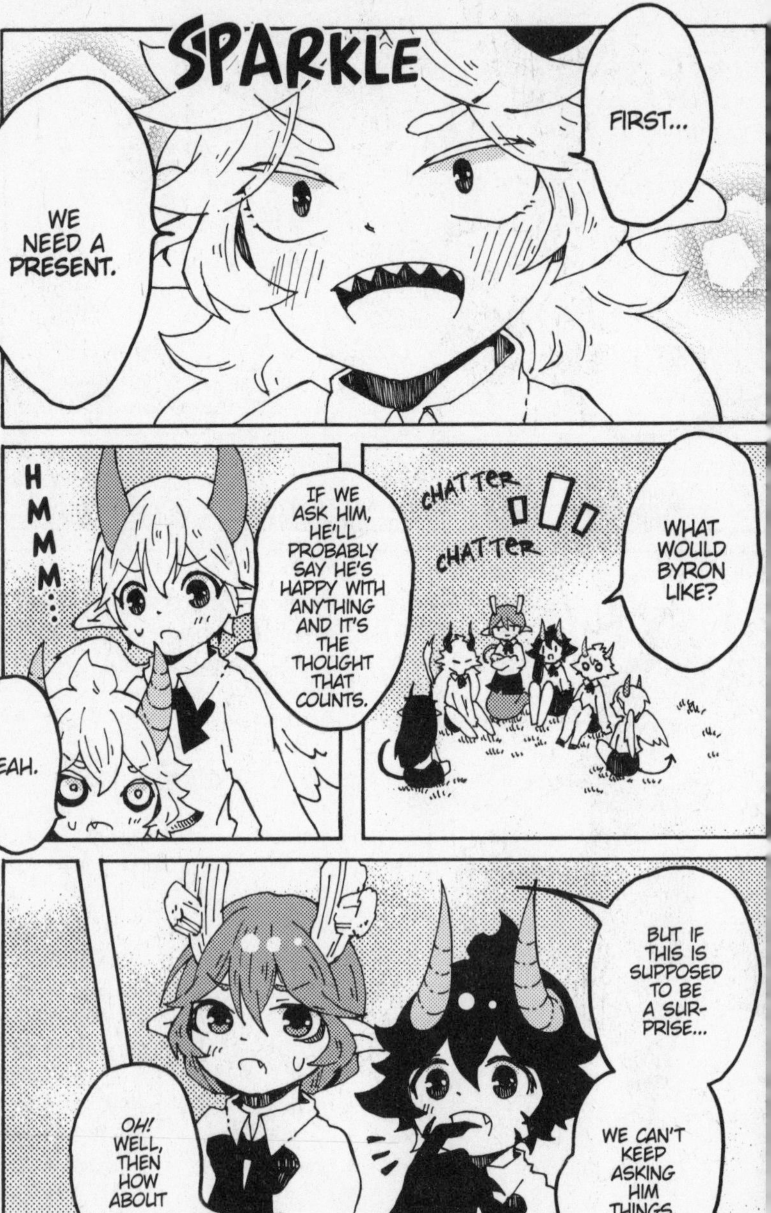
SPARKLE
FIRST...
WE NEED A PRESENT.
WHAT WOULD BYRON LIKE?
CHATTER CHATTER
IF WE ASK HIM, HE'LL PROBABLY SAY HE'S HAPPY WITH ANYTHING AND IT'S THE THOUGHT THAT COUNTS.
HMMM...
YEAH.
BUT IF THIS IS SUPPOSED TO BE A SUR-PRISE...
WE CAN'T KEEP ASKING HIM THINGS.
OH! WELL, THEN HOW ABOUT ...

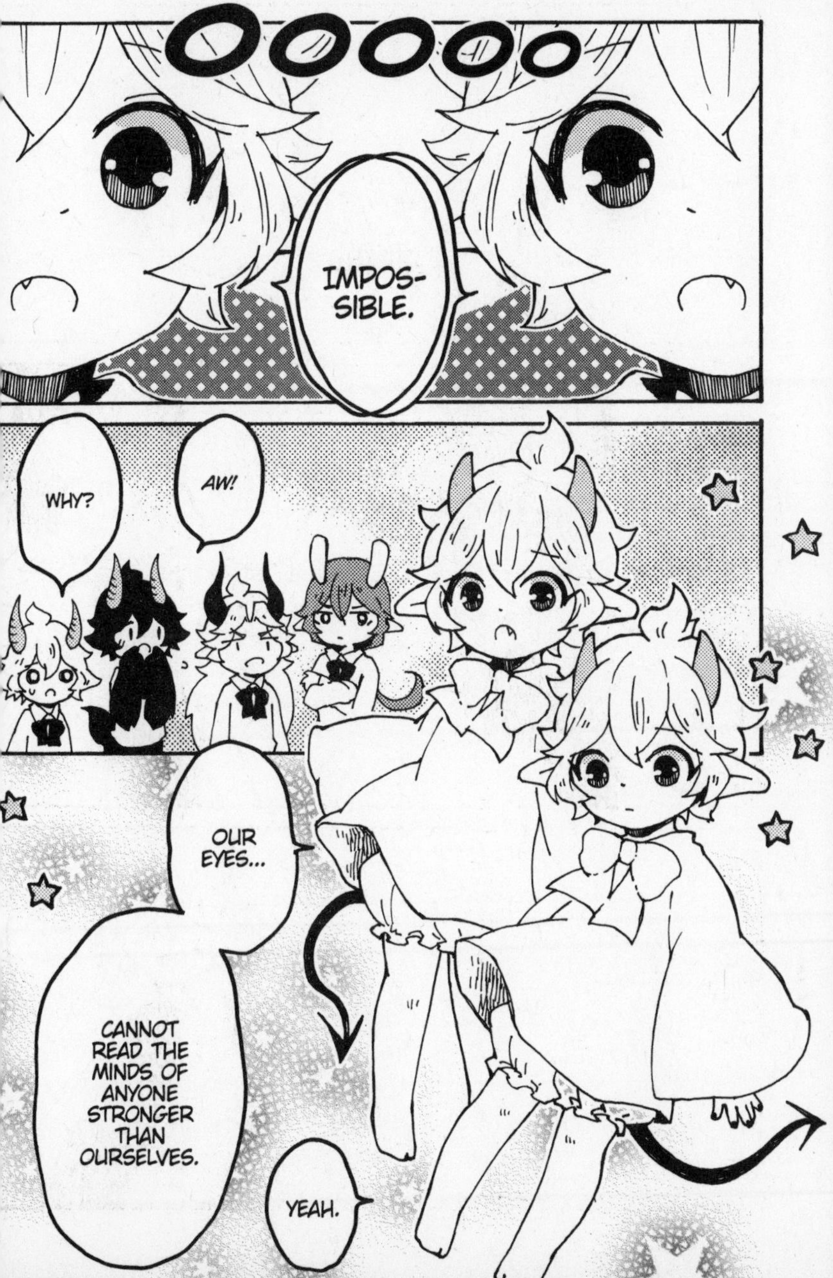
OOOOO
IMPOS-SIBLE.
AW!
WHY?
OUR EYES...
CANNOT READ THE MINDS OF ANYONE STRONGER THAN OURSELVES.
YEAH.

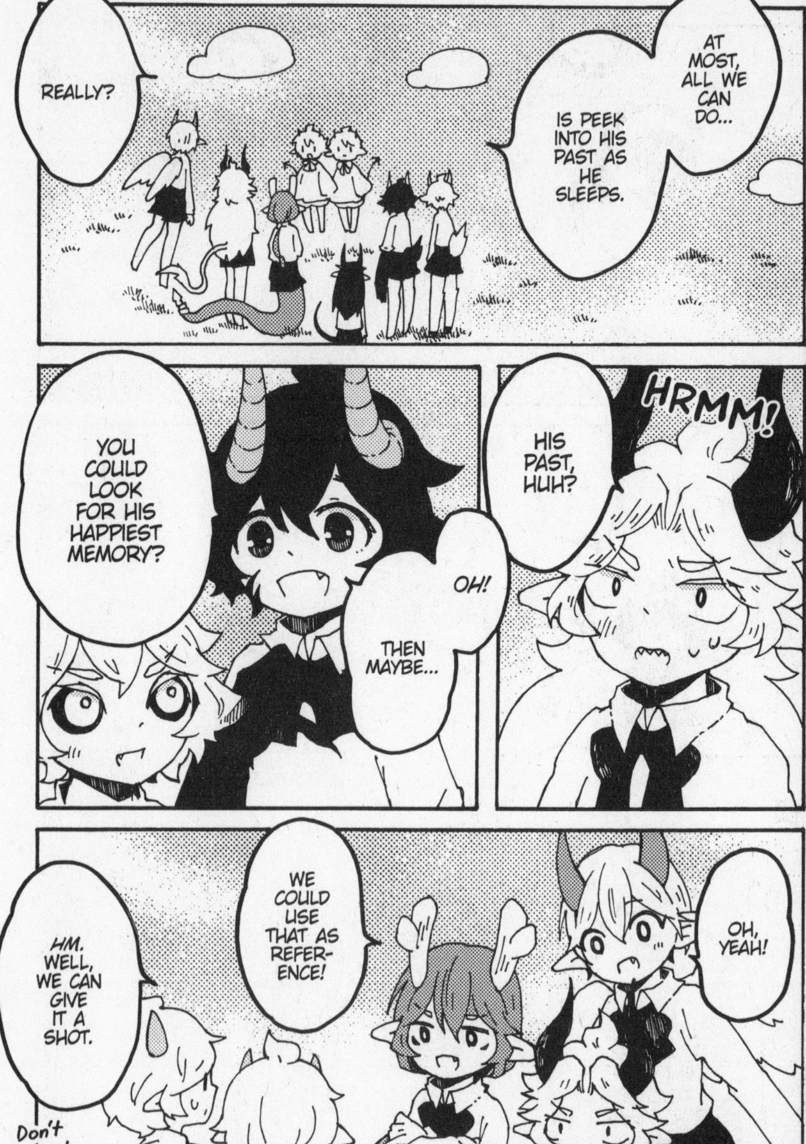
AT MOST, ALL WE CAN DO...
IS PEEK INTO HIS PAST AS HE SLEEPS.
REALLY?
HRMM!
HIS PAST, HUH?
OH!
THEN MAYBE...
YOU COULD LOOK FOR HIS HAPPIEST MEMORY?
OH, YEAH!
WE COULD USE THAT AS REFER-ENCE!
HM. WELL, WE CAN GIVE IT A SHOT.
Don't expect anything.

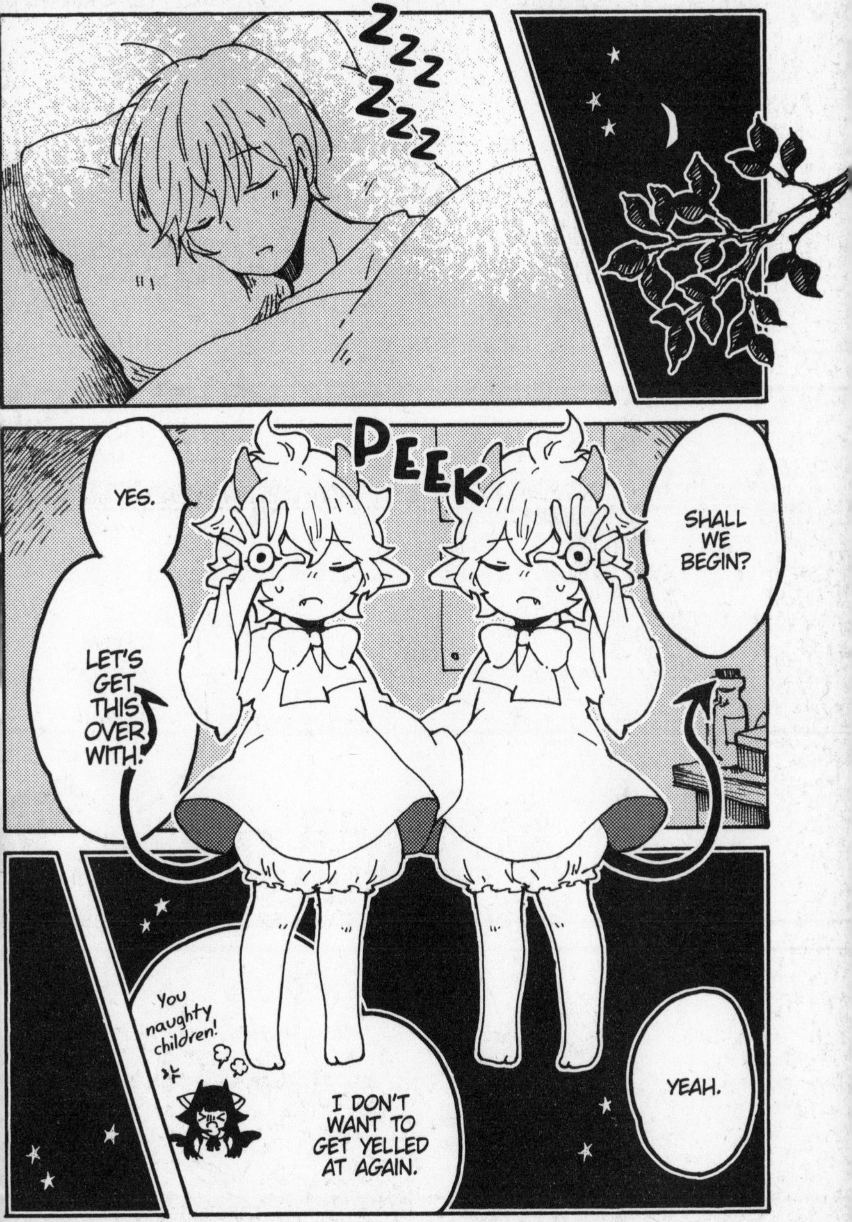
ZZZ
ZZZ
PEEK
SHALL WE BEGIN?
YES.
LET'S GET THIS OVER WITH!
YEAH.
I DON'T WANT TO GET YELLED AT AGAIN.
You naughty children!

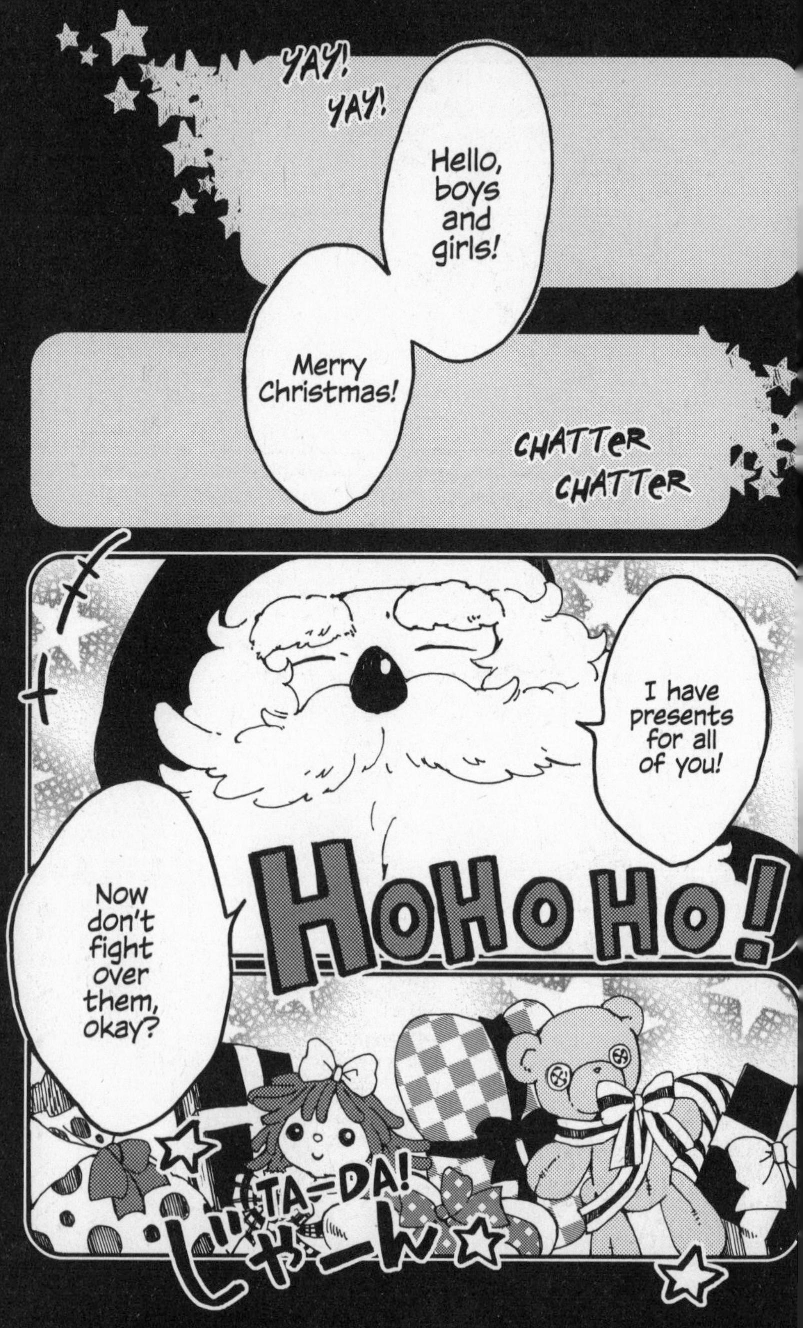
YAY!
YAY!
Hello, boys and girls!
Merry Christmas!
CHATTER
CHATTER
I have presents for all of you!
HOHOHO!
Now don't fight over them, okay?
TA-DA!
じゃーん

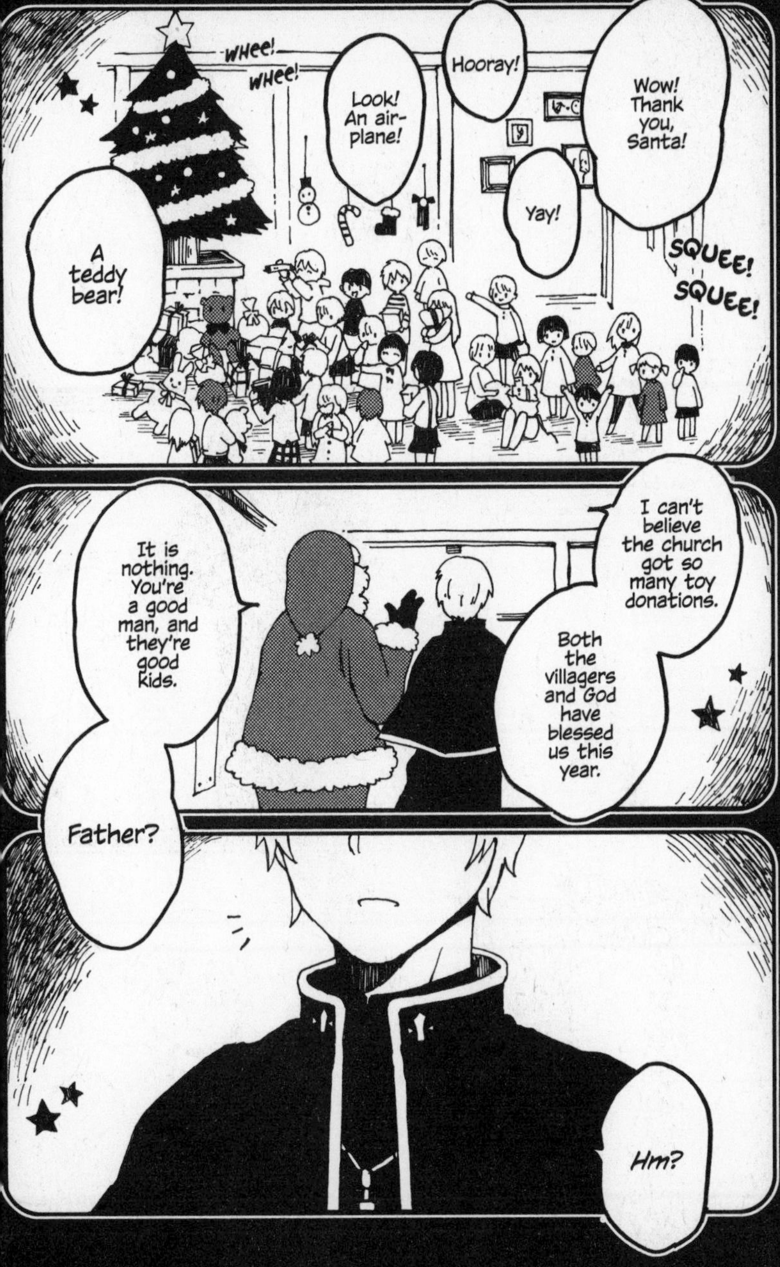
Wow! Thank you, Santa!
SQUEE! SQUEE!
Hooray!
Yay!
Look! An air-plane!
WHEE! WHEE!
A teddy bear!
I can't believe the church got so many toy donations.
Both the villagers and God have blessed us this year.
It is nothing. You're a good man, and they're good kids.
Father?
Hm?

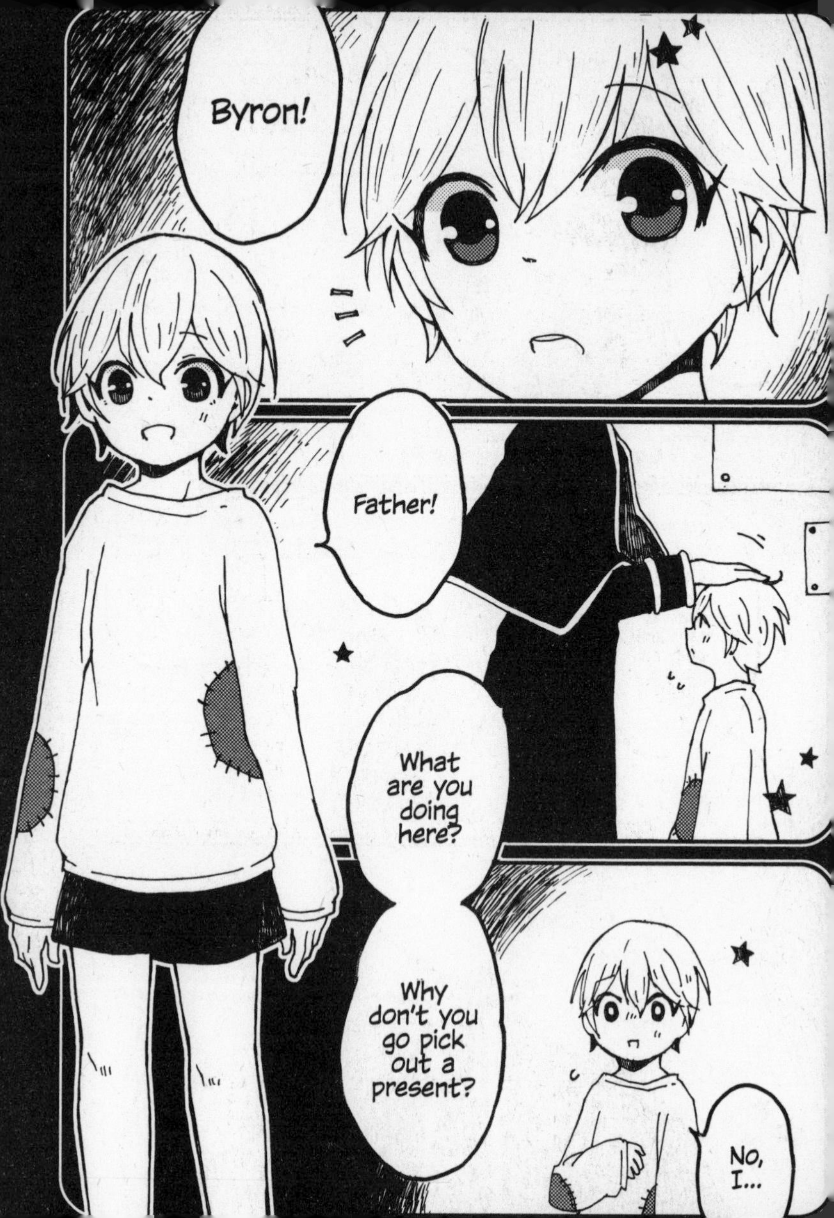
Byron!
Father!
What are you doing here?
Why don't you go pick out a present?
No, I...

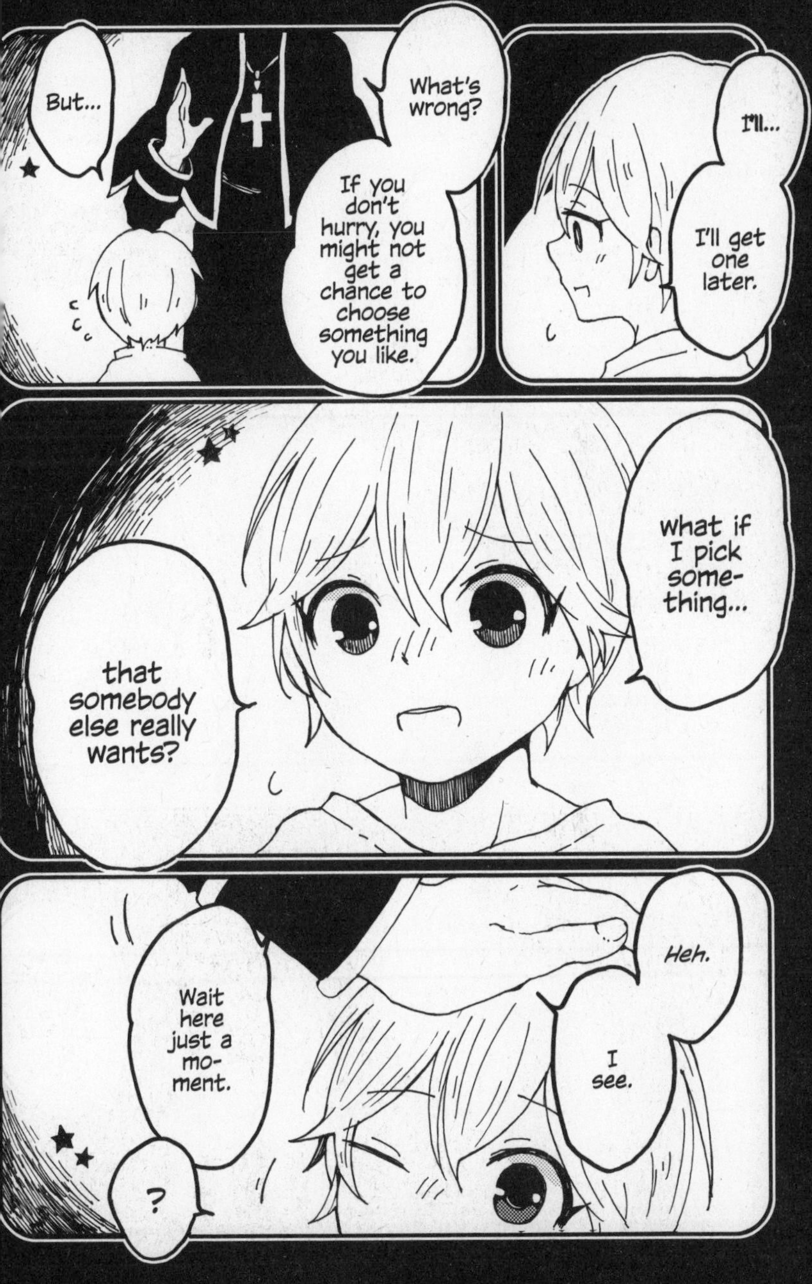
I'll...
I'll get one later.
What's wrong?
If you don't hurry, you might not get a chance to choose something you like.
But...
what if I pick some-thing...
that somebody else really wants?
Heh.
I see.
Wait here just a mo-ment.
?

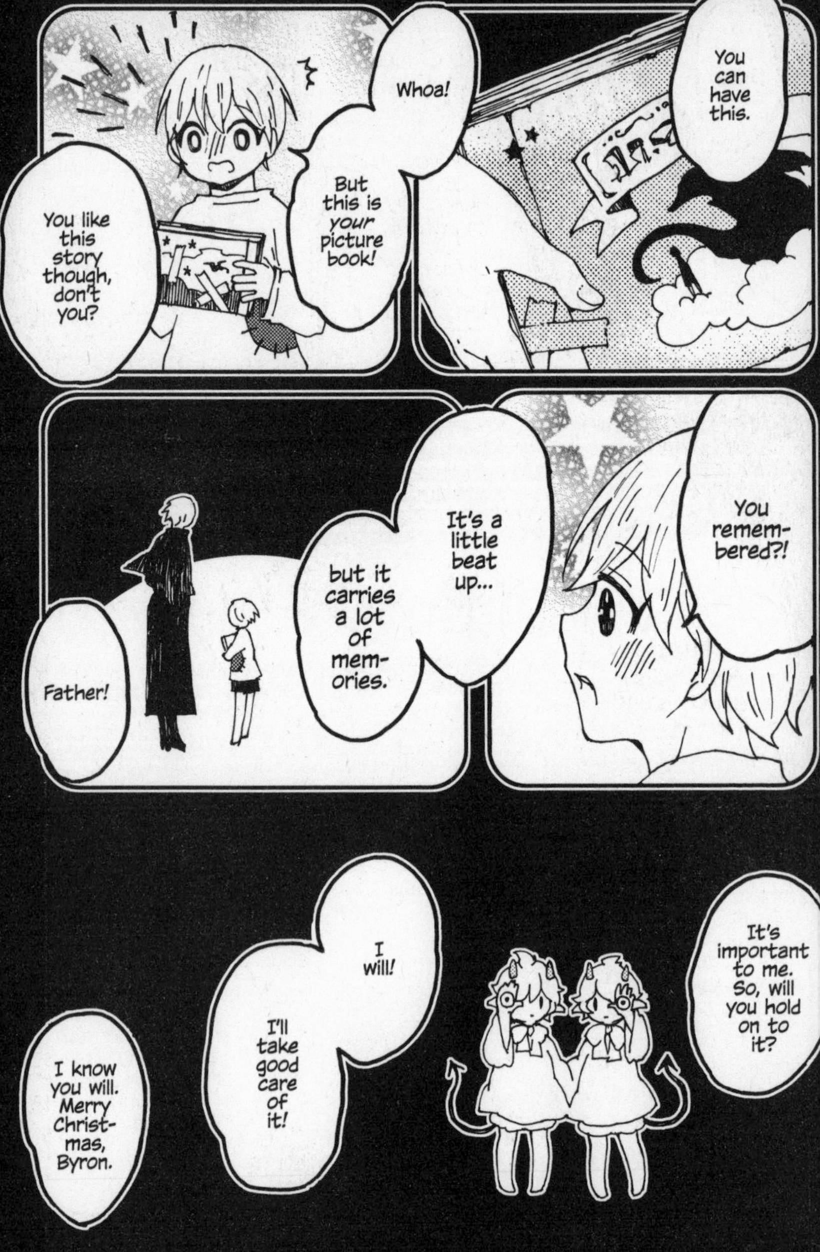
You can have this.
Whoa!
But this is *your* picture book!
You like this story though, don't you?
You remem-bered?!
It's a little beat up...
but it carries a lot of mem-ories.
Father!
It's important to me. So, will you hold on to it?
I will!
I'll take good care of it!
I know you will. Merry Christ-mas, Byron.

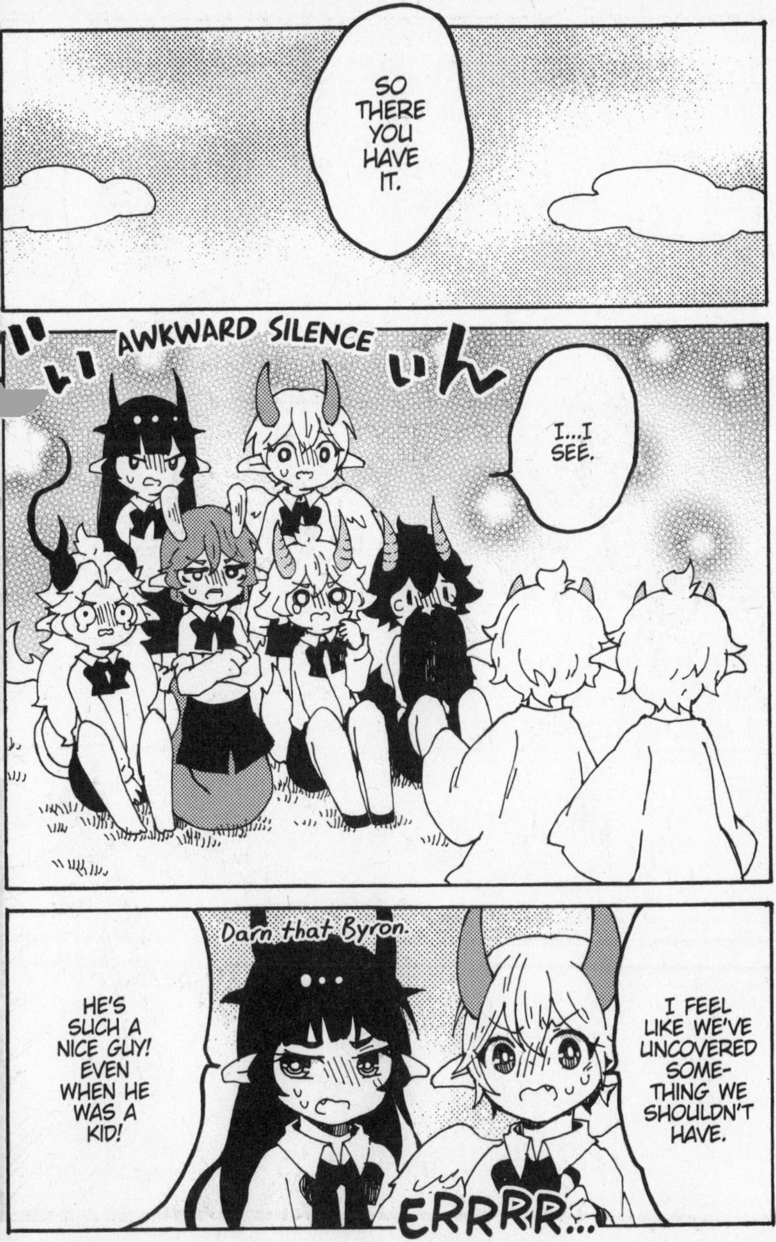
SO THERE YOU HAVE IT.
AWKWARD SILENCE
I...I SEE.
I FEEL LIKE WE'VE UNCOVERED SOME-THING WE SHOULDN'T HAVE.
Darn that Byron.
HE'S SUCH A NICE GUY! EVEN WHEN HE WAS A KID!
ERRRR...

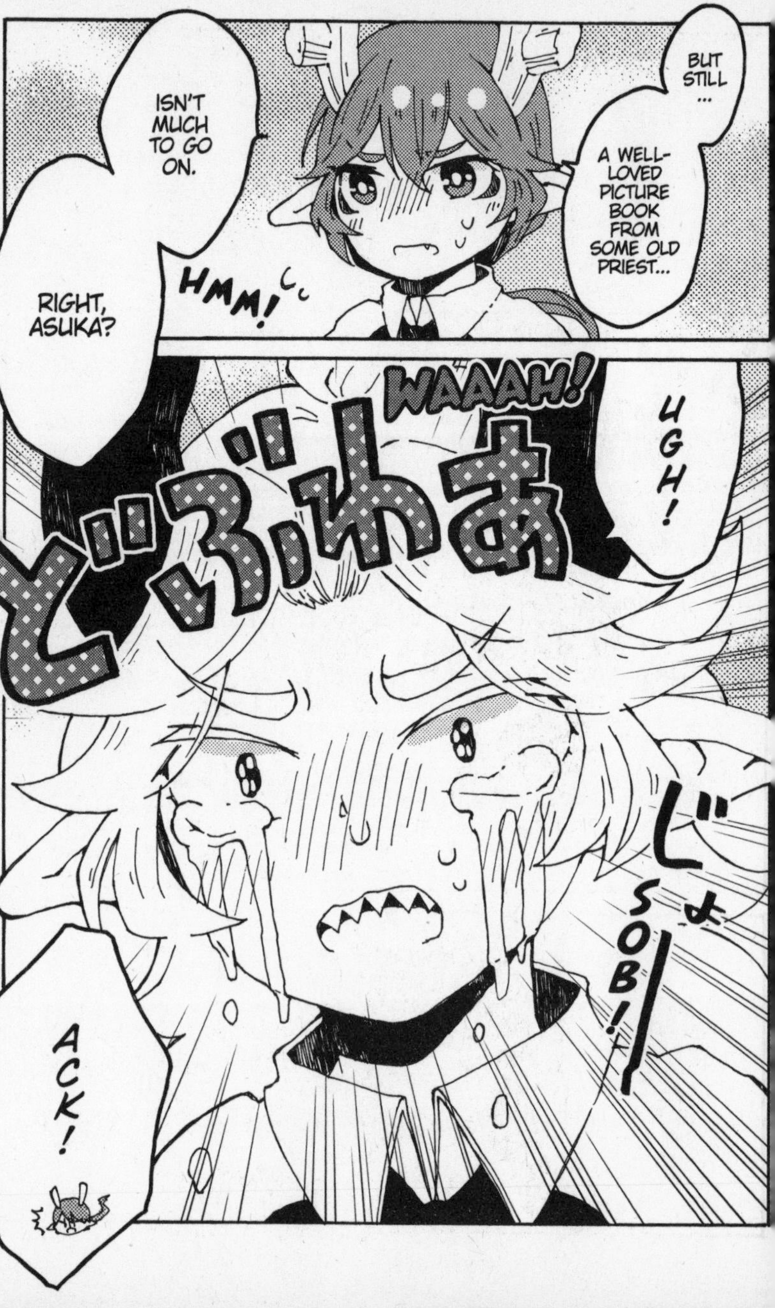
BUT STILL...
A WELL-LOVED PICTURE BOOK FROM SOME OLD PRIEST...
HMM!
ISN'T MUCH TO GO ON.
RIGHT, ASUKA?
WAAAH!
UGH!
どぶわあ
じょ
SOB!
ACK!

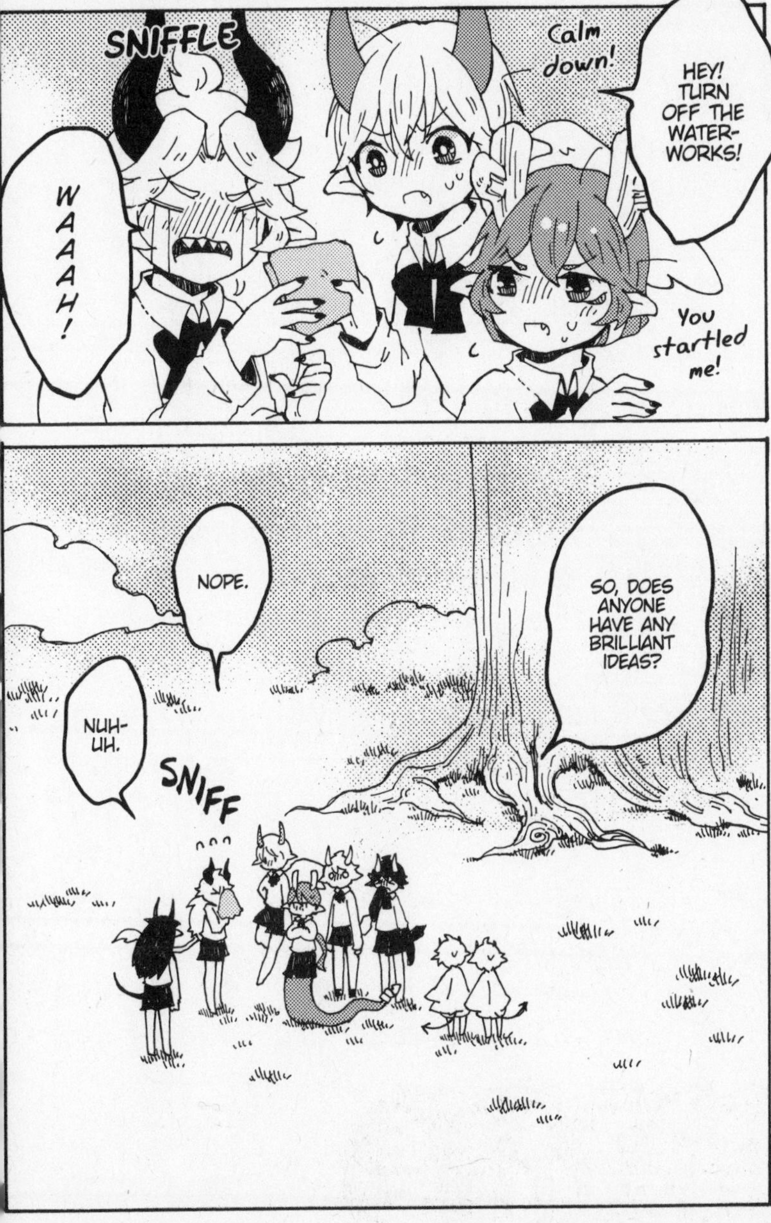
HEY! TURN OFF THE WATER-WORKS!
Calm down!
You startled me!
SNIFFLE
WAAAAH!
SO, DOES ANYONE HAVE ANY BRILLIANT IDEAS?
NOPE.
NUH-UH.
SNIFF

LITTLE DEVILS

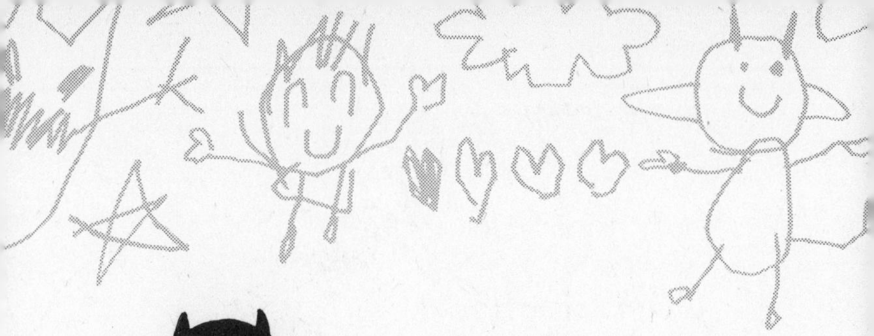

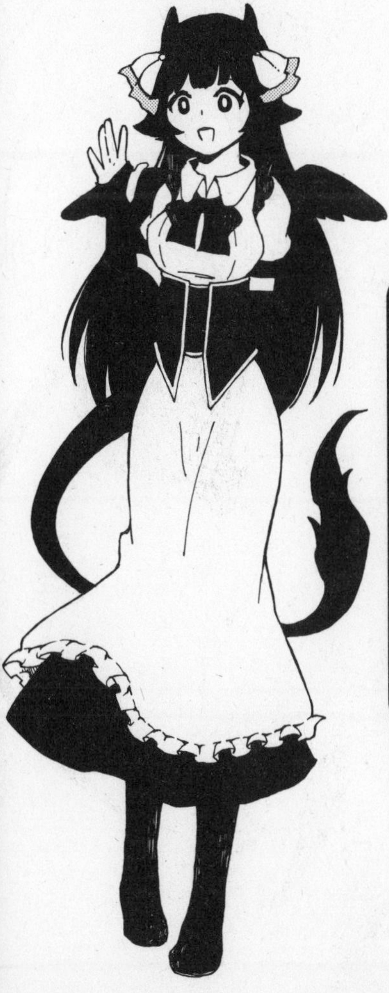

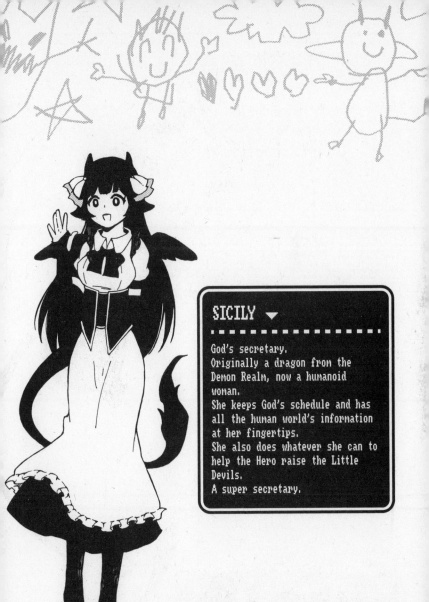

SICILY ▼

God's secretary.
Originally a dragon from the Demon Realm, now a humanoid woman.
She keeps God's schedule and has all the human world's information at her fingertips.
She also does whatever she can to help the Hero raise the Little Devils.
A super secretary.

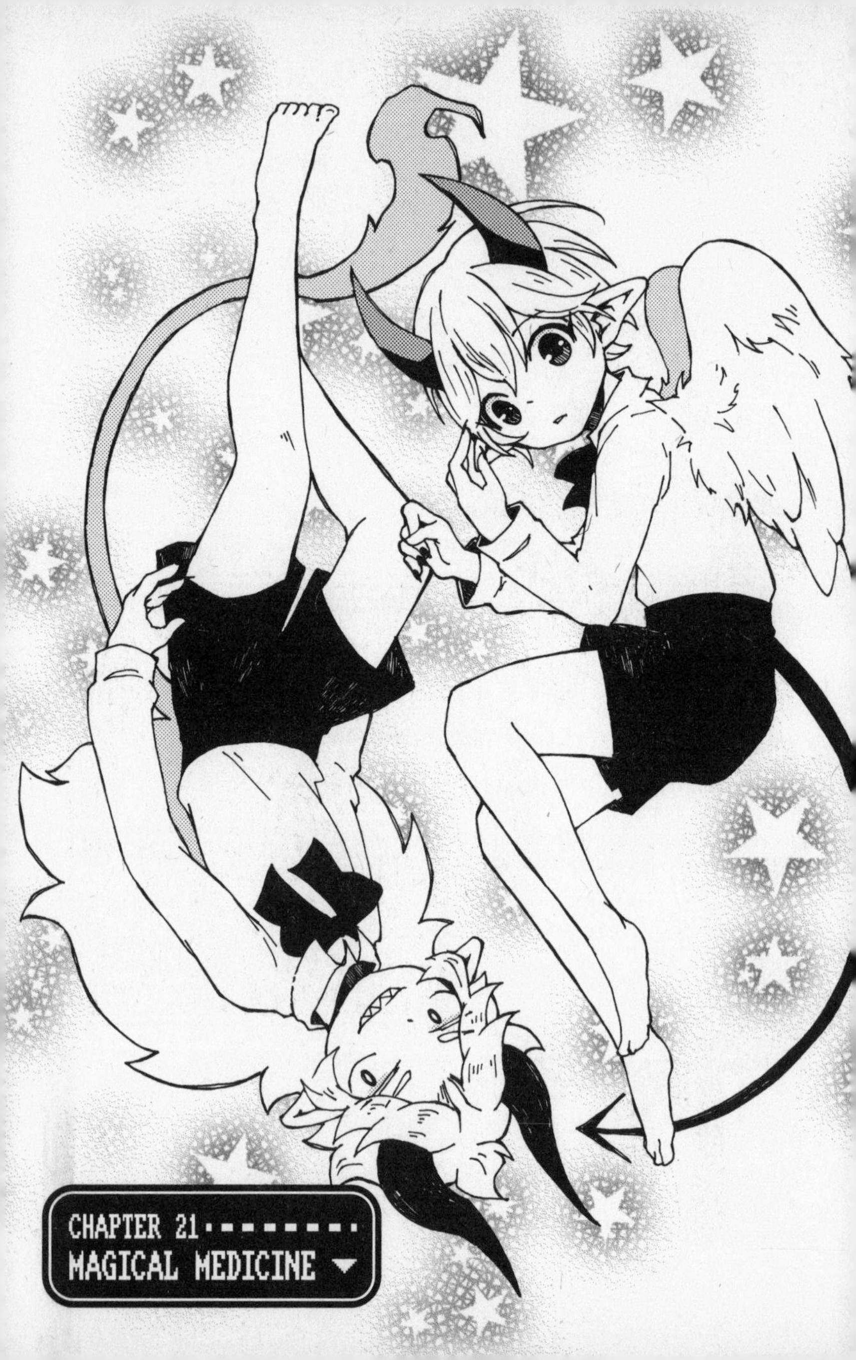
CHAPTER 21
MAGICAL MEDICINE

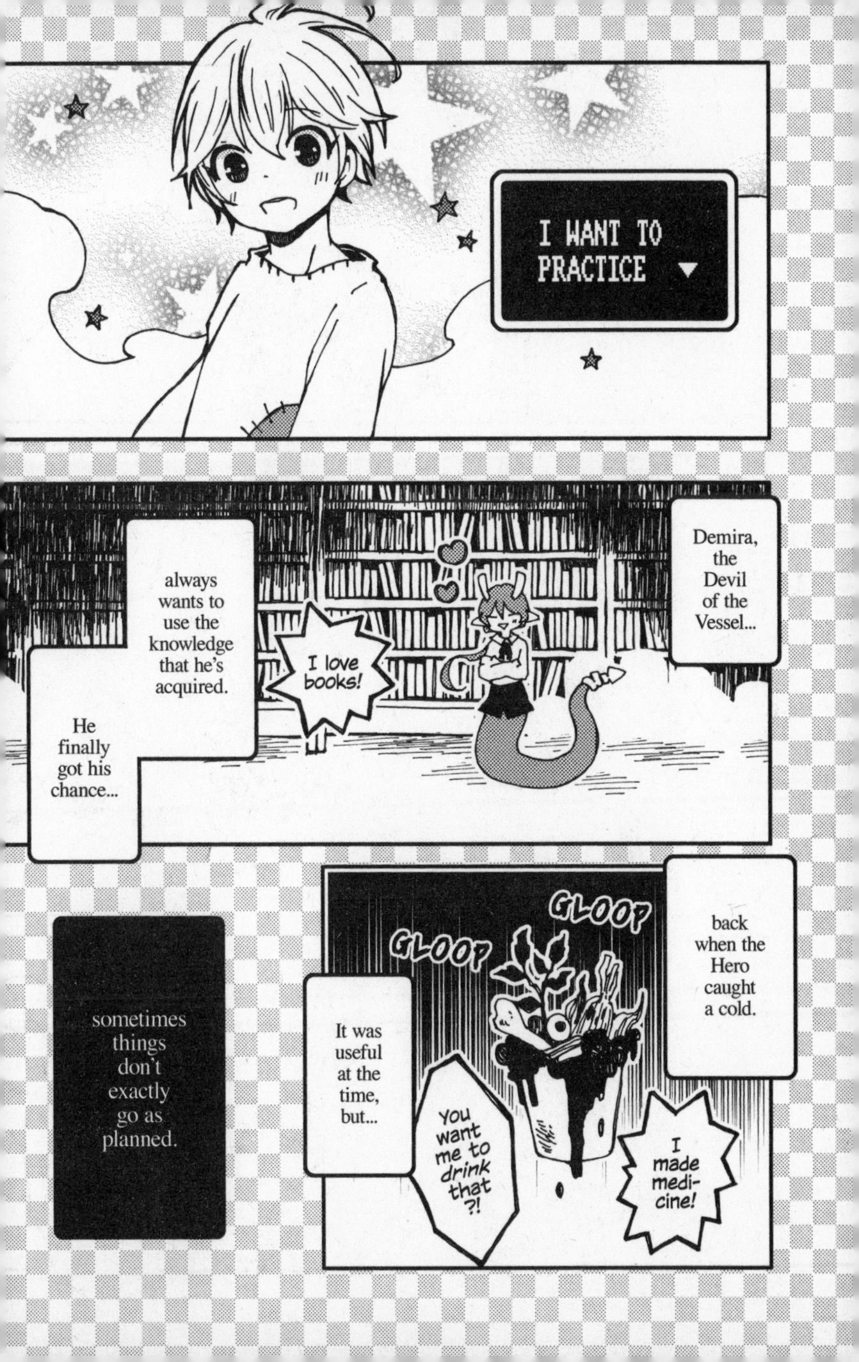
I WANT TO PRACTICE ▼
Demira, the Devil of the Vessel...
I love books!
always wants to use the knowledge that he's acquired.
He finally got his chance...
back when the Hero caught a cold.
GLOOP
GLOOP
I made medicine!
You want me to drink that?!
It was useful at the time, but...
sometimes things don't exactly go as planned.

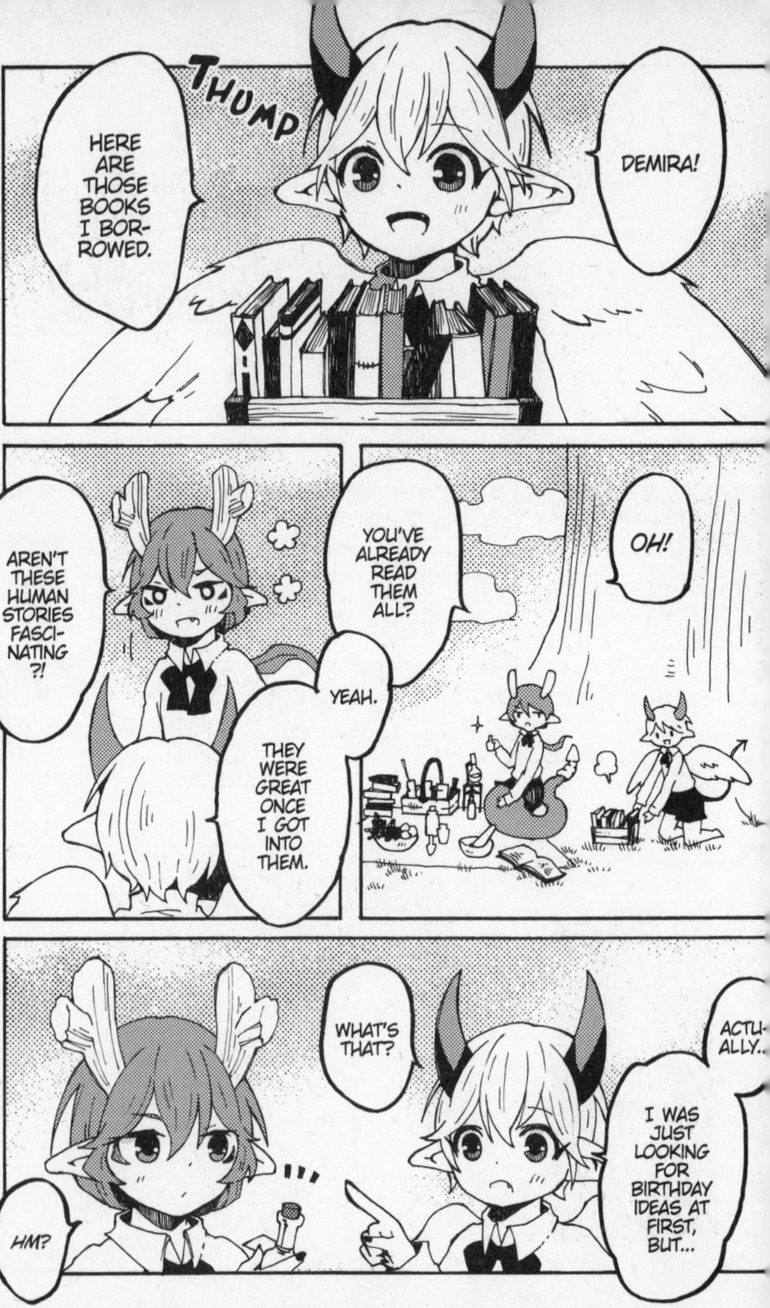
DEMIRA!
THUMP
HERE ARE THOSE BOOKS I BORROWED.
OH!
YOU'VE ALREADY READ THEM ALL?
AREN'T THESE HUMAN STORIES FASCINATING?!
YEAH.
THEY WERE GREAT ONCE I GOT INTO THEM.
ACTUALLY...
WHAT'S THAT?
I WAS JUST LOOKING FOR BIRTHDAY IDEAS AT FIRST, BUT...
HM?

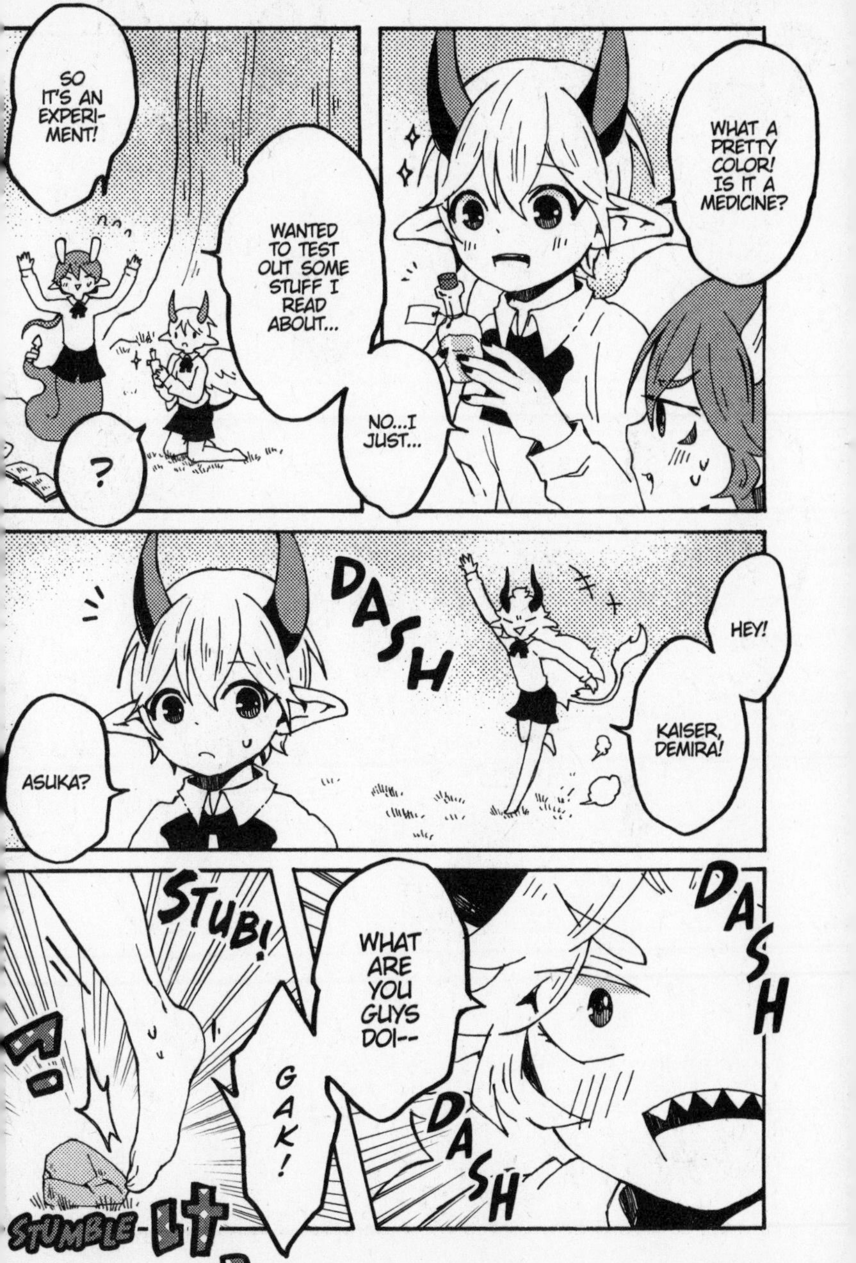
WHAT A PRETTY COLOR! IS IT A MEDICINE?
NO...I JUST...
WANTED TO TEST OUT SOME STUFF I READ ABOUT...
SO IT'S AN EXPERIMENT!
?
HEY!
KAISER, DEMIRA!
DASH
ASUKA?
DASH
DASH
WHAT ARE YOU GUYS DOI--
GAK!
STUB!
STUMBLE

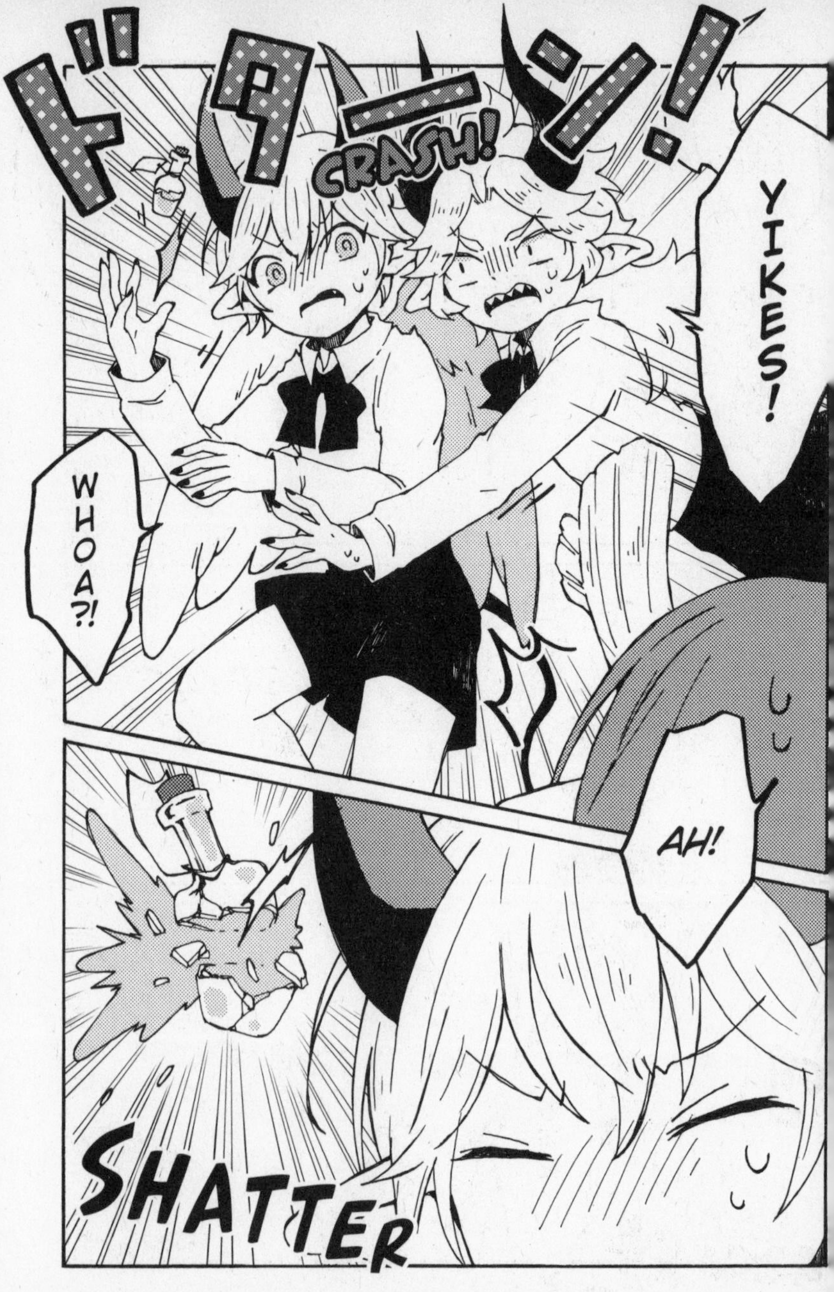
ドターン!
CRASH!
YIKES!
WHOA?!
AH!
SHATTER

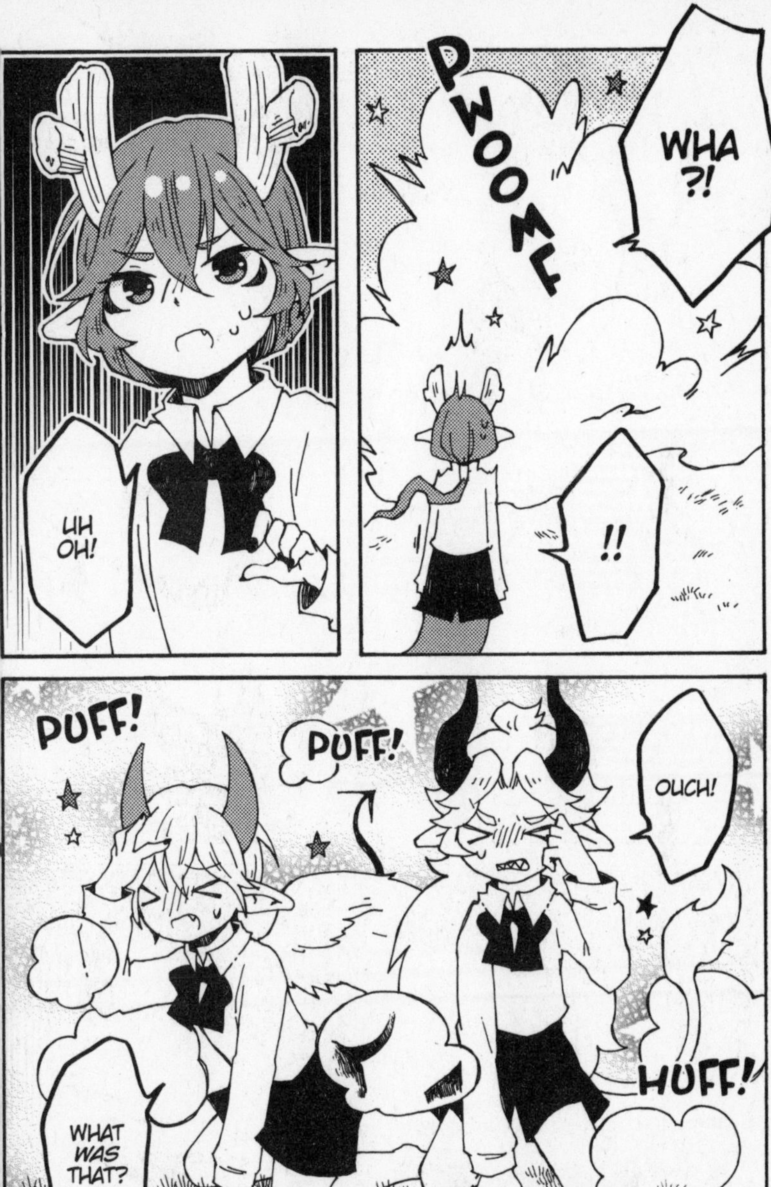
PWOOMF
WHA ?!
!!
UH OH!
OUCH!
PUFF!
PUFF!
HUFF!
WHAT *WAS* THAT?

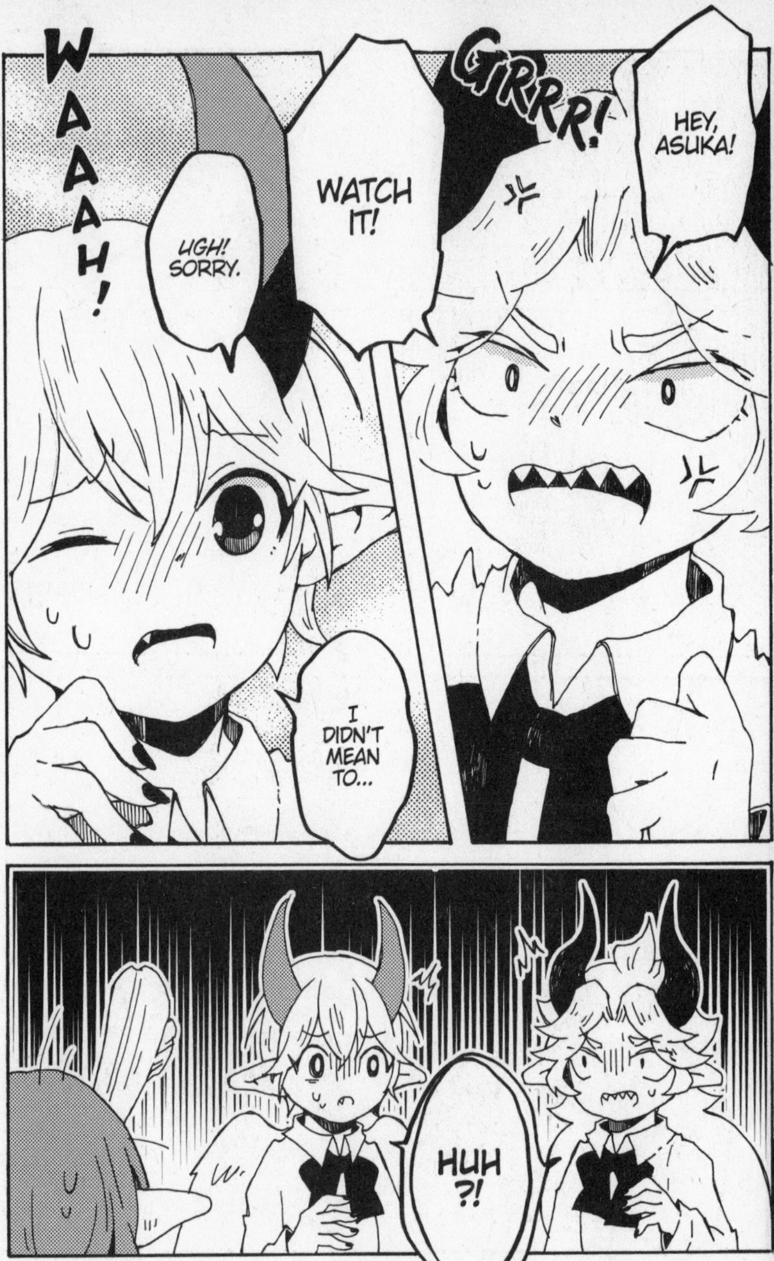
HEY, ASUKA!
GRRRR!
WATCH IT!
WAAAAH!
UGH! SORRY.
I DIDN'T MEAN TO...
HUH?!

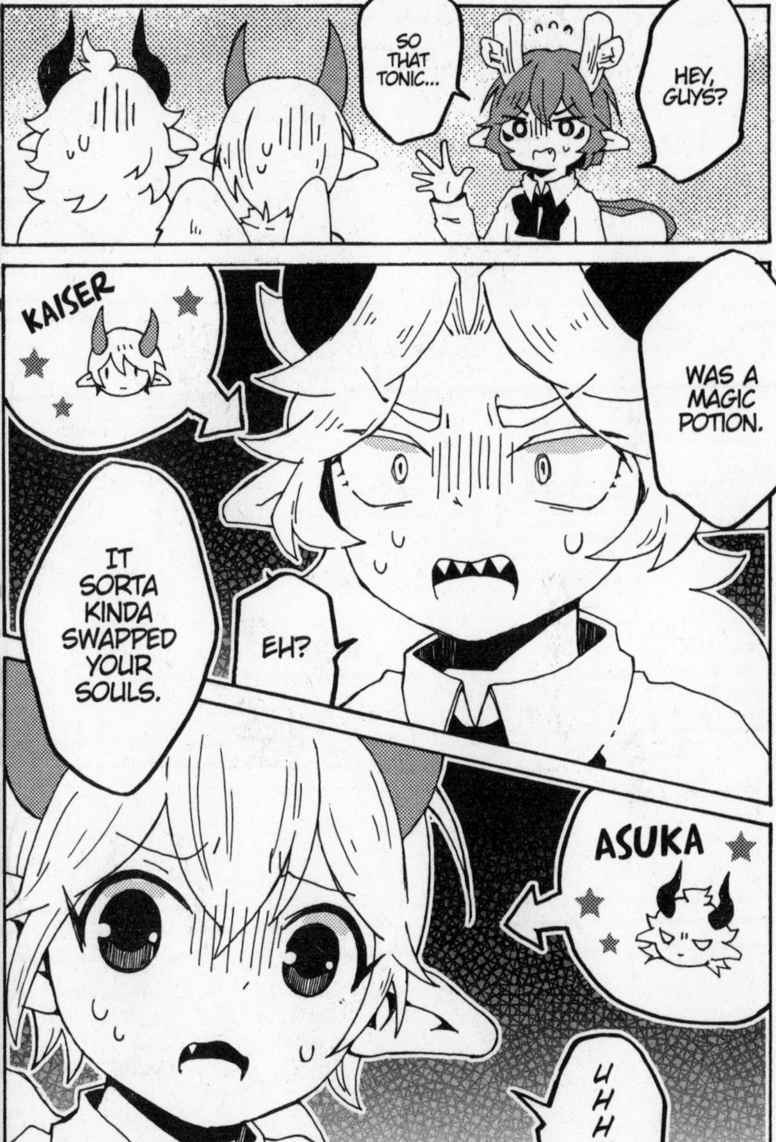
HEY, GUYS?
SO THAT TONIC...
WAS A MAGIC POTION.
KAISER
IT SORTA KINDA SWAPPED YOUR SOULS.
EH?
ASUKA
UHHHH?

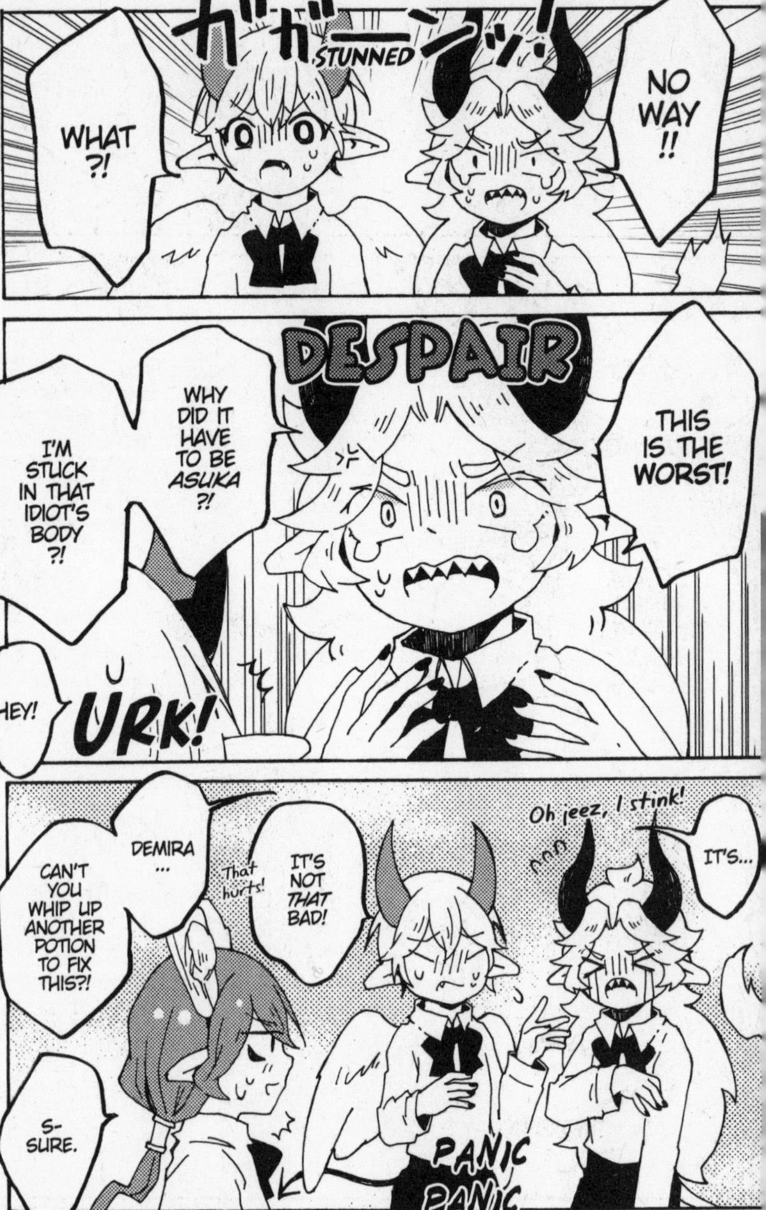
NO WAY!!
ガガーンッ!
STUNNED
WHAT?!
DESPAIR
THIS IS THE WORST!
WHY DID IT HAVE TO BE ASUKA?!
I'M STUCK IN THAT IDIOT'S BODY?!
URK!
HEY!
IT'S...
Oh jeez, I stink!
IT'S NOT THAT BAD!
That hurts!
DEMIRA...
CAN'T YOU WHIP UP ANOTHER POTION TO FIX THIS?!
PANIC PANIC
S-SURE.

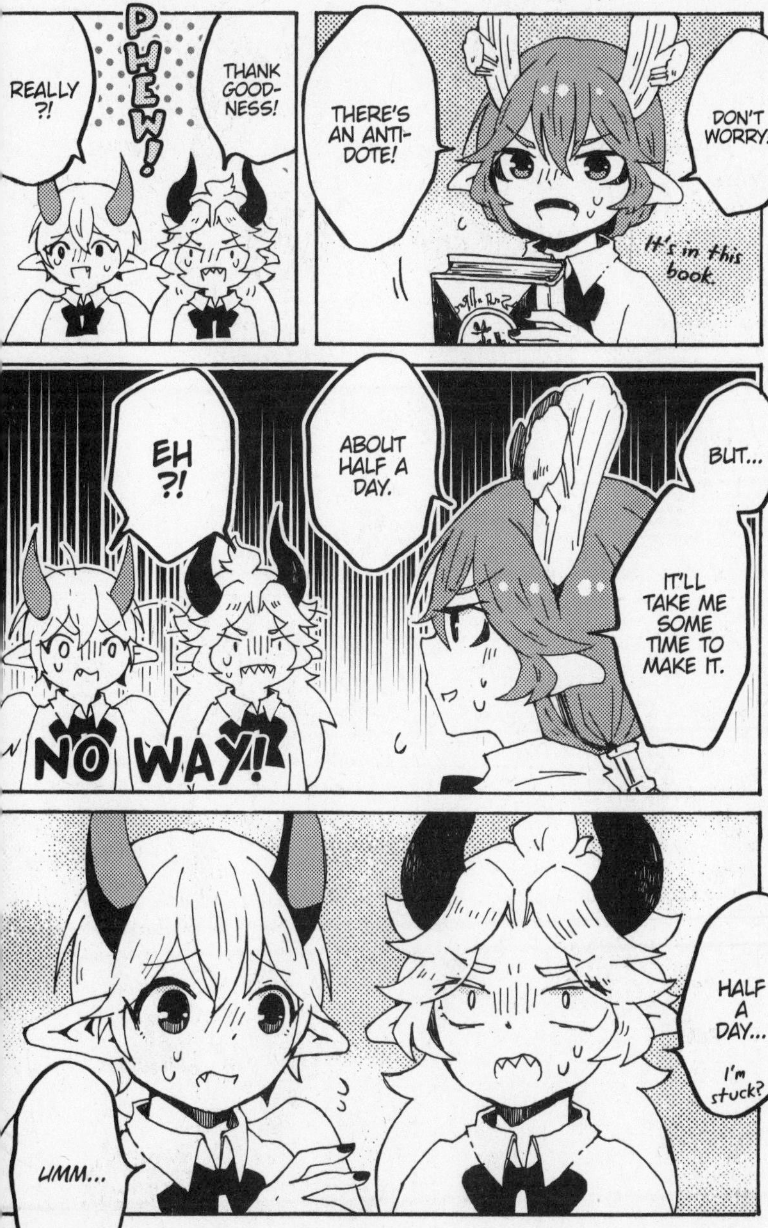
DON'T WORRY!
THERE'S AN ANTI-DOTE!
It's in this book.
THANK GOODNESS!
PHEW!
REALLY ?!
BUT...
IT'LL TAKE ME SOME TIME TO MAKE IT.
ABOUT HALF A DAY.
EH ?!
NO WAY!
HALF A DAY...
I'm stuck?
UMM...

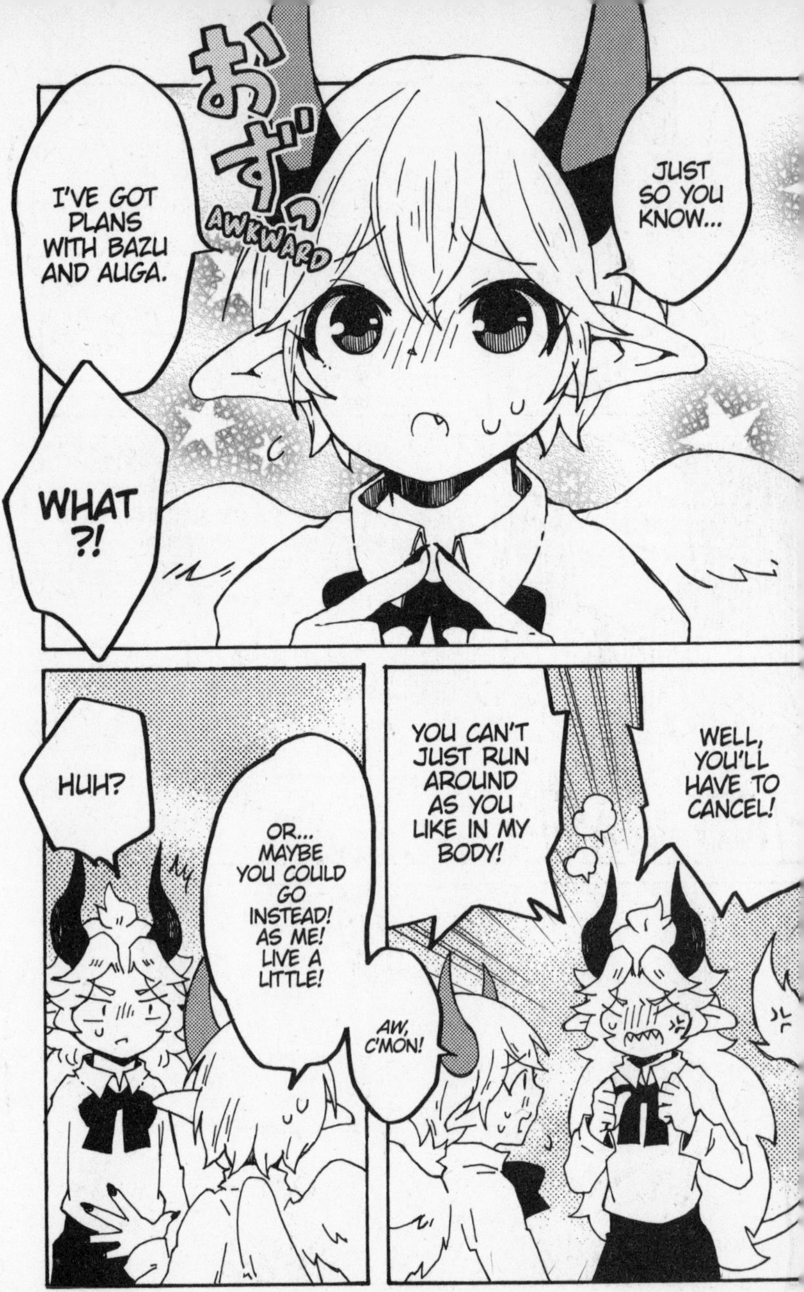
JUST SO YOU KNOW...
I'VE GOT PLANS WITH BAZU AND AUGA.
おずっ
AWKWARD
WHAT ?!
WELL, YOU'LL HAVE TO CANCEL!
YOU CAN'T JUST RUN AROUND AS YOU LIKE IN MY BODY!
AW, C'MON!
OR... MAYBE YOU COULD GO INSTEAD! AS ME! LIVE A LITTLE!
HUH?

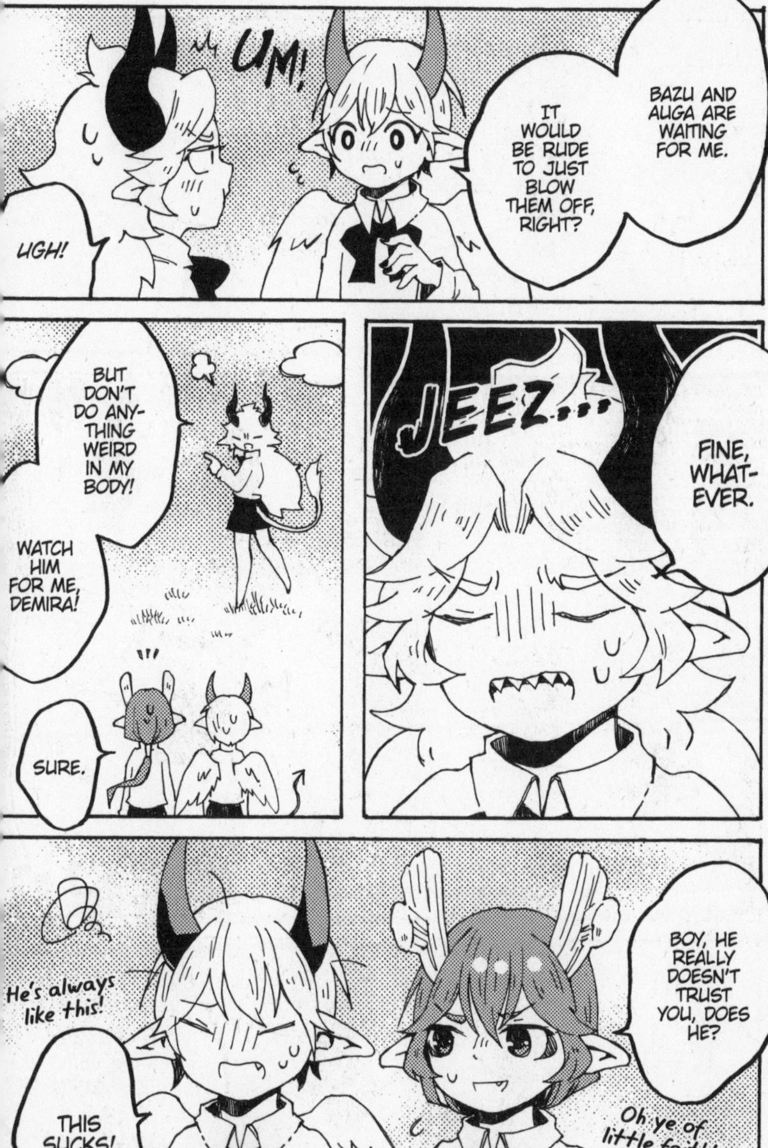
BAZU AND AUGA ARE WAITING FOR ME.
IT WOULD BE RUDE TO JUST BLOW THEM OFF, RIGHT?
UM!
UGH!
JEEZ...
FINE, WHAT-EVER.
BUT DON'T DO ANY-THING WEIRD IN MY BODY!
WATCH HIM FOR ME, DEMIRA!
SURE.
BOY, HE REALLY DOESN'T TRUST YOU, DOES HE?
Oh ye of little faith!
He's always like this!
THIS SUCKS!

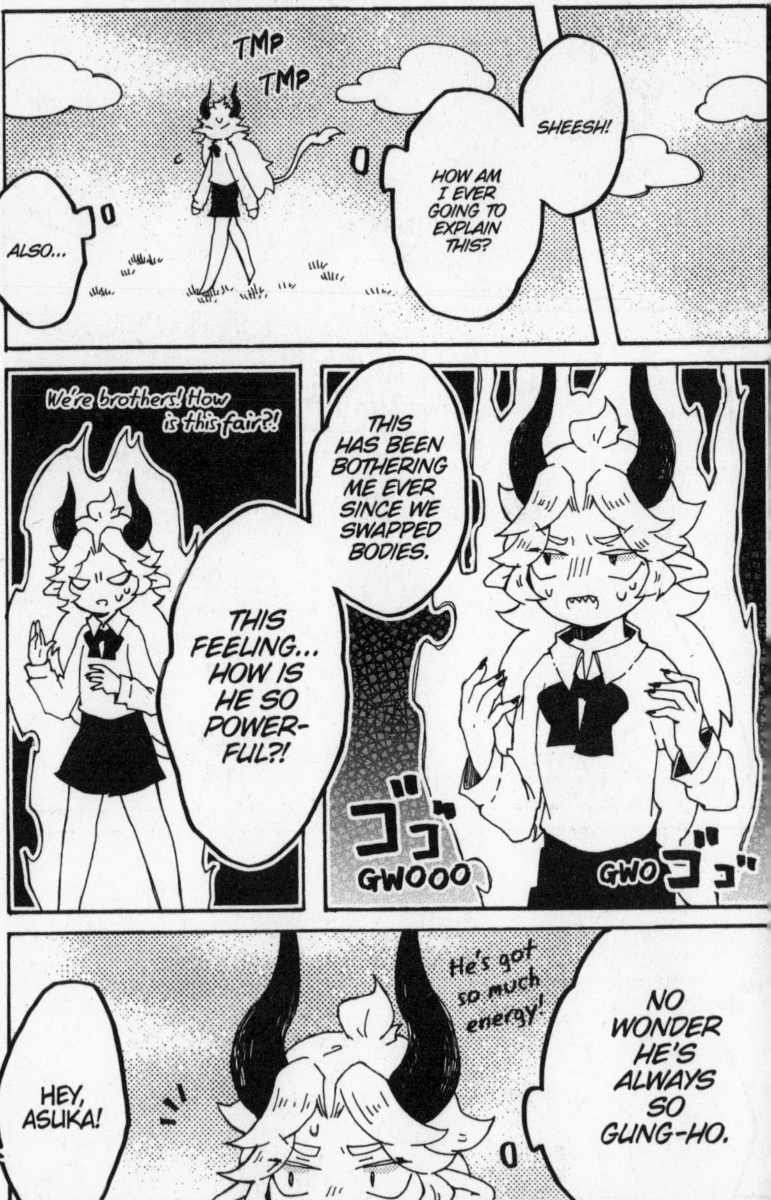
SHEESH!
HOW AM I EVER GOING TO EXPLAIN THIS?
TMP TMP
ALSO...
THIS HAS BEEN BOTHERING ME EVER SINCE WE SWAPPED BODIES.
GWO
GWOOO
THIS FEELING... HOW IS HE SO POWER-FUL?!
We're brothers! How is this fair?!
NO WONDER HE'S ALWAYS SO GUNG-HO.
He's got so much energy!
HEY, ASUKA!

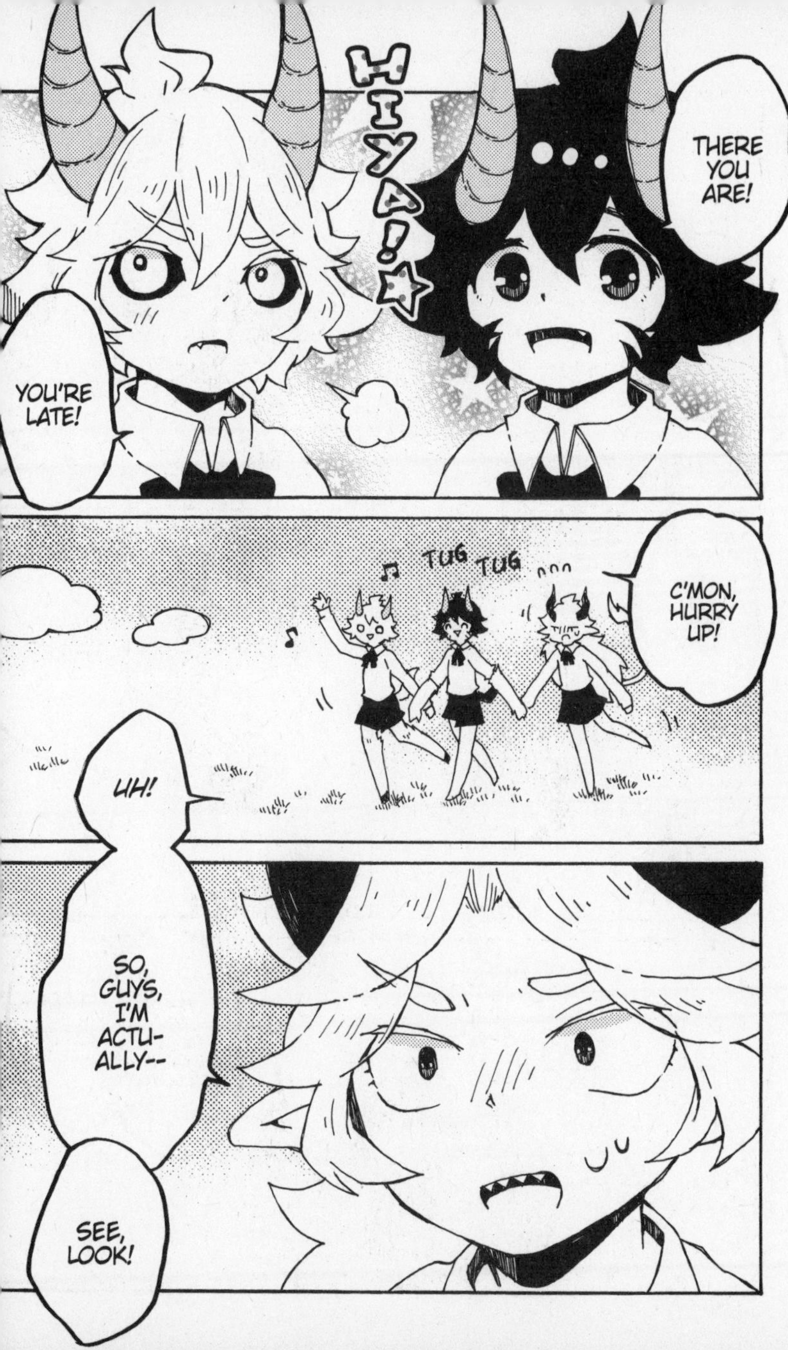
THERE YOU ARE!
HIYA!
YOU'RE LATE!
C'MON, HURRY UP!
TUG TUG
UH!
SO, GUYS, I'M ACTU-ALLY--
SEE, LOOK!

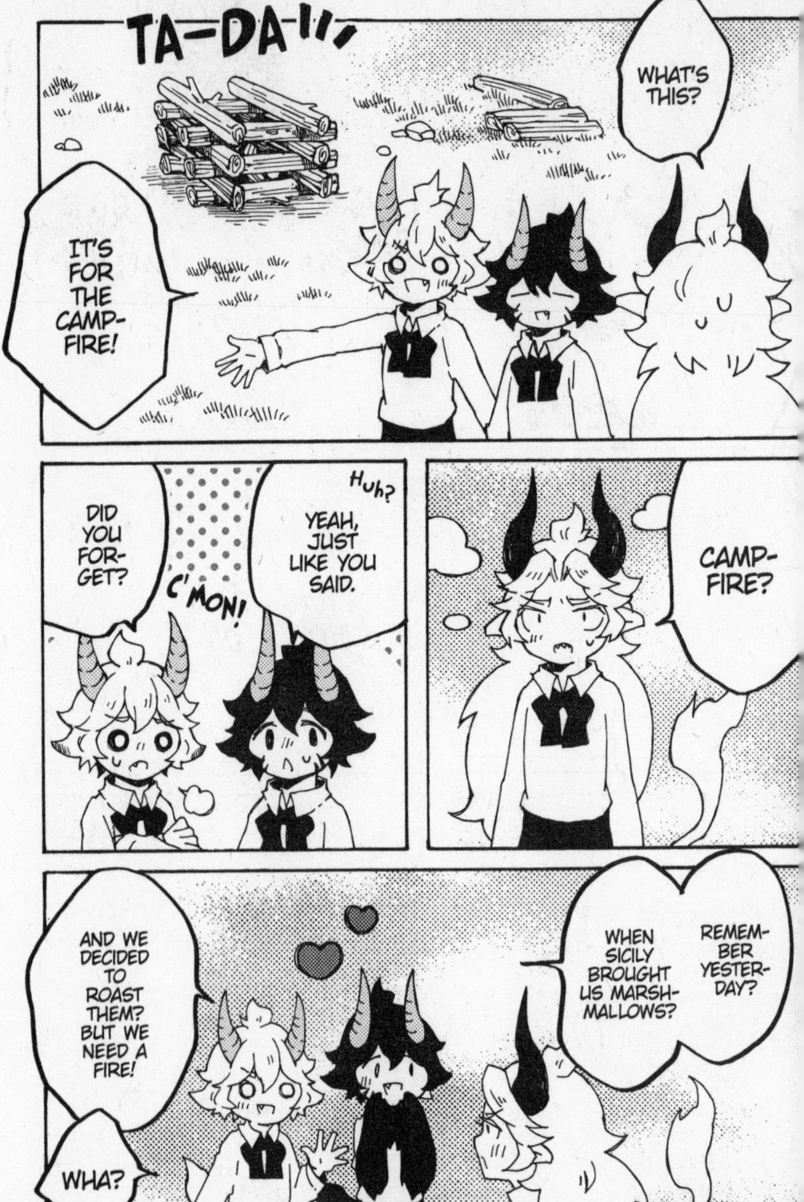
TA-DA!!!
WHAT'S THIS?
IT'S FOR THE CAMP-FIRE!
CAMP-FIRE?
Huh?
YEAH, JUST LIKE YOU SAID.
DID YOU FOR-GET?
C'MON!
REMEM-BER YESTER-DAY?
WHEN SICILY BROUGHT US MARSH-MALLOWS?
AND WE DECIDED TO ROAST THEM? BUT WE NEED A FIRE!
WHA?

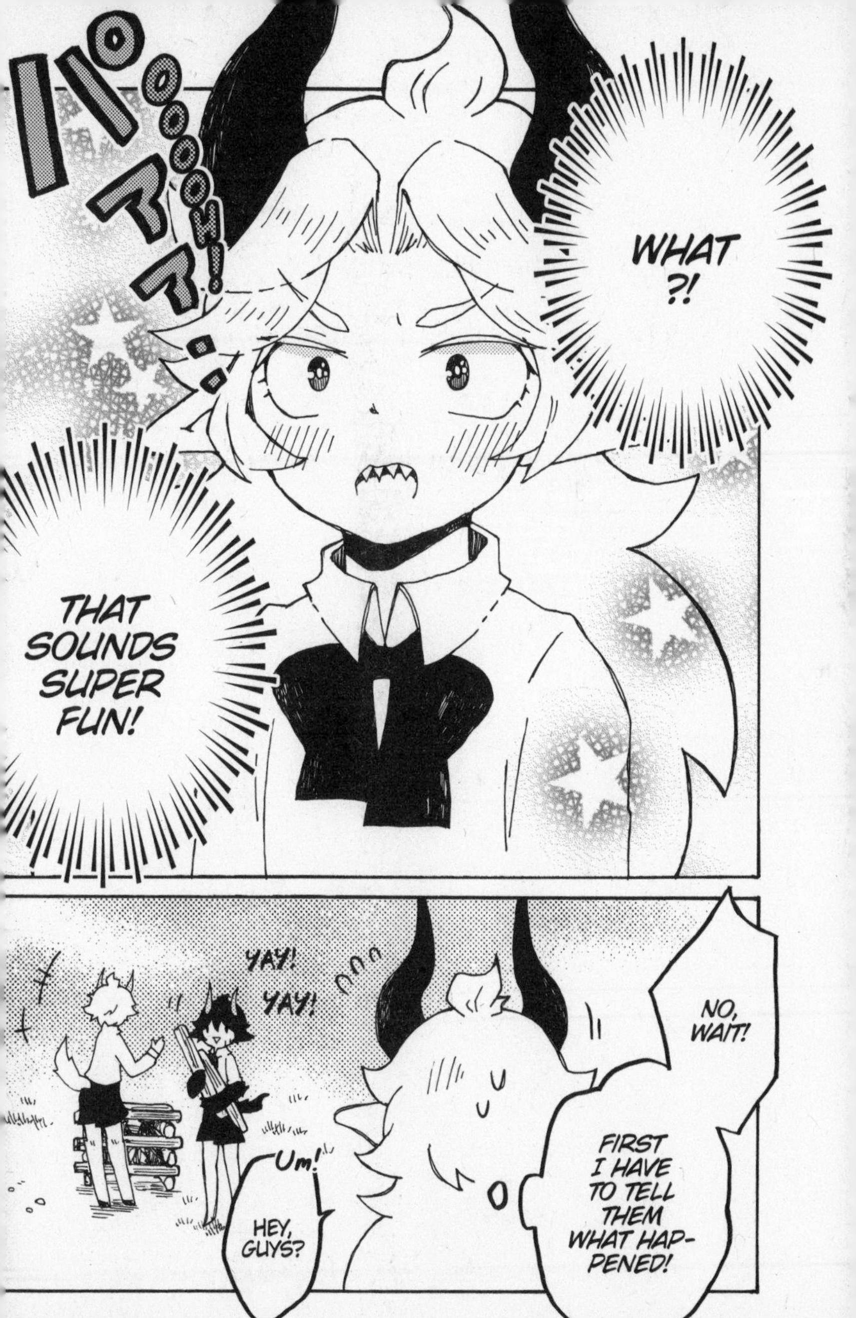
WHAT ?!
パアア..
OOOOH!
THAT SOUNDS SUPER FUN!
NO, WAIT!
FIRST I HAVE TO TELL THEM WHAT HAP-PENED!
Um!
HEY, GUYS?
YAY! YAY!

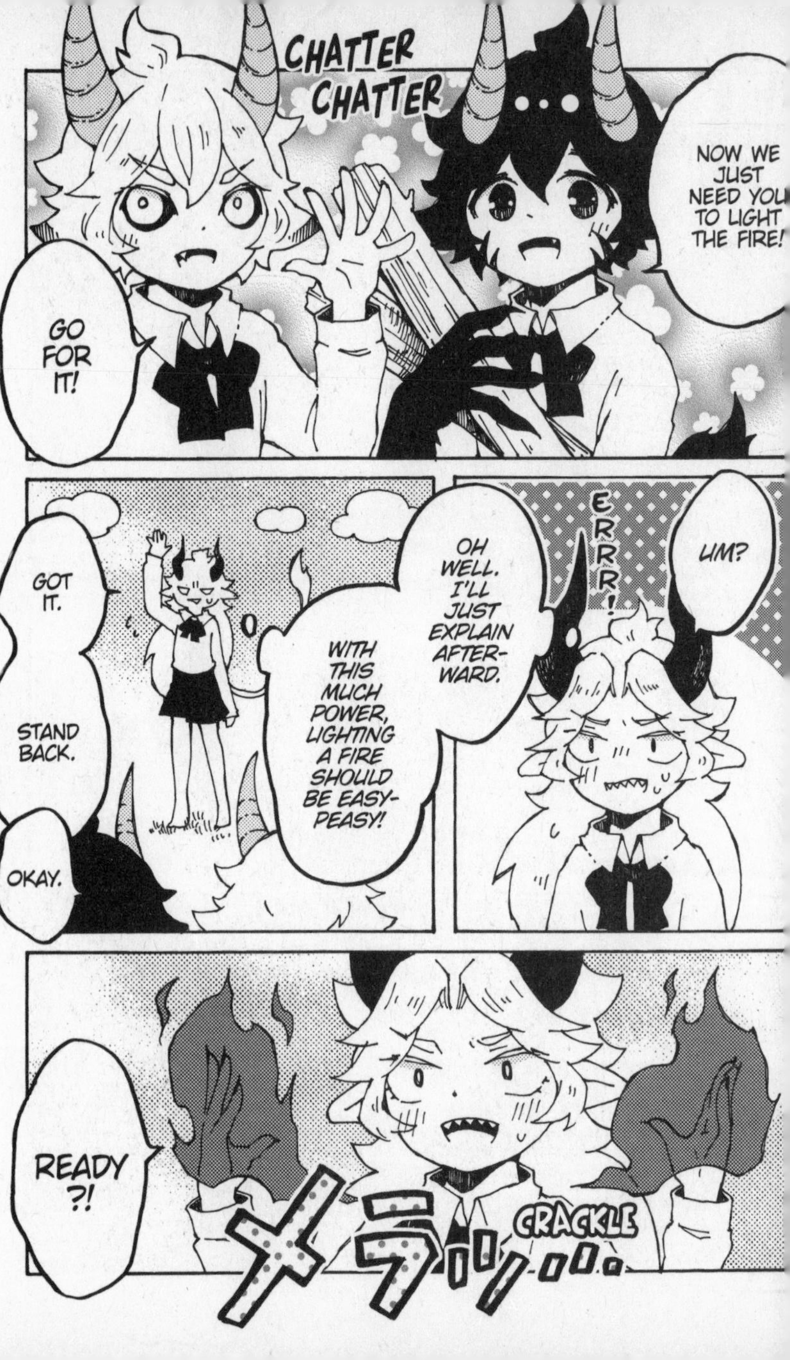
CHATTER CHATTER
NOW WE JUST NEED YOU TO LIGHT THE FIRE!
GO FOR IT!
UM?
ERRR!
OH WELL. I'LL JUST EXPLAIN AFTER-WARD.
WITH THIS MUCH POWER, LIGHTING A FIRE SHOULD BE EASY-PEASY!
GOT IT. STAND BACK.
OKAY.
READY?!
CRACKLE

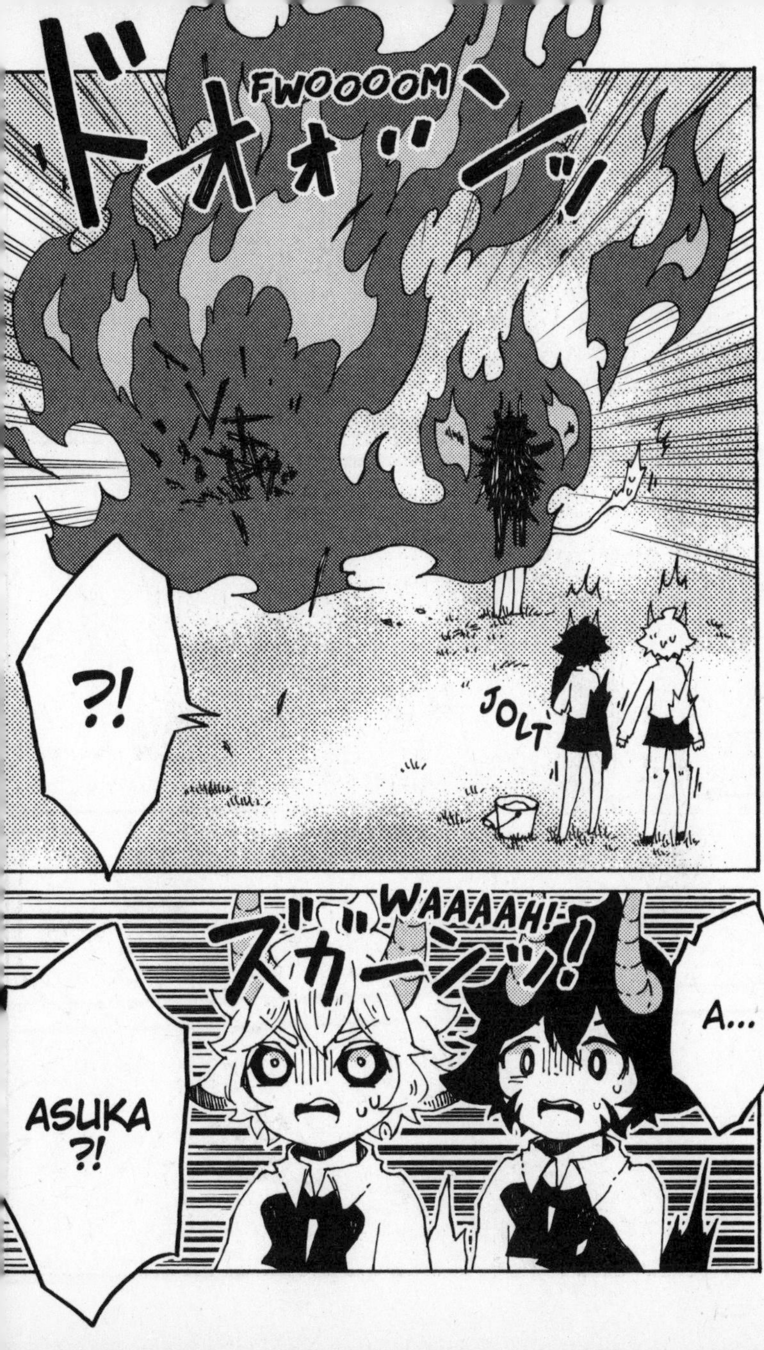
FWOOOOM
JOLT
?!
A...
WAAAAH!
ASUKA ?!

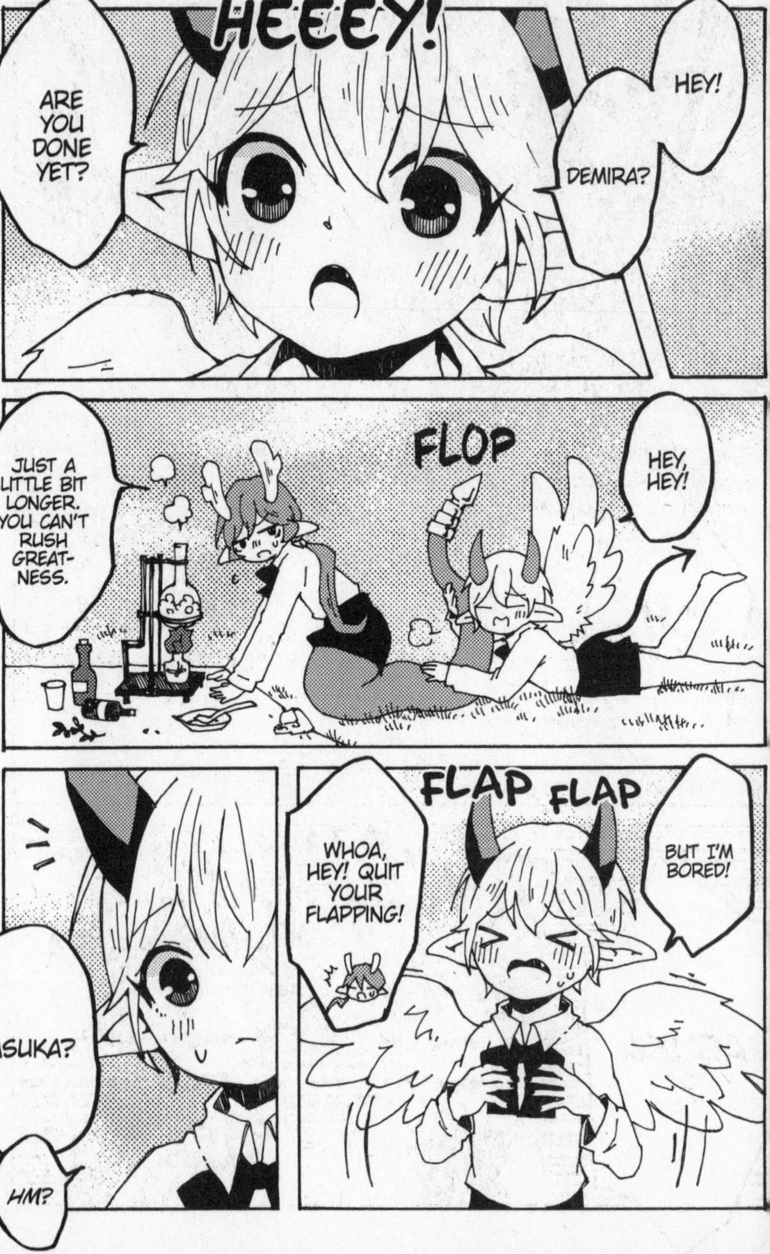
HEEEY!
HEY!
DEMIRA?
ARE YOU DONE YET?
HEY, HEY!
FLOP
JUST A LITTLE BIT LONGER. YOU CAN'T RUSH GREAT-NESS.
FLAP FLAP
BUT I'M BORED!
WHOA, HEY! QUIT YOUR FLAPPING!
ASUKA?
HM?

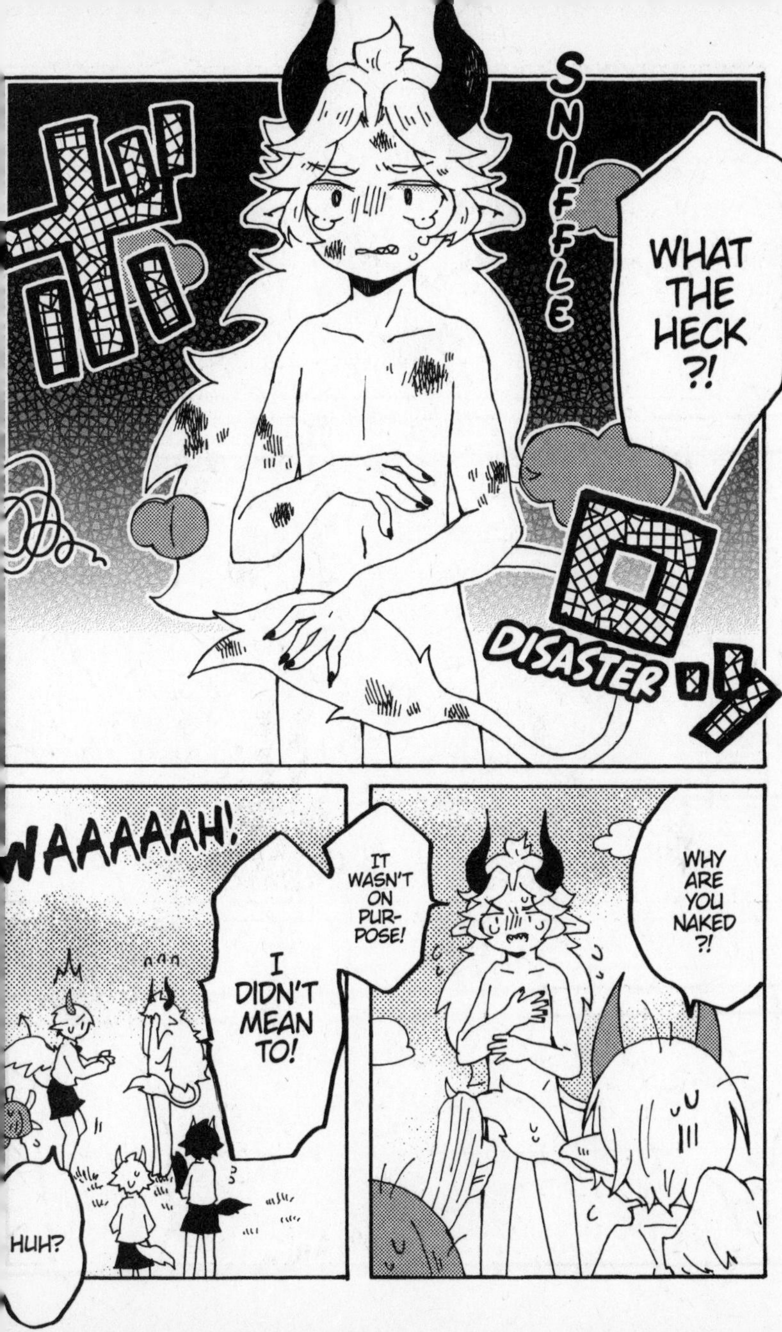
SNIFFLE
WHAT THE HECK?!
DISASTER
WHY ARE YOU NAKED?!
IT WASN'T ON PUR-POSE!
I DIDN'T MEAN TO!
WAAAAAH!
HUH?

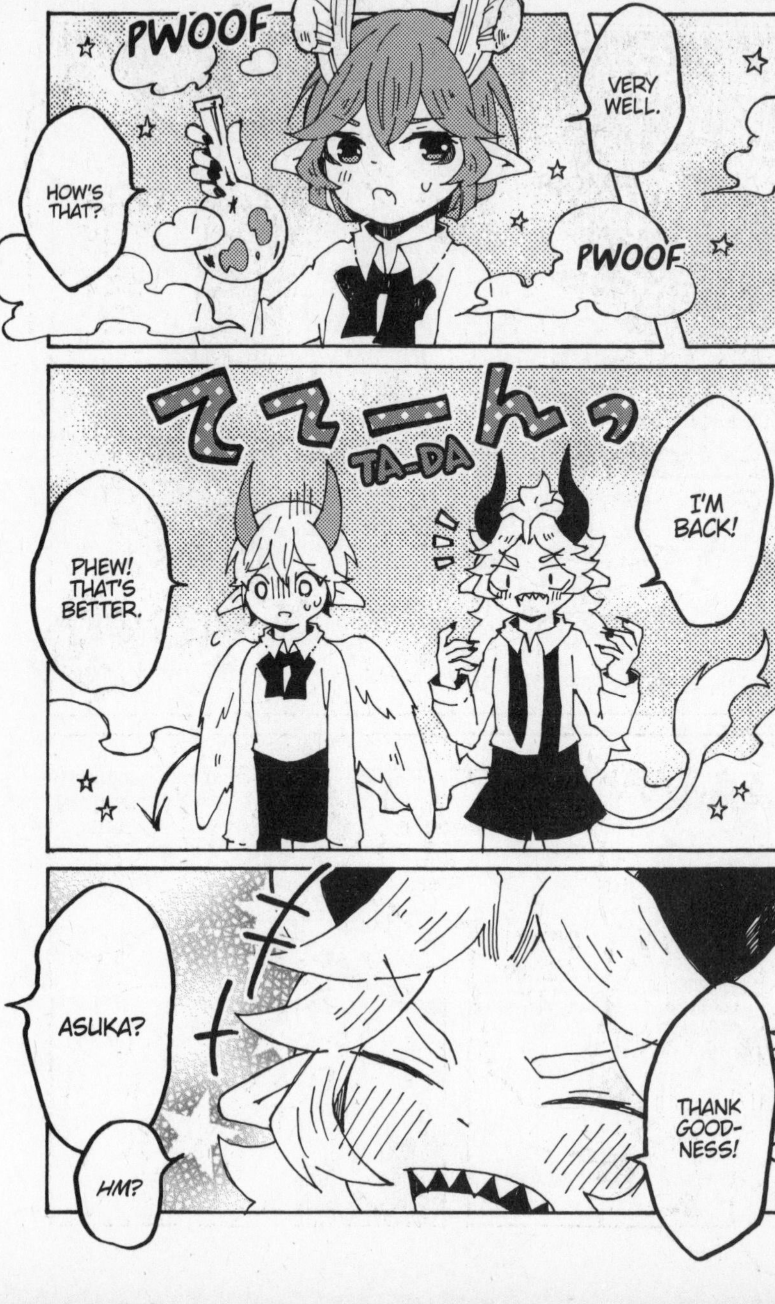
VERY WELL.
PWOOF
HOW'S THAT?
PWOOF
ててーんっ
TA-DA
I'M BACK!
PHEW! THAT'S BETTER.
THANK GOOD-NESS!
ASUKA?
HM?

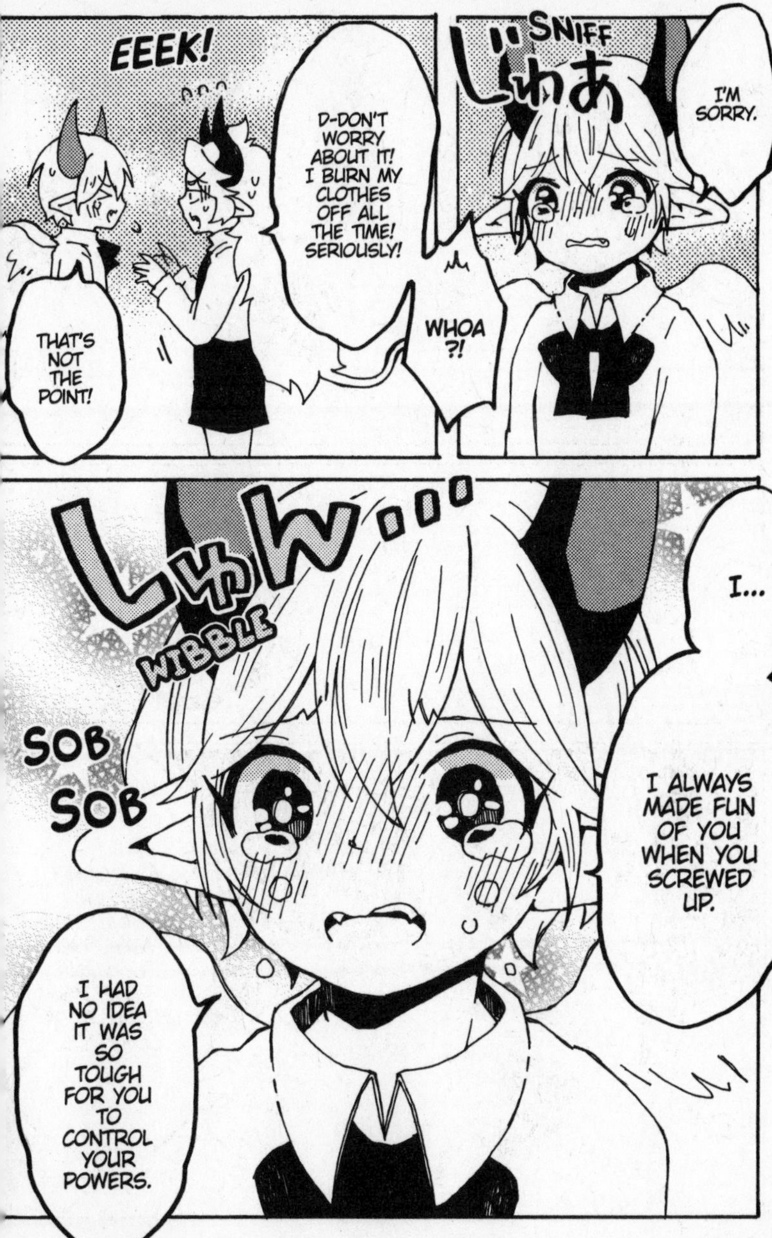

じゅあ SNIFF
I'M SORRY.
WHOA ?!
D-DON'T WORRY ABOUT IT! I BURN MY CLOTHES OFF ALL THE TIME! SERIOUSLY!
EEEK!
THAT'S NOT THE POINT!
I...
I ALWAYS MADE FUN OF YOU WHEN YOU SCREWED UP.
しゅん... WIBBLE
SOB SOB
I HAD NO IDEA IT WAS SO TOUGH FOR YOU TO CONTROL YOUR POWERS.

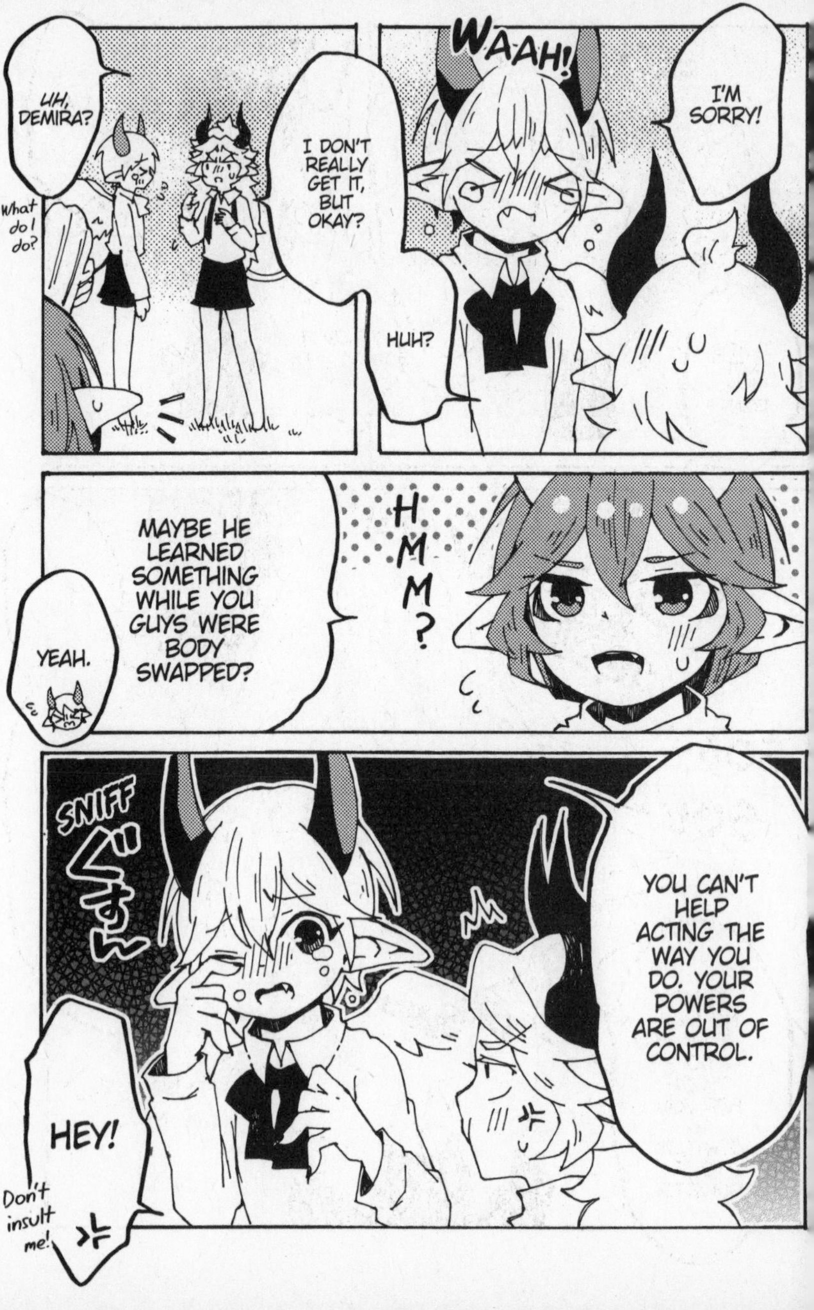
WAAH!
I'M SORRY!
HUH?
I DON'T REALLY GET IT, BUT OKAY?
UH, DEMIRA?
What do I do?
HMM?
MAYBE HE LEARNED SOMETHING WHILE YOU GUYS WERE BODY SWAPPED?
YEAH.
YOU CAN'T HELP ACTING THE WAY YOU DO. YOUR POWERS ARE OUT OF CONTROL.
SNIFF
ぐすん
HEY!
Don't insult me!

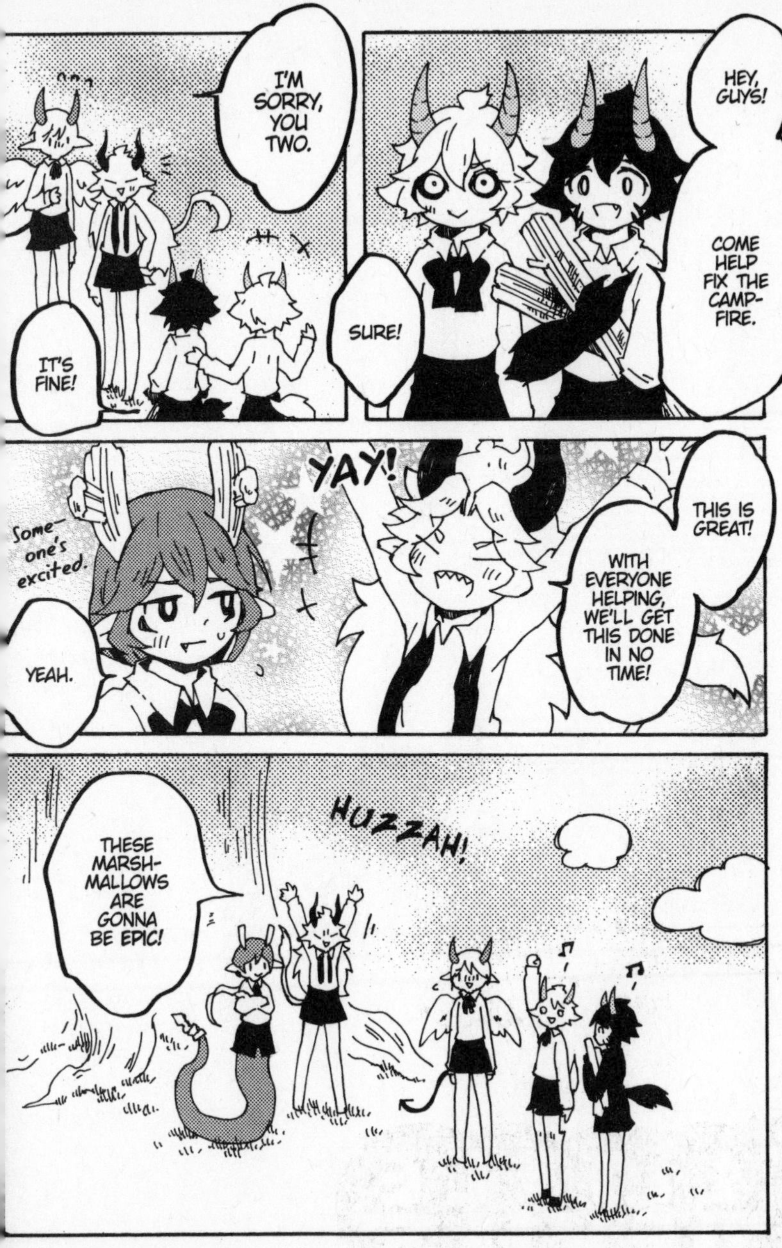
HEY, GUYS!
COME HELP FIX THE CAMP-FIRE.
SURE!
I'M SORRY, YOU TWO.
IT'S FINE!
THIS IS GREAT!
WITH EVERYONE HELPING, WE'LL GET THIS DONE IN NO TIME!
YAY!
Some-one's excited.
YEAH.
HUZZAH!
THESE MARSH-MALLOWS ARE GONNA BE EPIC!

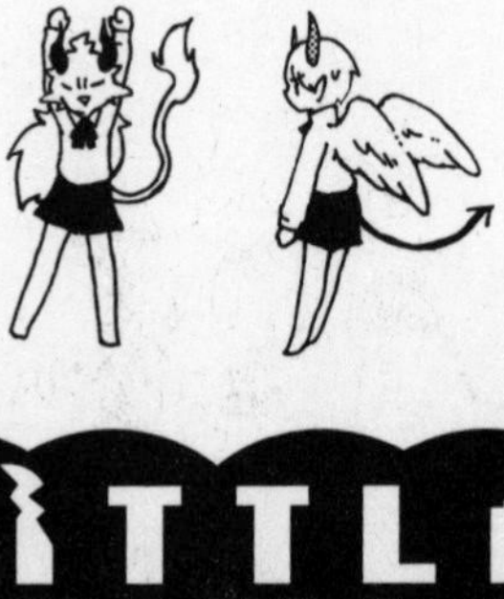

LITTLE DEVILS

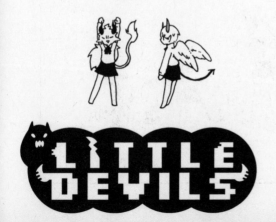

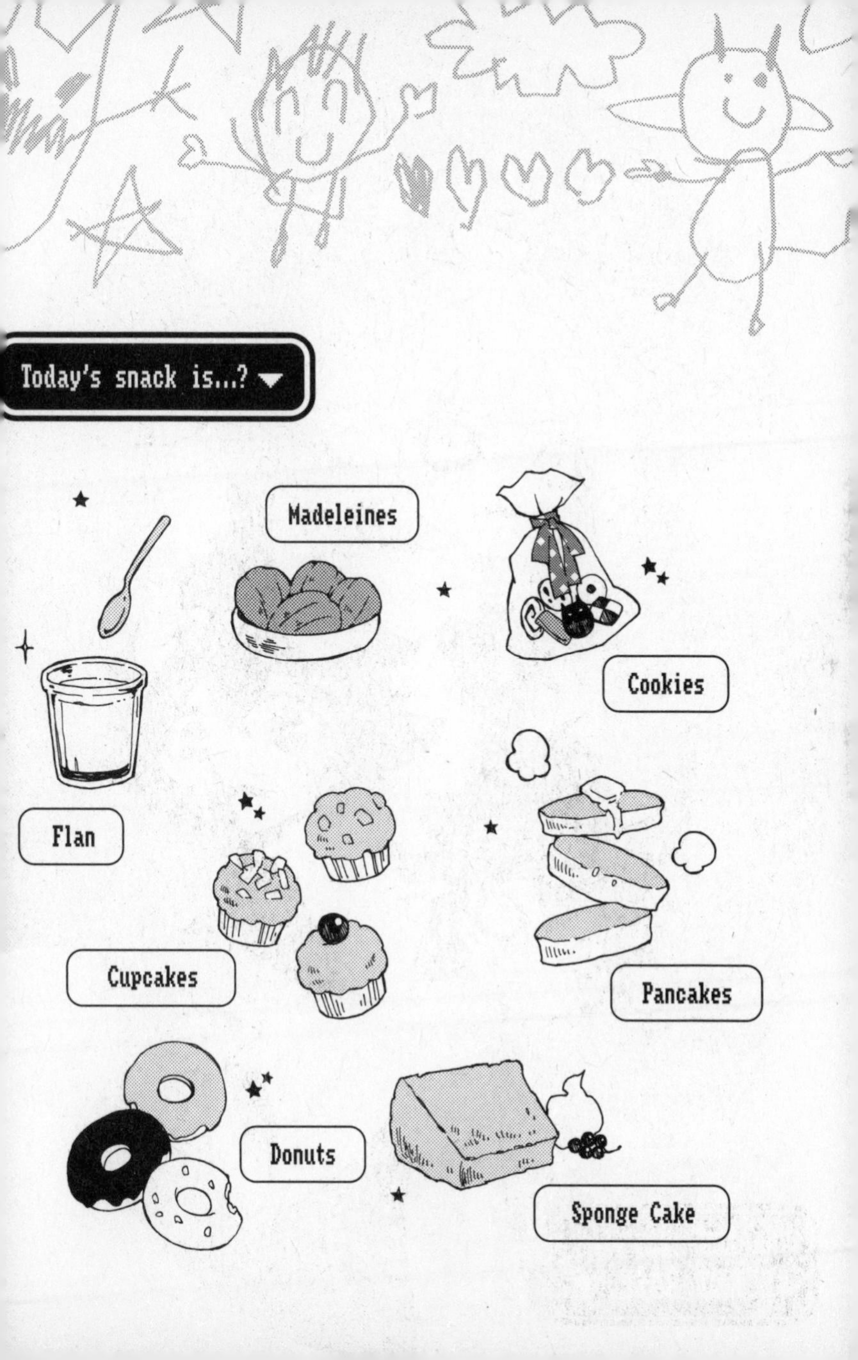
Today's snack is...?
Madeleines
Cookies
Flan
Cupcakes
Pancakes
Donuts
Sponge Cake

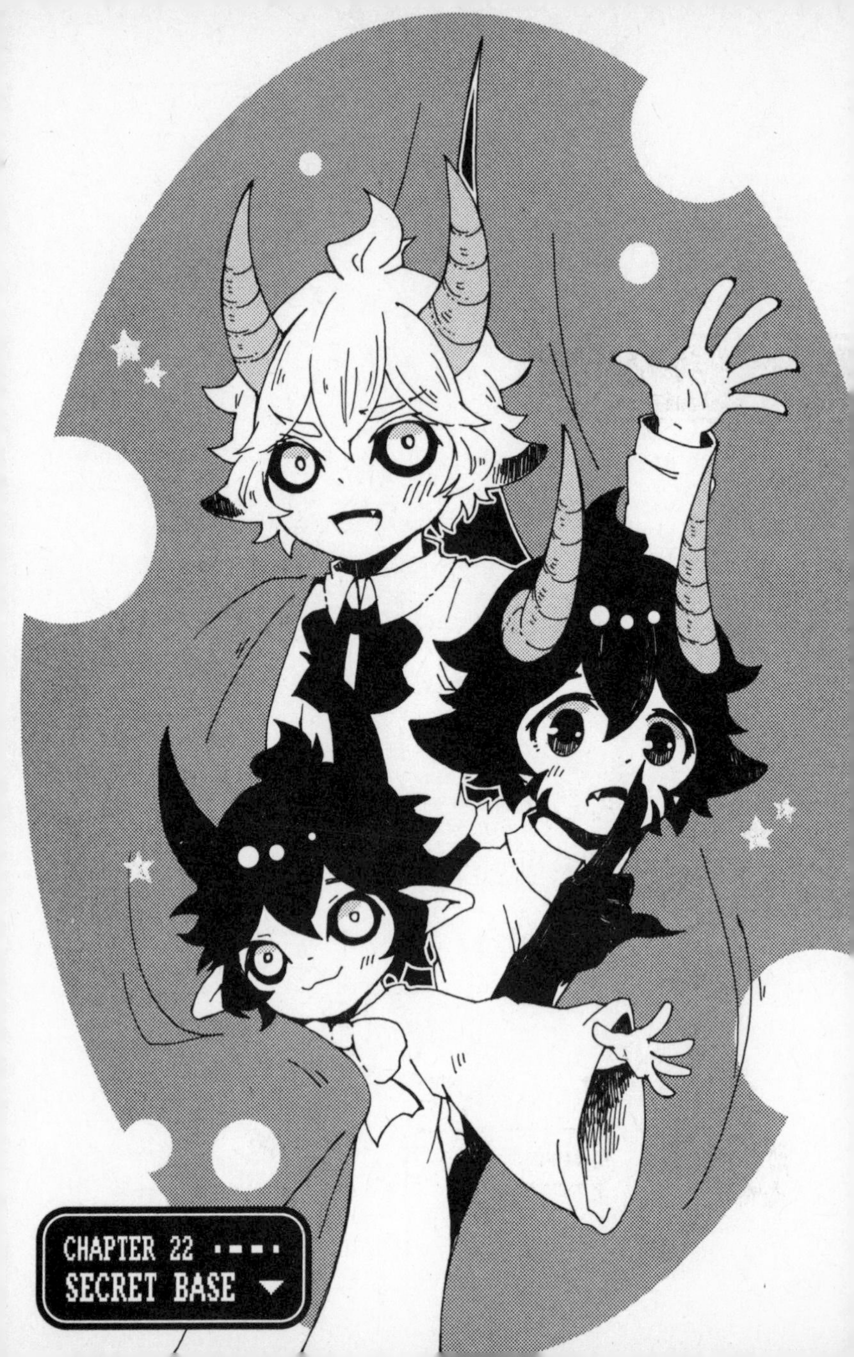
CHAPTER 22
SECRET BASE

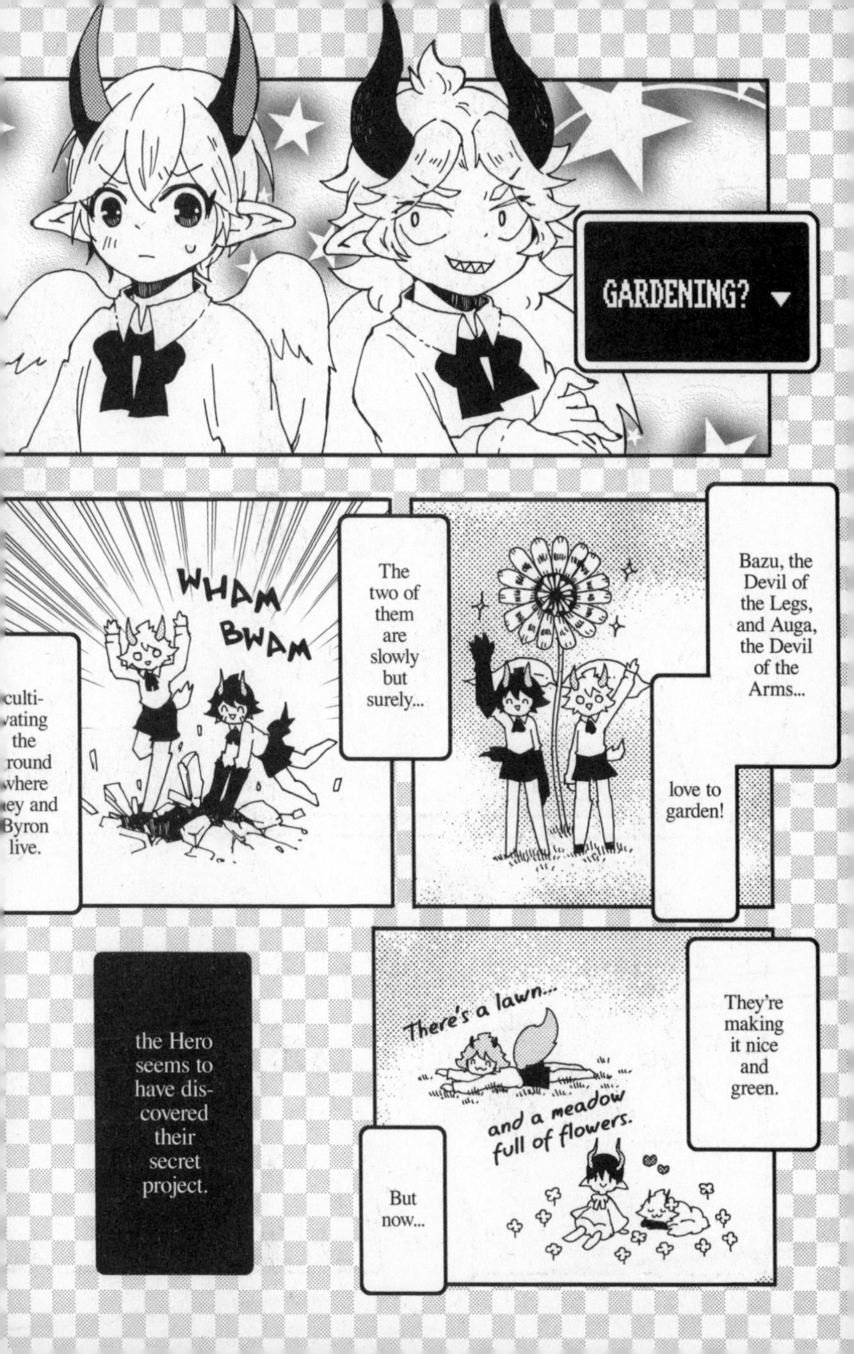
GARDENING?
Bazu, the Devil of the Legs, and Auga, the Devil of the Arms...
love to garden!
The two of them are slowly but surely...
WHAM
BWAM
culti-vating the round where ey and Byron live.
They're making it nice and green.
There's a lawn...
and a meadow full of flowers.
But now...
the Hero seems to have dis-covered their secret project.

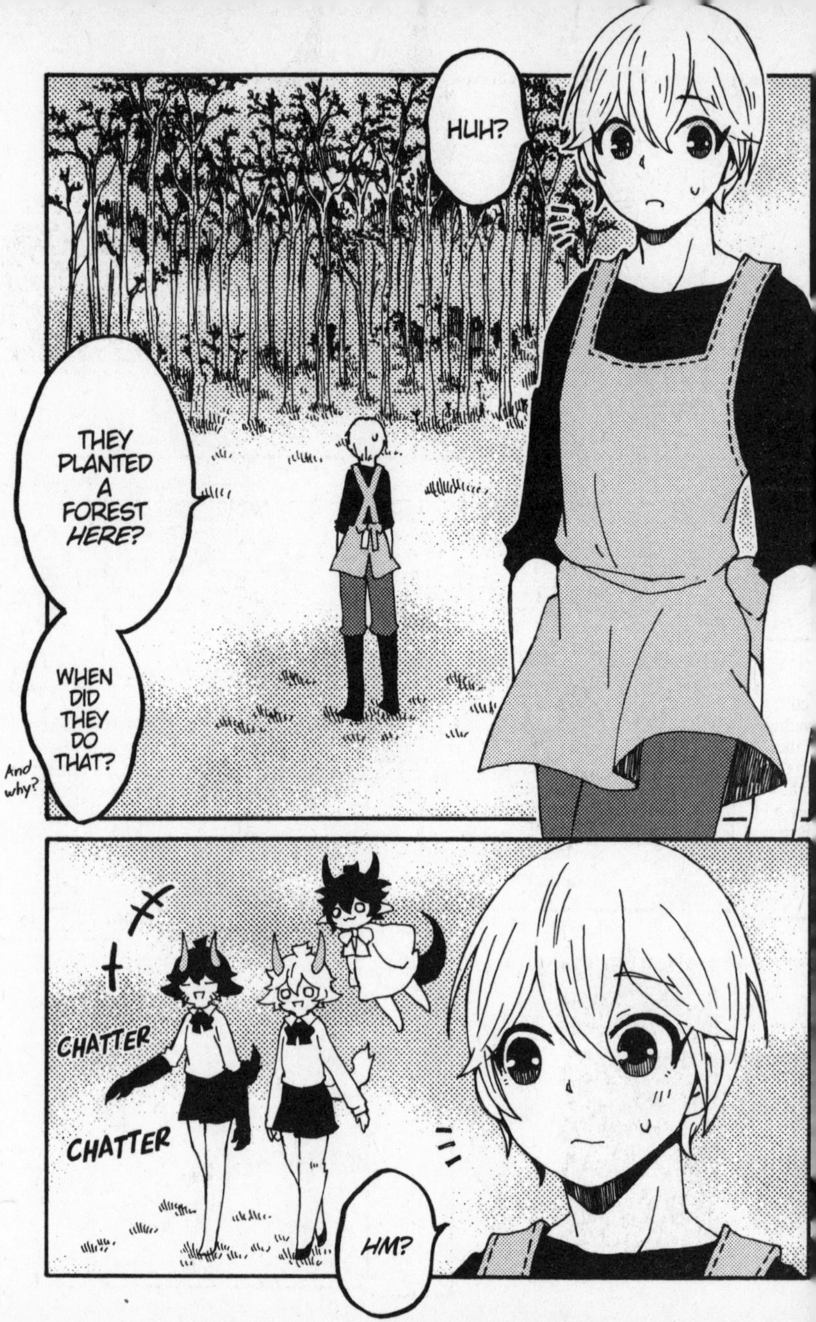
HUH?
THEY PLANTED A FOREST *HERE?*
WHEN DID THEY DO THAT?
And why?
HM?
CHATTER
CHATTER

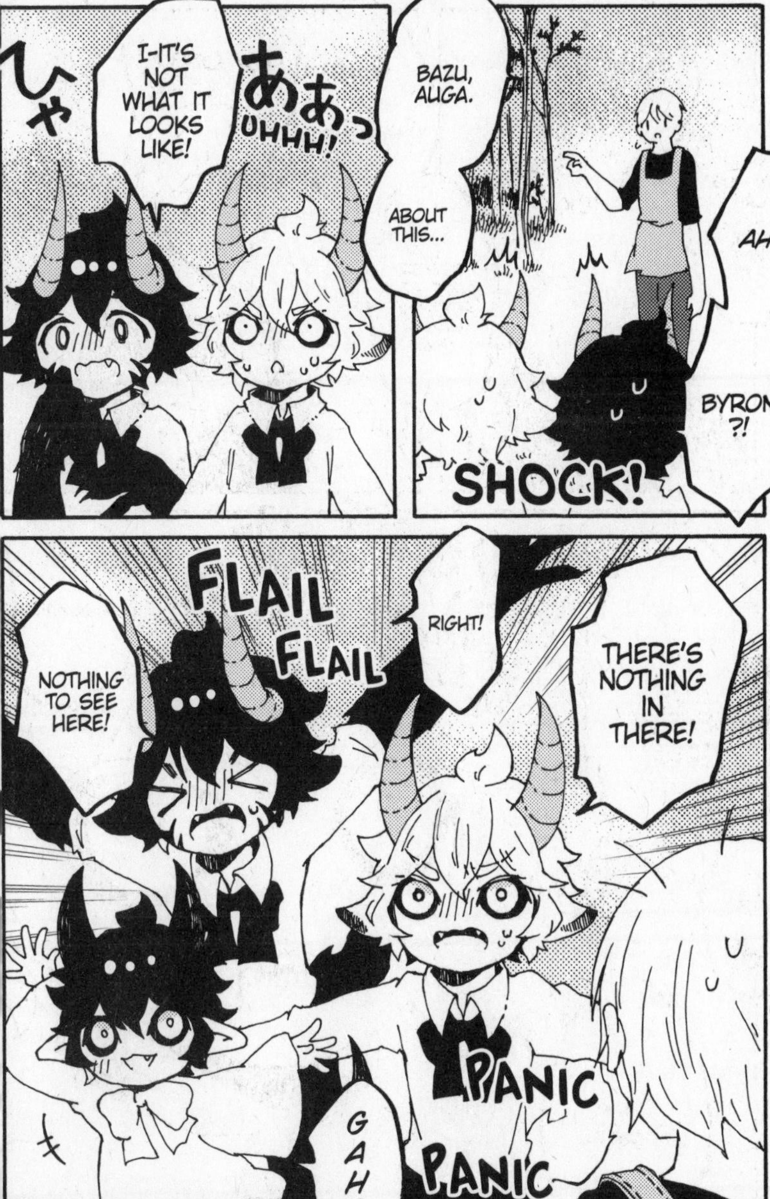
AH!
BYRON ?!
BAZU, AUGA.
ABOUT THIS...
SHOCK!
あぁっ
UHHH!
I-IT'S NOT WHAT IT LOOKS LIKE!
ひゃ
THERE'S NOTHING IN THERE!
RIGHT!
FLAIL FLAIL
NOTHING TO SEE HERE!
PANIC PANIC
GAH!
キ

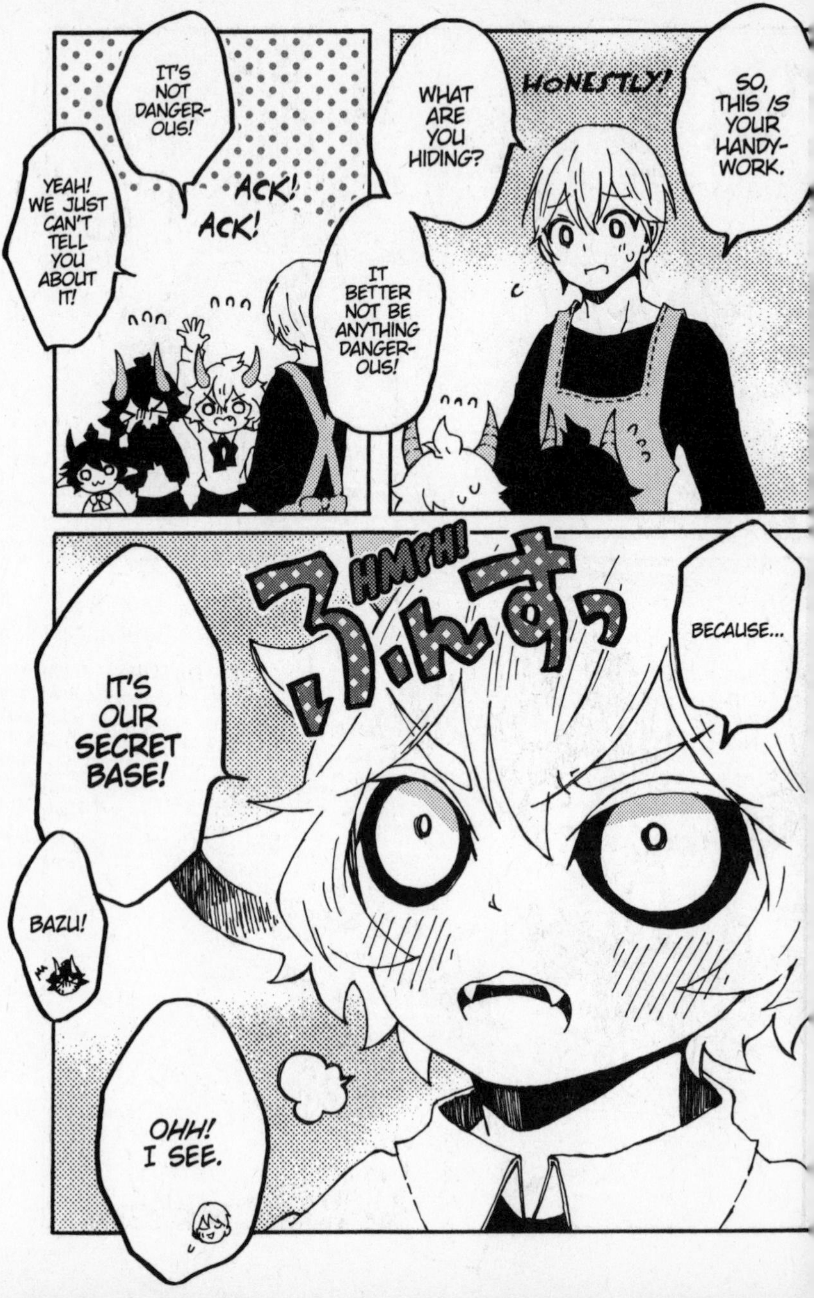
SO, THIS IS YOUR HANDY-WORK.
HONESTLY!
WHAT ARE YOU HIDING?
IT BETTER NOT BE ANYTHING DANGER-OUS!
IT'S NOT DANGER-OUS!
ACK! ACK!
YEAH! WE JUST CAN'T TELL YOU ABOUT IT!
BECAUSE...
ふんすっ
HMPH!
IT'S OUR SECRET BASE!
BAZU!
OHH! I SEE.

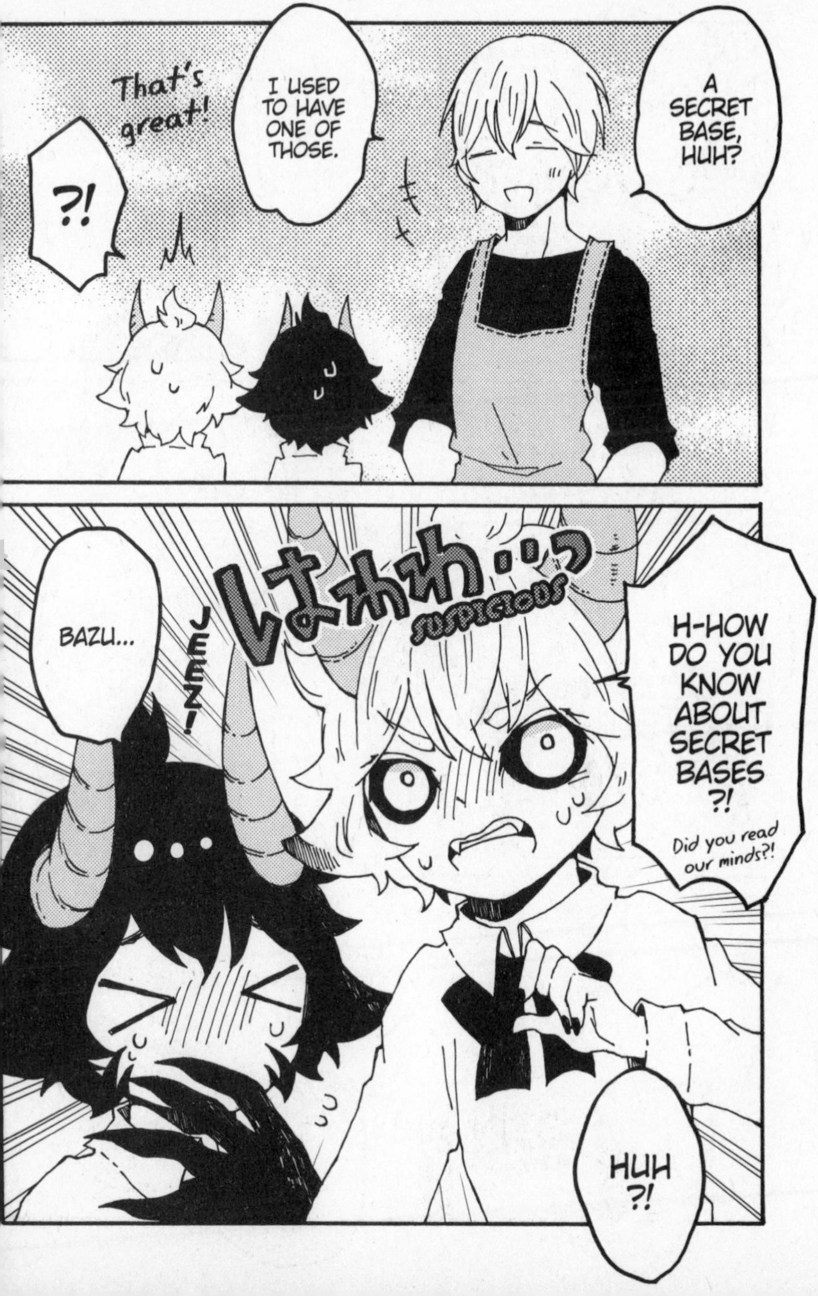
A SECRET BASE, HUH?
I USED TO HAVE ONE OF THOSE.
That's great!
?!
H-HOW DO YOU KNOW ABOUT SECRET BASES?!
Did you read our minds?!
SUSPICIOUS
JEEZ!
BAZU...
HUH?!

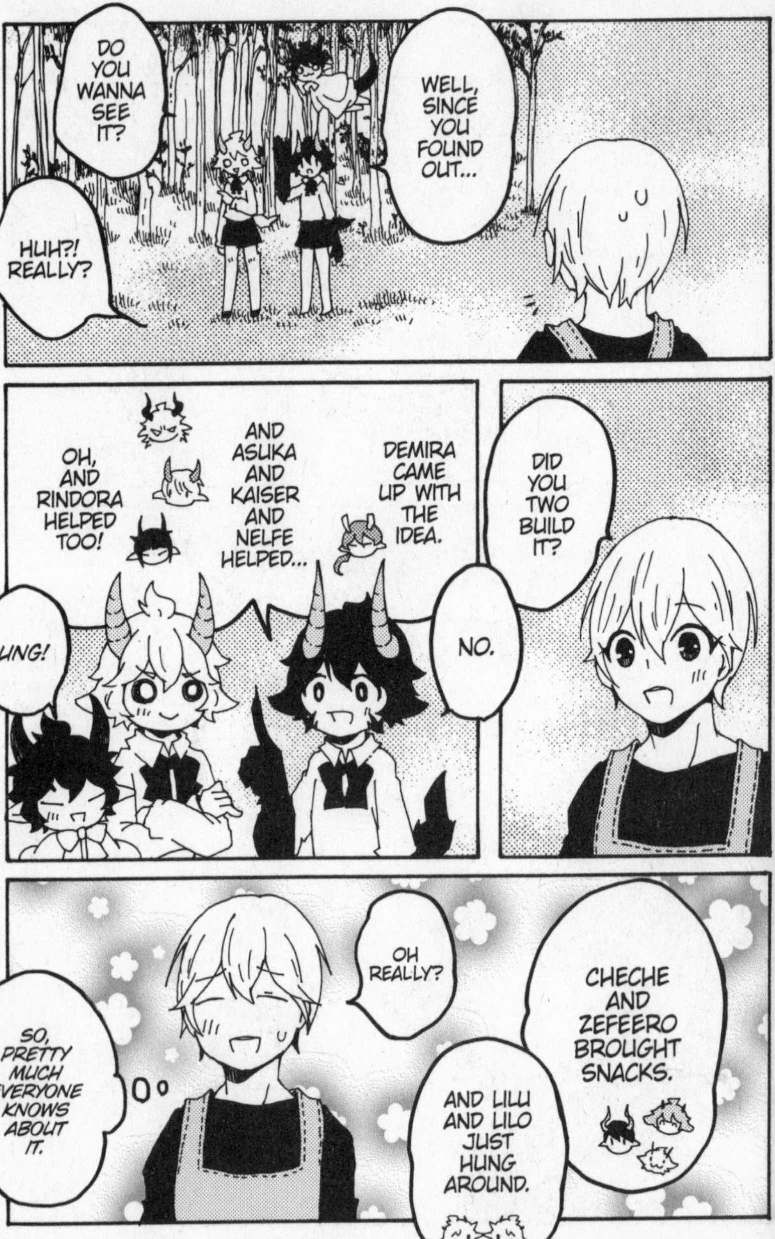
WELL, SINCE YOU FOUND OUT...
DO YOU WANNA SEE IT?
HUH?! REALLY?
DID YOU TWO BUILD IT?
NO.
DEMIRA CAME UP WITH THE IDEA.
AND ASUKA AND KAISER AND NELFE HELPED...
OH, AND RINDORA HELPED TOO!
UNG!
CHECHE AND ZEFEERO BROUGHT SNACKS.
AND LILU AND LILO JUST HUNG AROUND.
OH REALLY?
SO, PRETTY MUCH EVERYONE KNOWS ABOUT IT.

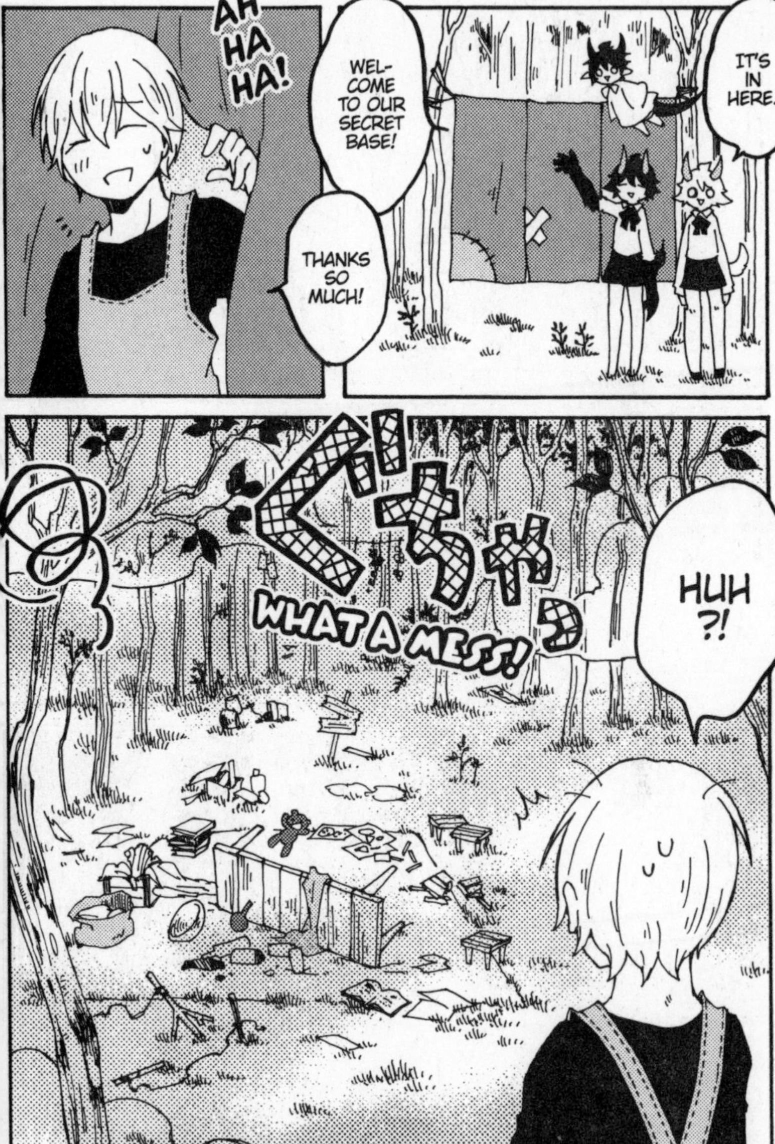
IT'S IN HERE.
WEL-COME TO OUR SECRET BASE!
THANKS SO MUCH!
AH HA HA!
ぐちゃっ
WHAT A MESS!
HUH?!

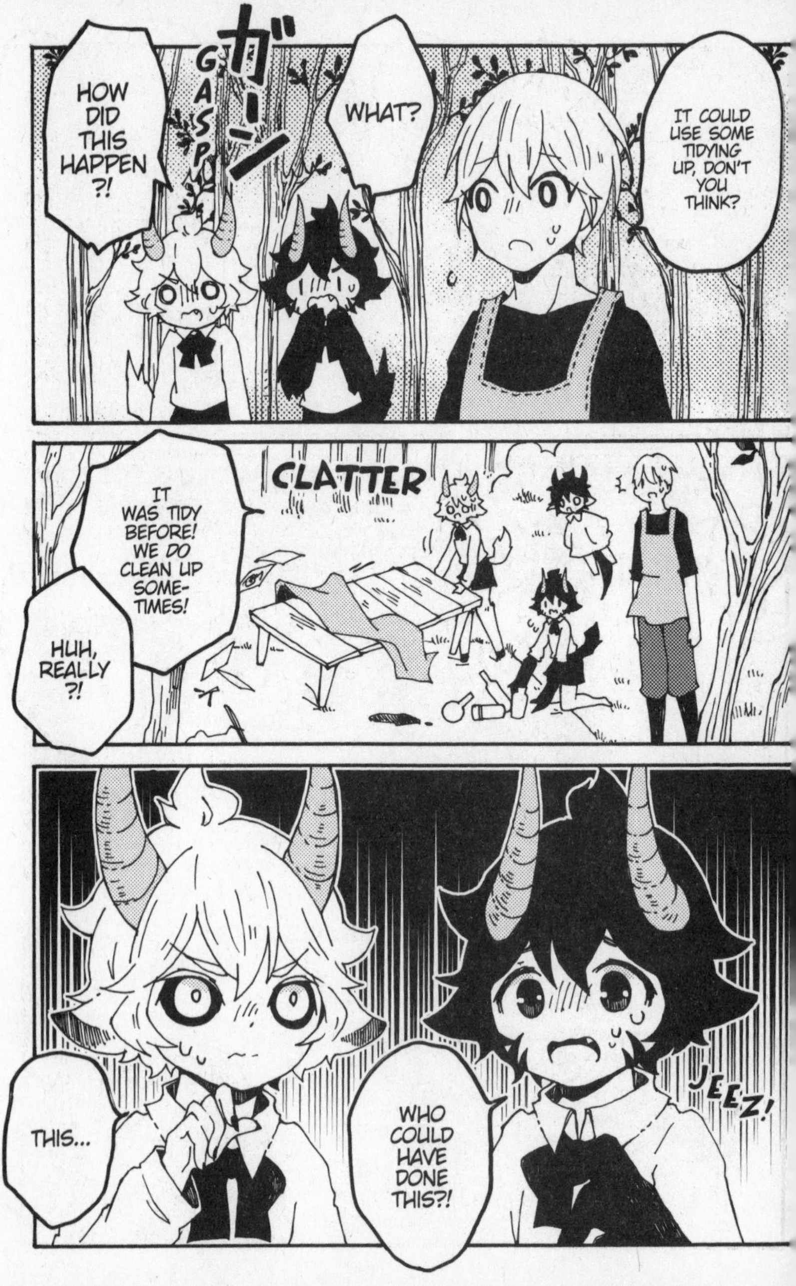

IT COULD USE SOME TIDYING UP, DON'T YOU THINK?
WHAT?
GASP
HOW DID THIS HAPPEN?!
CLATTER
IT WAS TIDY BEFORE! WE DO CLEAN UP SOME-TIMES!
HUH, REALLY?!
JEEZ!
WHO COULD HAVE DONE THIS?!
THIS...

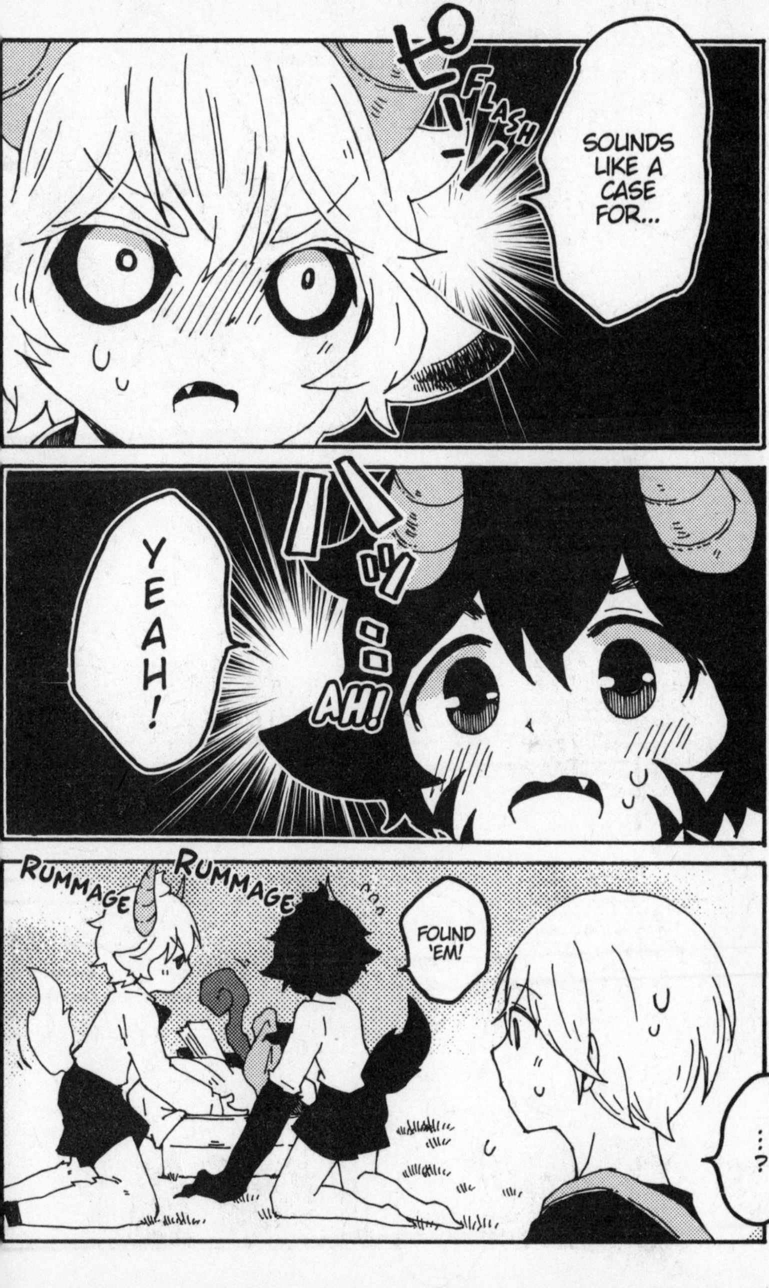
FLASH
SOUNDS LIKE A CASE FOR...
AH!
YEAH!
FOUND 'EM!
RUMMAGE RUMMAGE
...?

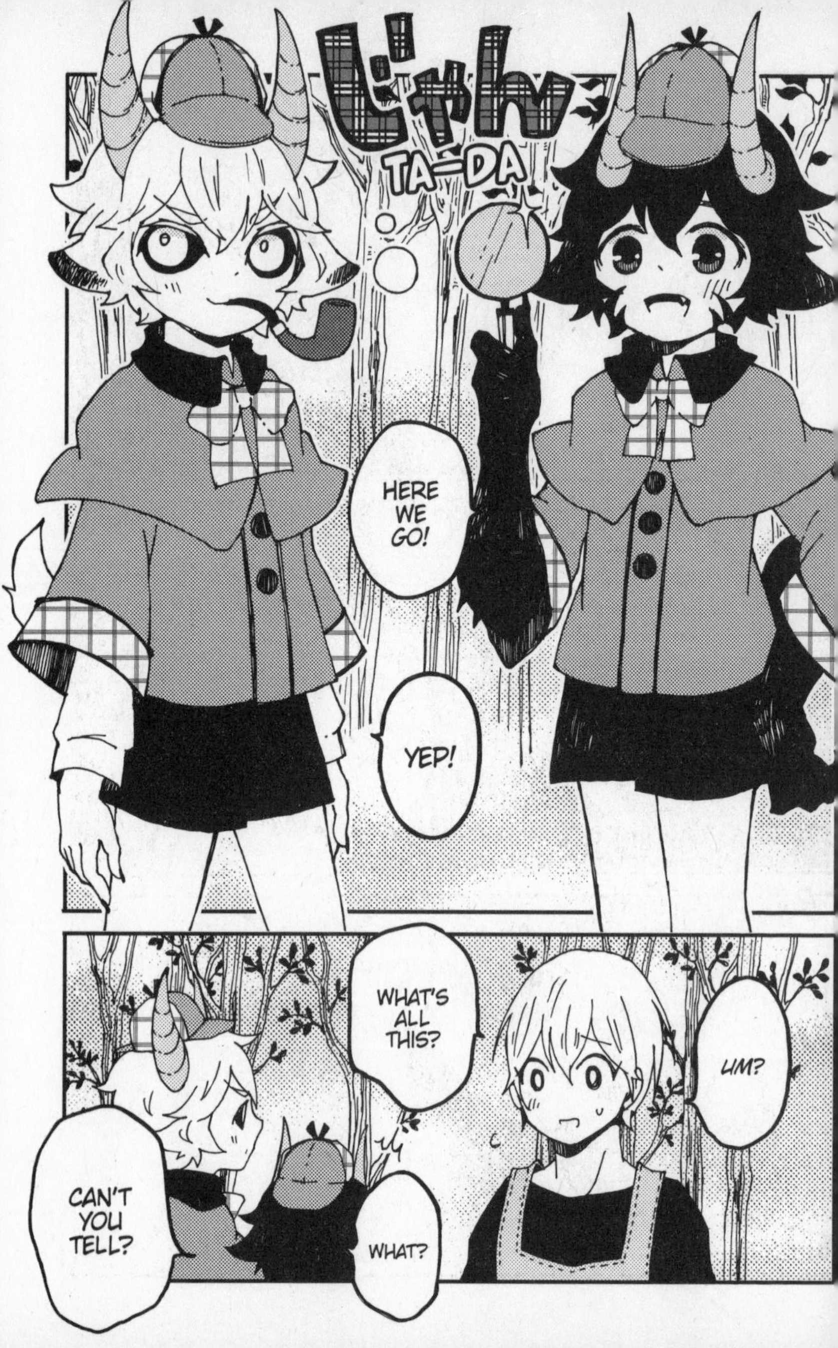
じゃん
TA-DA
HERE WE GO!
YEP!
UM?
WHAT'S ALL THIS?
WHAT?
CAN'T YOU TELL?

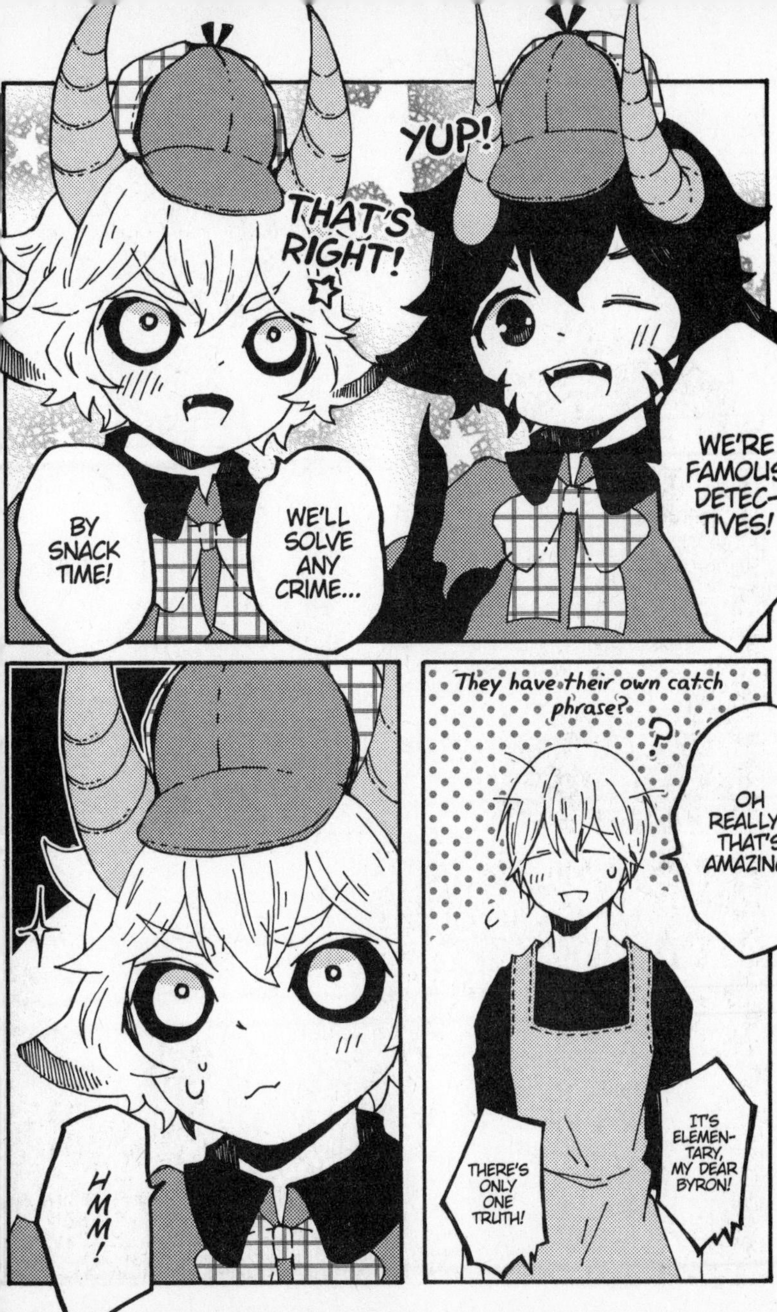
WE'RE FAMOUS DETECTIVES!
YUP!
THAT'S RIGHT!
WE'LL SOLVE ANY CRIME...
BY SNACK TIME!
They have their own catch phrase?
OH REALLY? THAT'S AMAZING!
IT'S ELEMENTARY, MY DEAR BYRON!
THERE'S ONLY ONE TRUTH!
HMM!

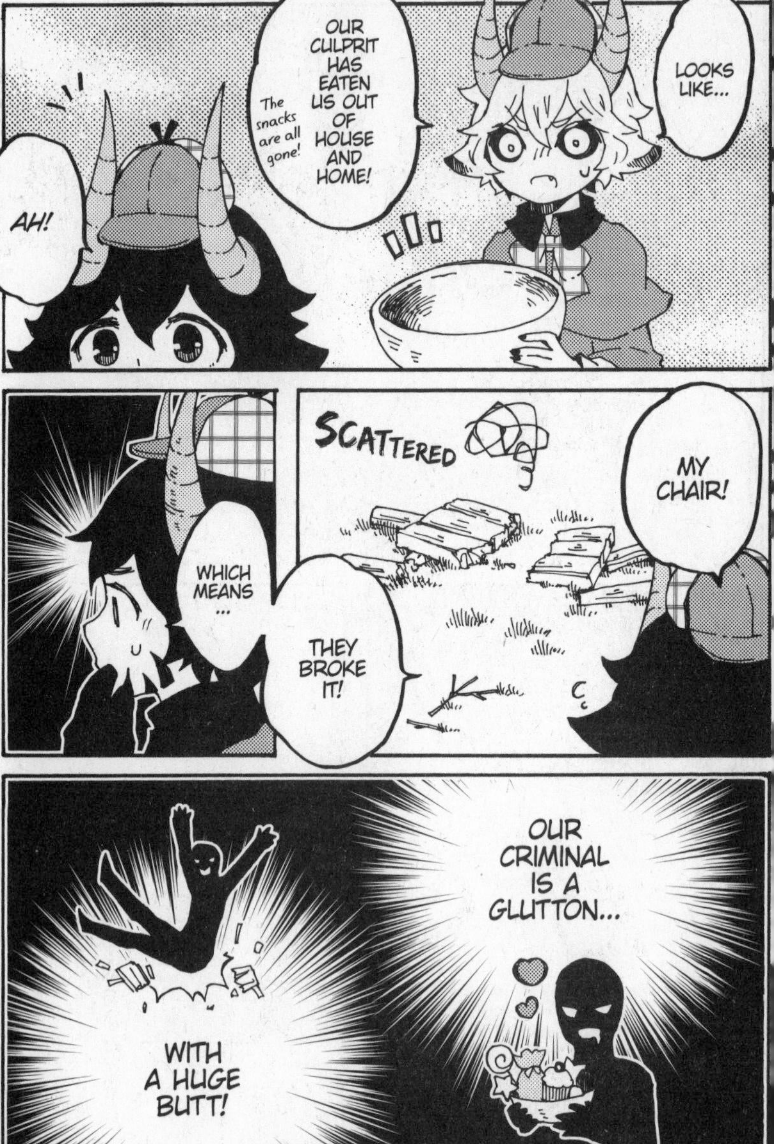
LOOKS LIKE...
OUR CULPRIT HAS EATEN US OUT OF HOUSE AND HOME!
The snacks are all gone!
AH!
MY CHAIR!
SCATTERED
THEY BROKE IT!
WHICH MEANS ...
OUR CRIMINAL IS A GLUTTON...
WITH A HUGE BUTT!

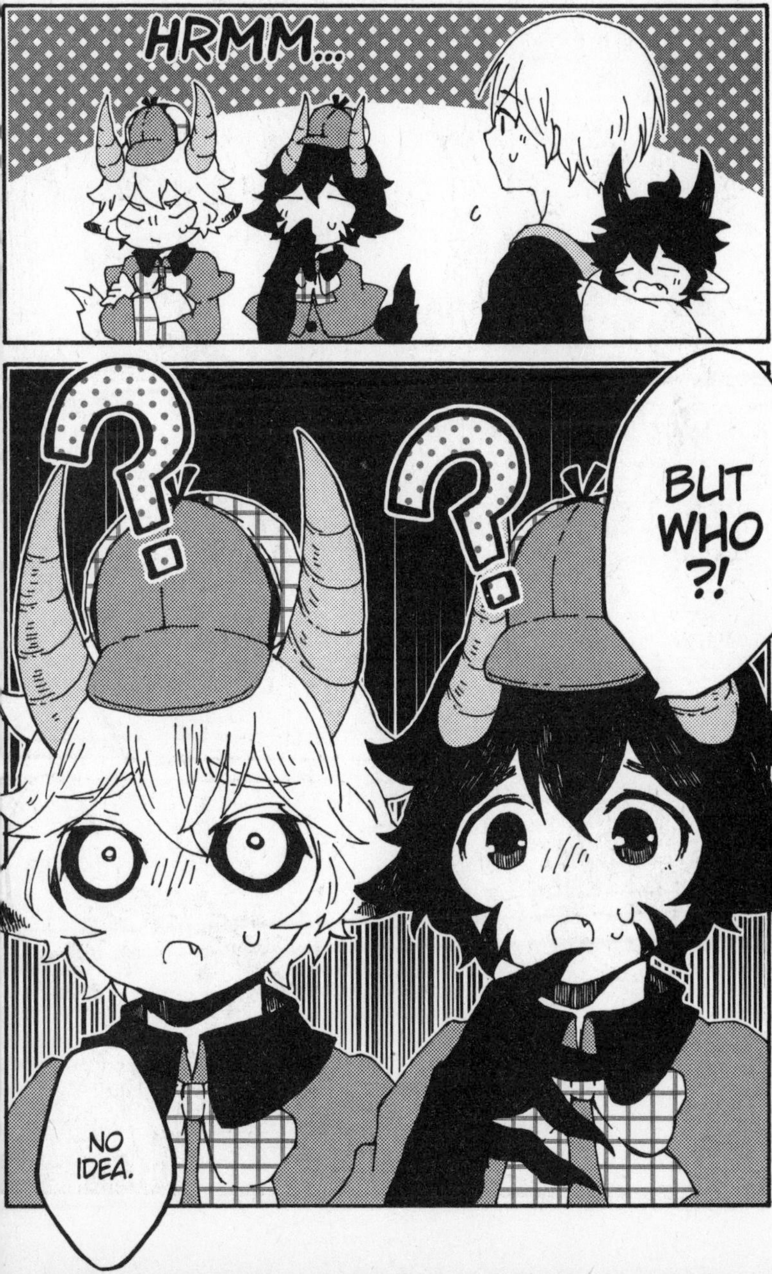
HRMM...
BUT WHO ?!
NO IDEA.

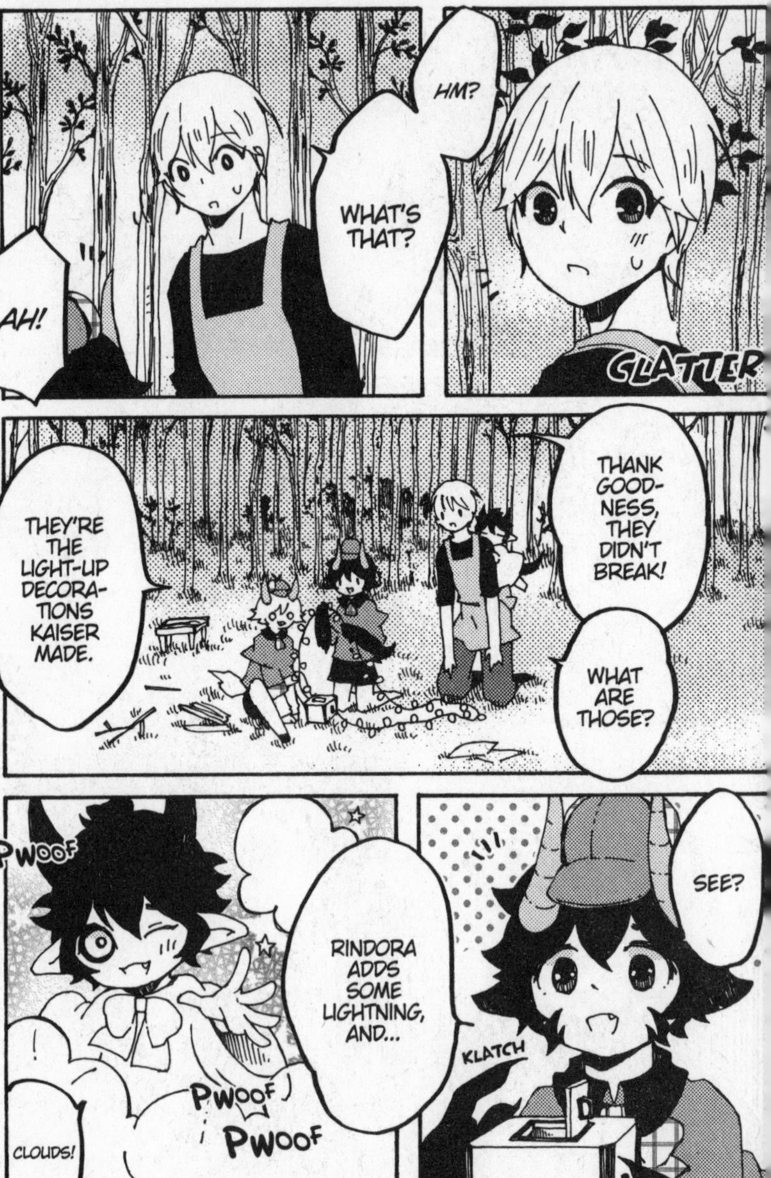
HM?
CLATTER
WHAT'S THAT?
AH!
THANK GOOD-NESS, THEY DIDN'T BREAK!
WHAT ARE THOSE?
THEY'RE THE LIGHT-UP DECORA-TIONS KAISER MADE.
SEE?
KLATCH
RINDORA ADDS SOME LIGHTNING, AND...
PWOOF
PWOOF
PWOOF
CLOUDS!

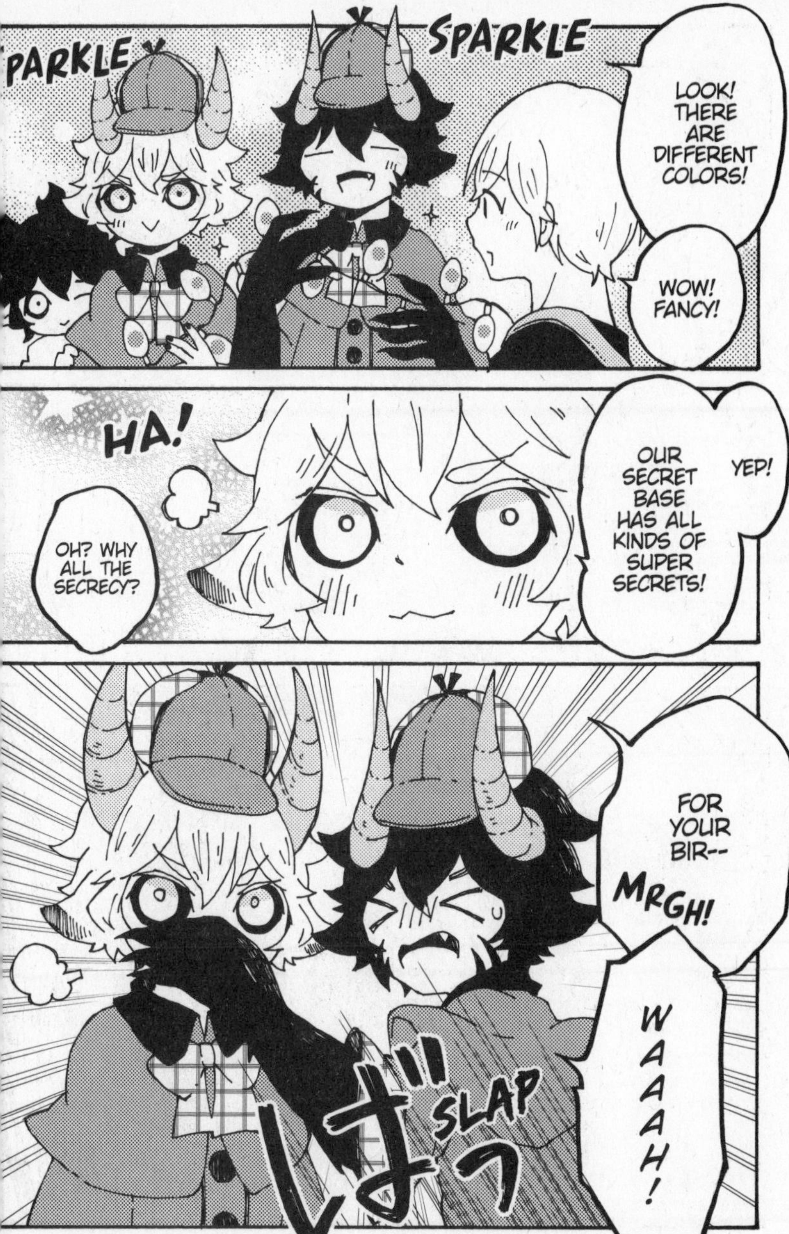
LOOK! THERE ARE DIFFERENT COLORS!
SPARKLE
WOW! FANCY!
PARKLE
OUR SECRET BASE HAS ALL KINDS OF SUPER SECRETS!
YEP!
HA!
OH? WHY ALL THE SECRECY?
FOR YOUR BIR--
MRGH!
WAAAAH!
SLAP

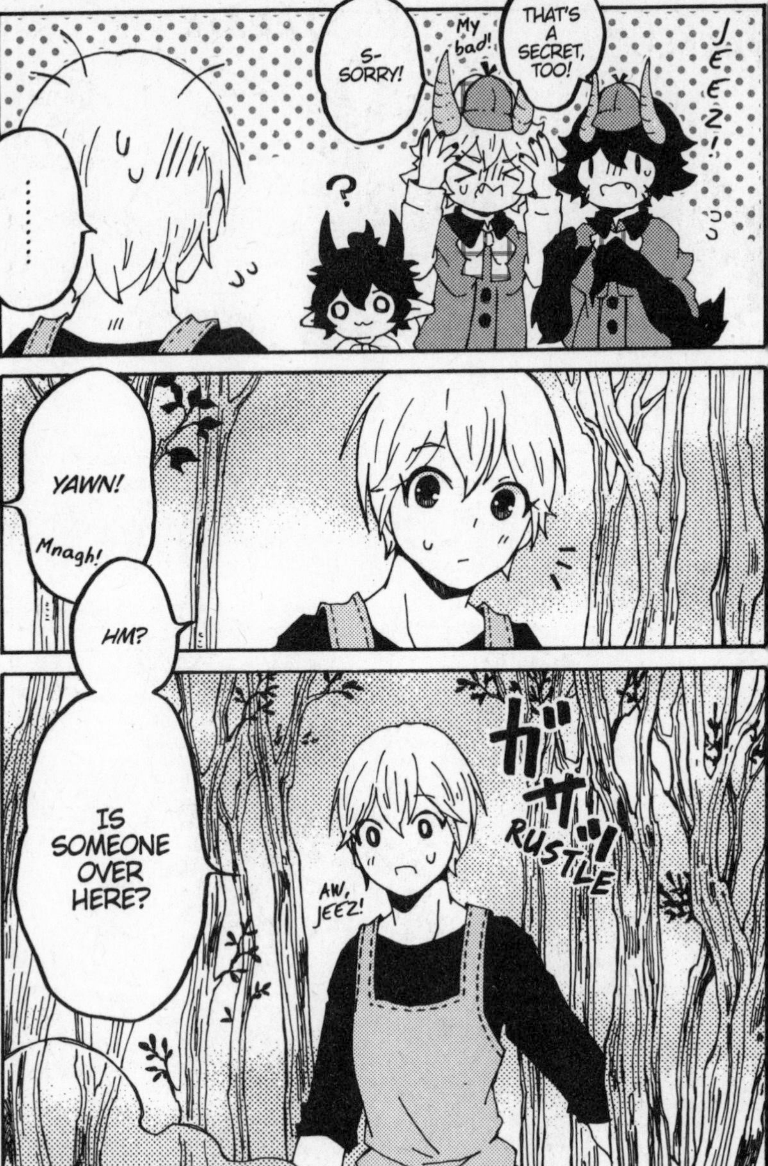
JEEZ!
THAT'S A SECRET, TOO!
My bad!
S-SORRY!
?
......
YAWN!
Mnagh!
HM?
ガサッ
RUSTLE
AW, JEEZ!
IS SOMEONE OVER HERE?

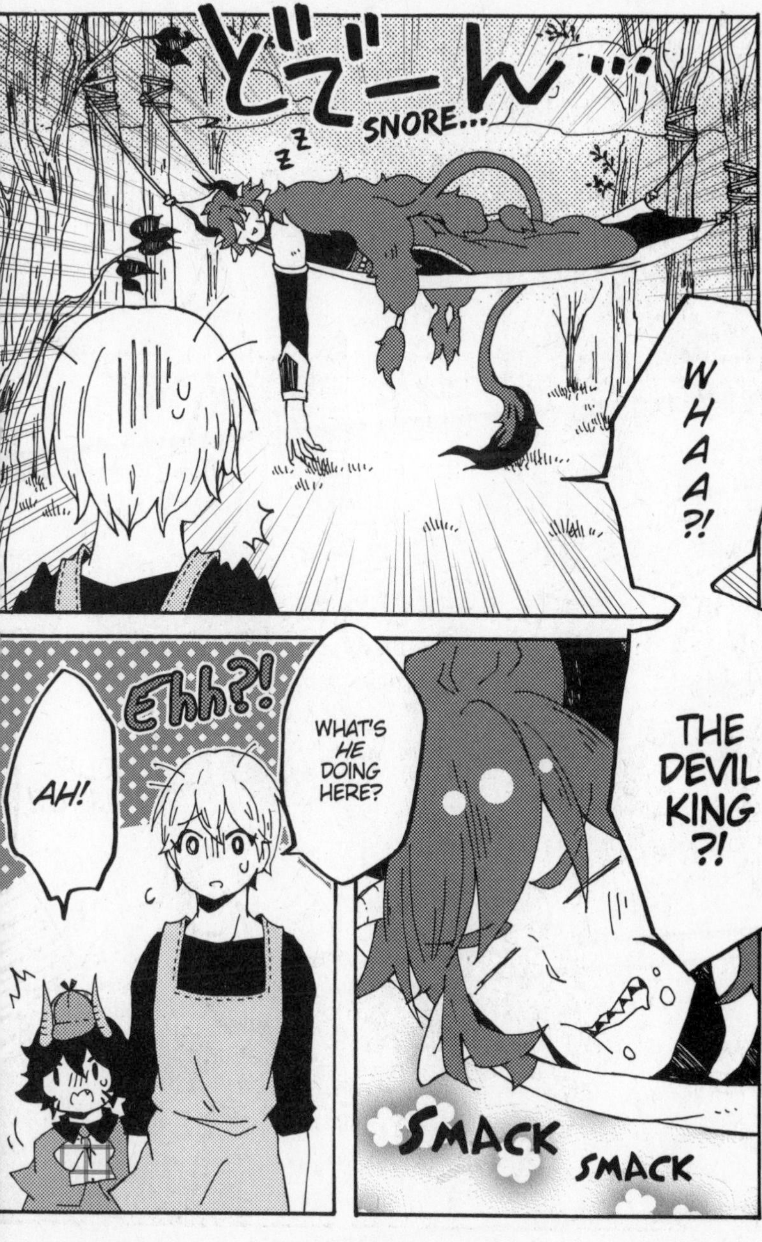
どでーん…
SNORE...
Z Z Z
WHAAA?! THE DEVIL KING?!
SMACK
SMACK
WHAT'S HE DOING HERE?
Ehh?!
AH!

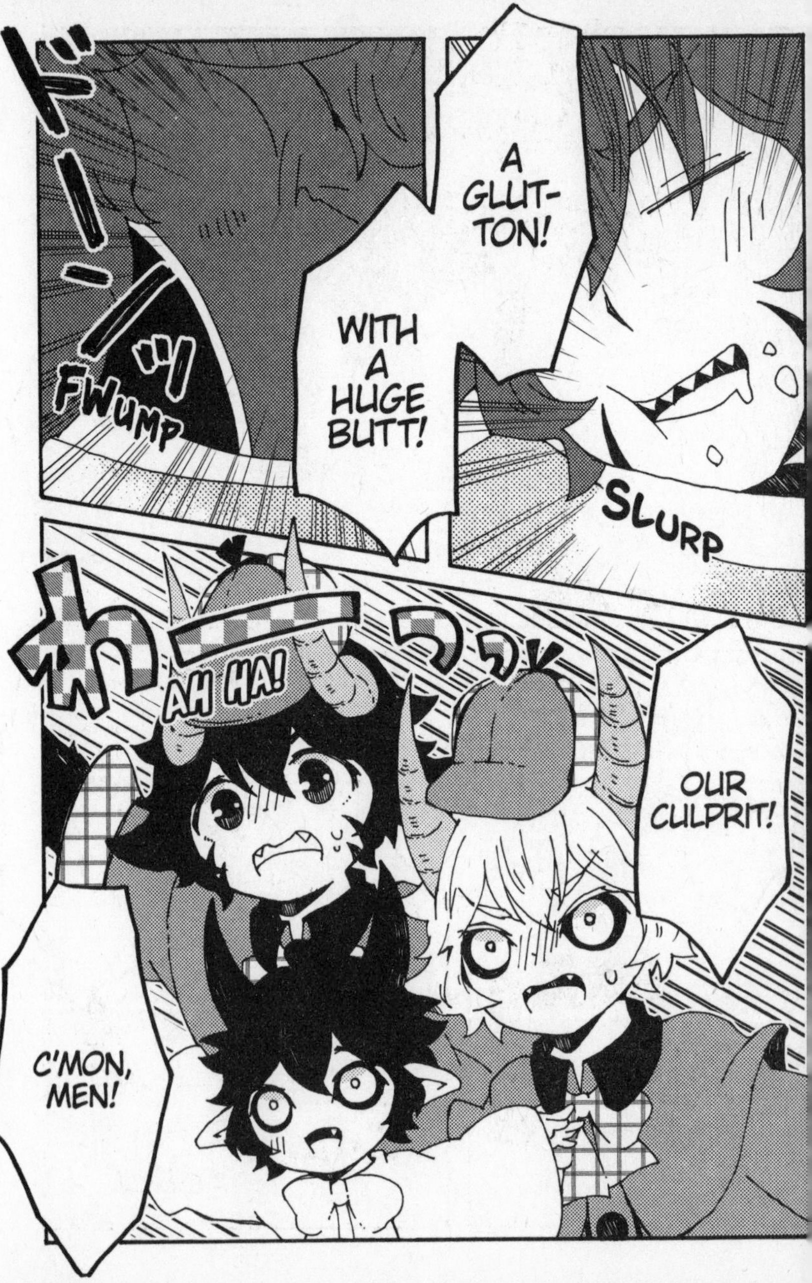
A GLUT-TON!
WITH A HUGE BUTT!
SLURP
ドーーーッ
FWUMP
OUR CULPRIT!
わーっっ
AH HA!
C'MON, MEN!

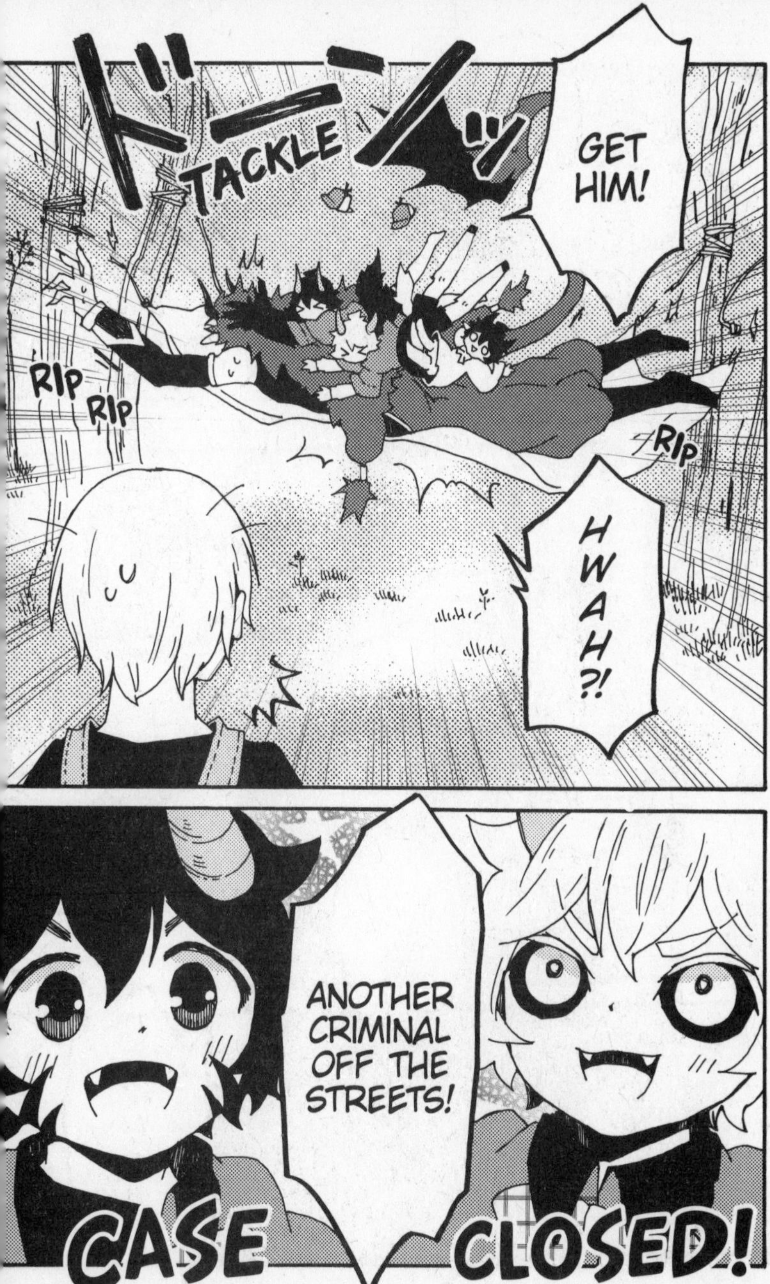
GET HIM!
ドーンッ
TACKLE
RIP
RIP
RIP
HWAH?!
ANOTHER CRIMINAL OFF THE STREETS!
CASE CLOSED!

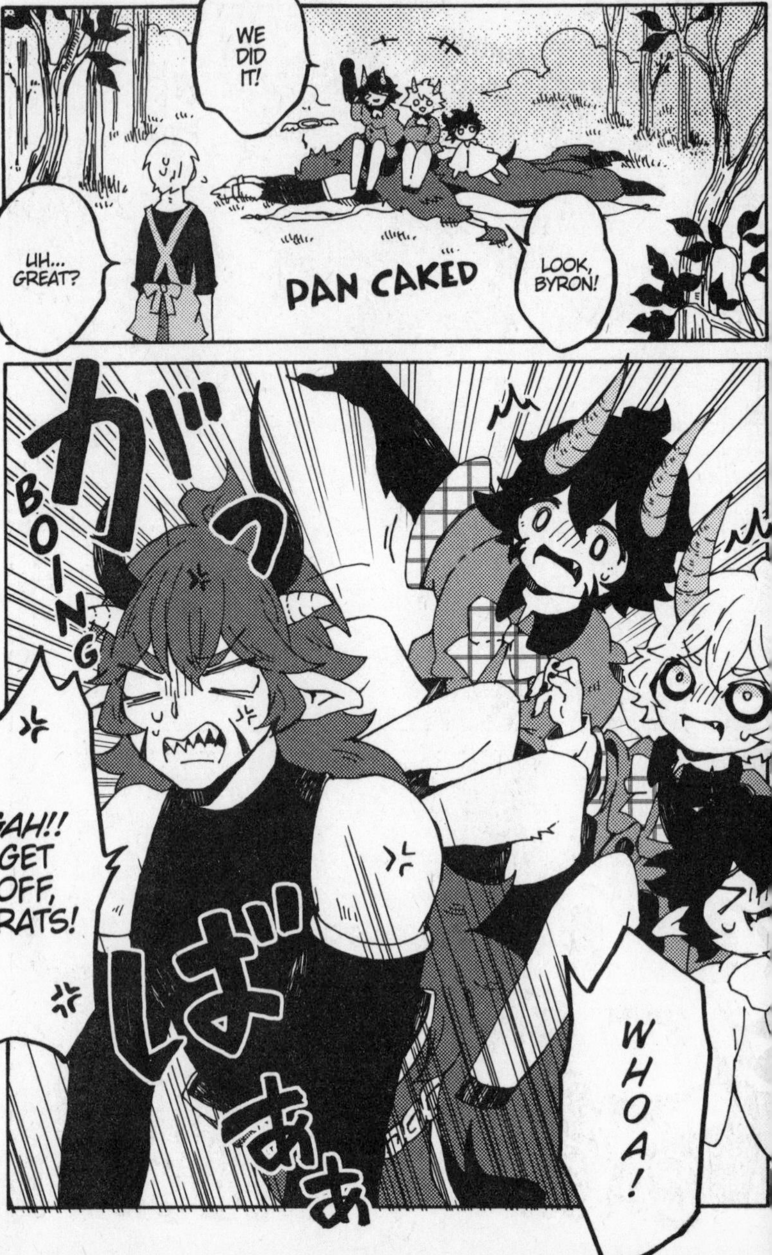
WE DID IT!
LOOK, BYRON!
PAN CAKED
UH... GREAT?
WHOA!
がっ
BOING
GAH!! GET OFF, BRATS!

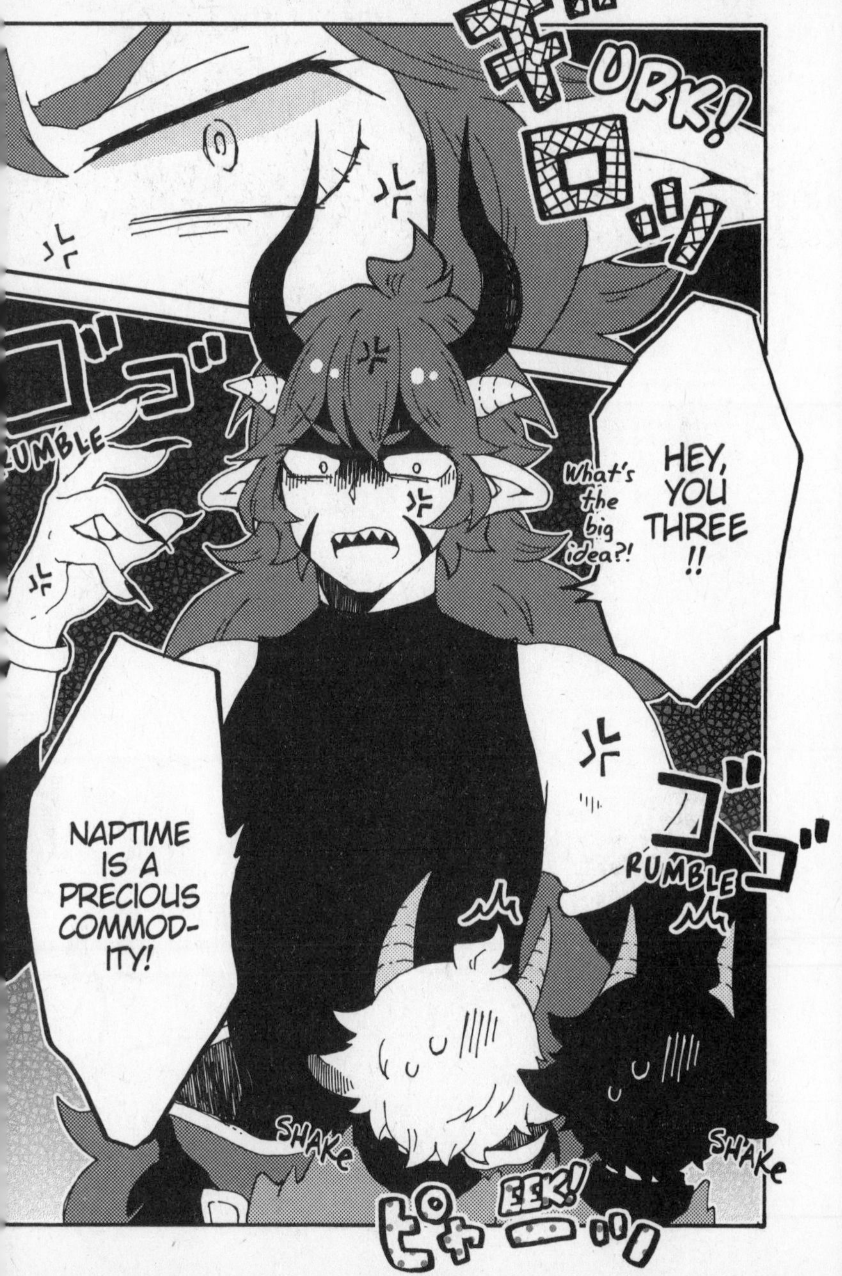
ギロッ
URK!
HEY, YOU THREE !!
What's the big idea?!
ゴゴ
RUMBLE
ゴゴ
RUMBLE
NAPTIME IS A PRECIOUS COMMOD-ITY!
SHAKE
ぴゃー
EEK!
SHAKE

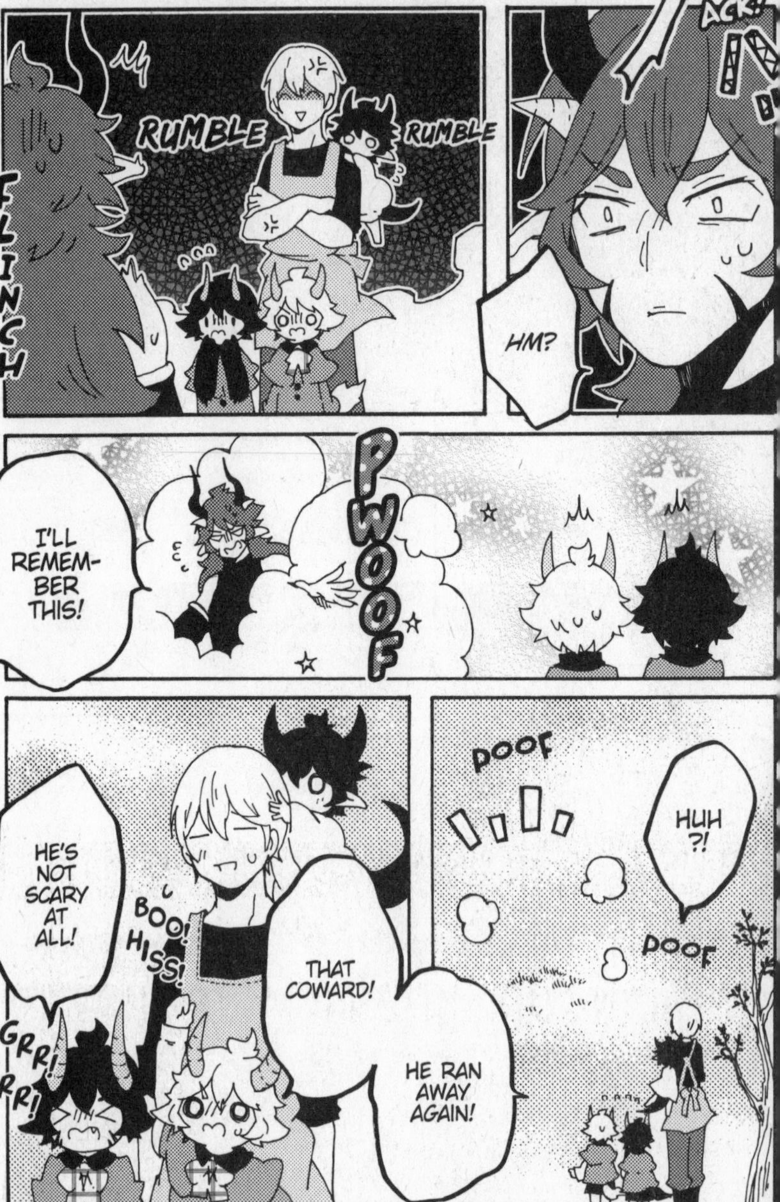
ACK!
HM?
RUMBLE
RUMBLE
FLINCH
PWOOF
I'LL REMEMBER THIS!
POOF
HUH?!
POOF
THAT COWARD!
HE RAN AWAY AGAIN!
BOO! HISS!
HE'S NOT SCARY AT ALL!
GRR! GRR!

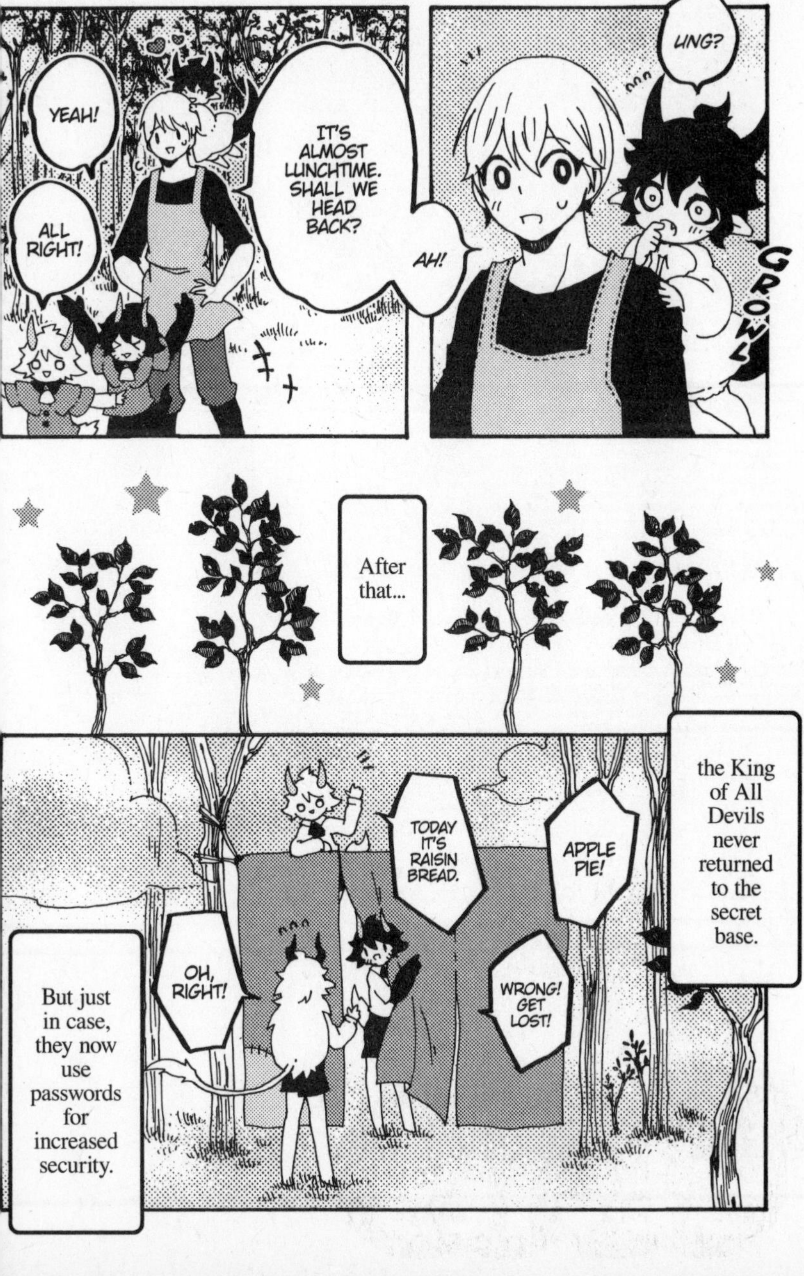
UNG?
GROWL
AH!
IT'S ALMOST LUNCHTIME. SHALL WE HEAD BACK?
YEAH!
ALL RIGHT!
After that...
the King of All Devils never returned to the secret base.
APPLE PIE!
TODAY IT'S RAISIN BREAD.
WRONG! GET LOST!
OH, RIGHT!
But just in case, they now use passwords for increased security.

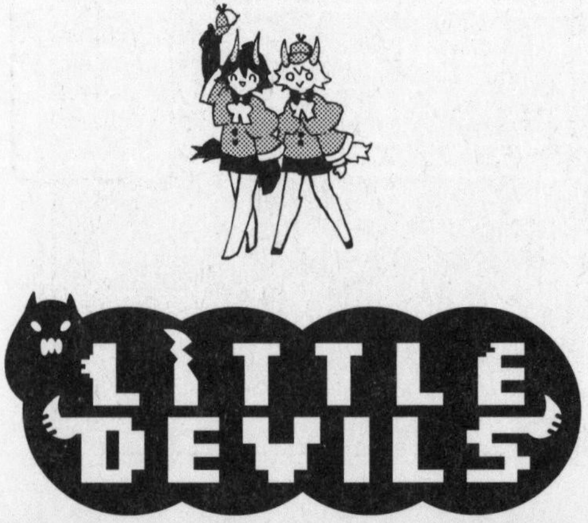

LITTLE DEVILS

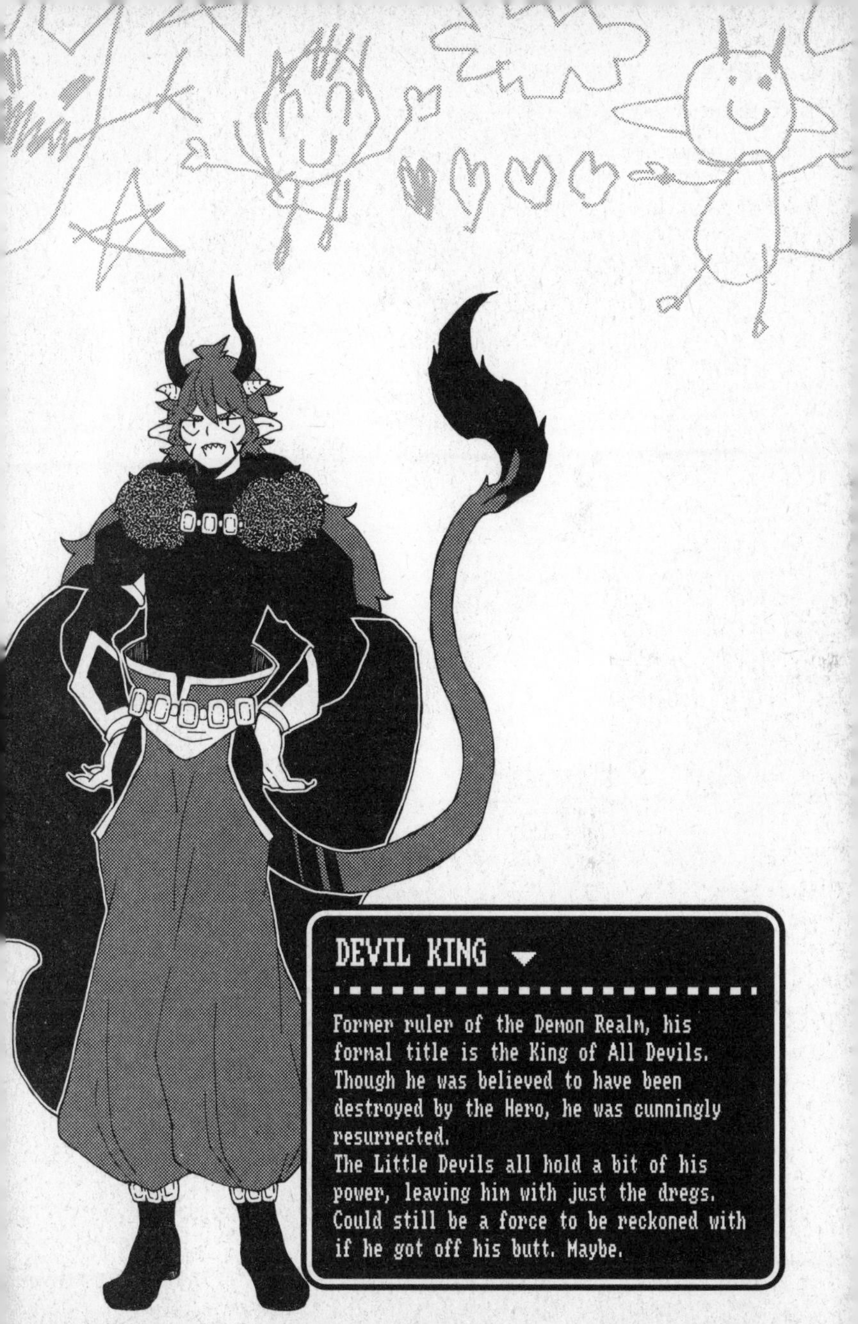

DEVIL KING

Former ruler of the Demon Realm, his formal title is the King of All Devils. Though he was believed to have been destroyed by the Hero, he was cunningly resurrected.
The Little Devils all hold a bit of his power, leaving him with just the dregs. Could still be a force to be reckoned with if he got off his butt. Maybe.

CHAPTER 23 ·····
SEARCHING ▼

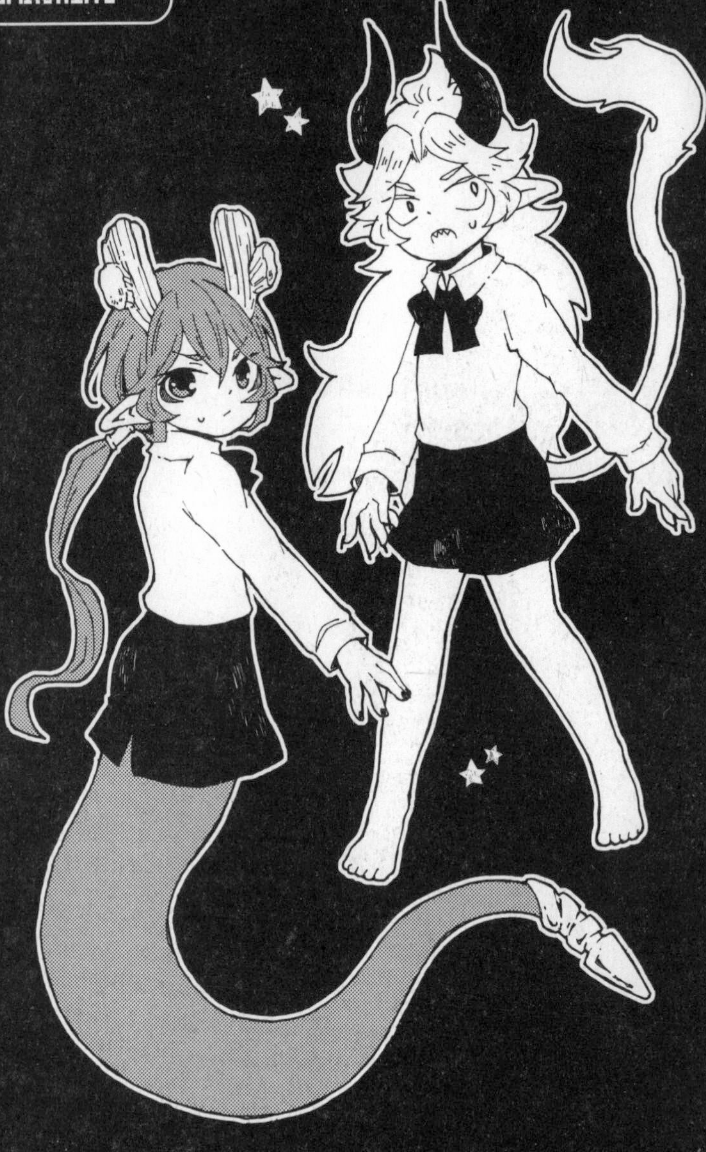

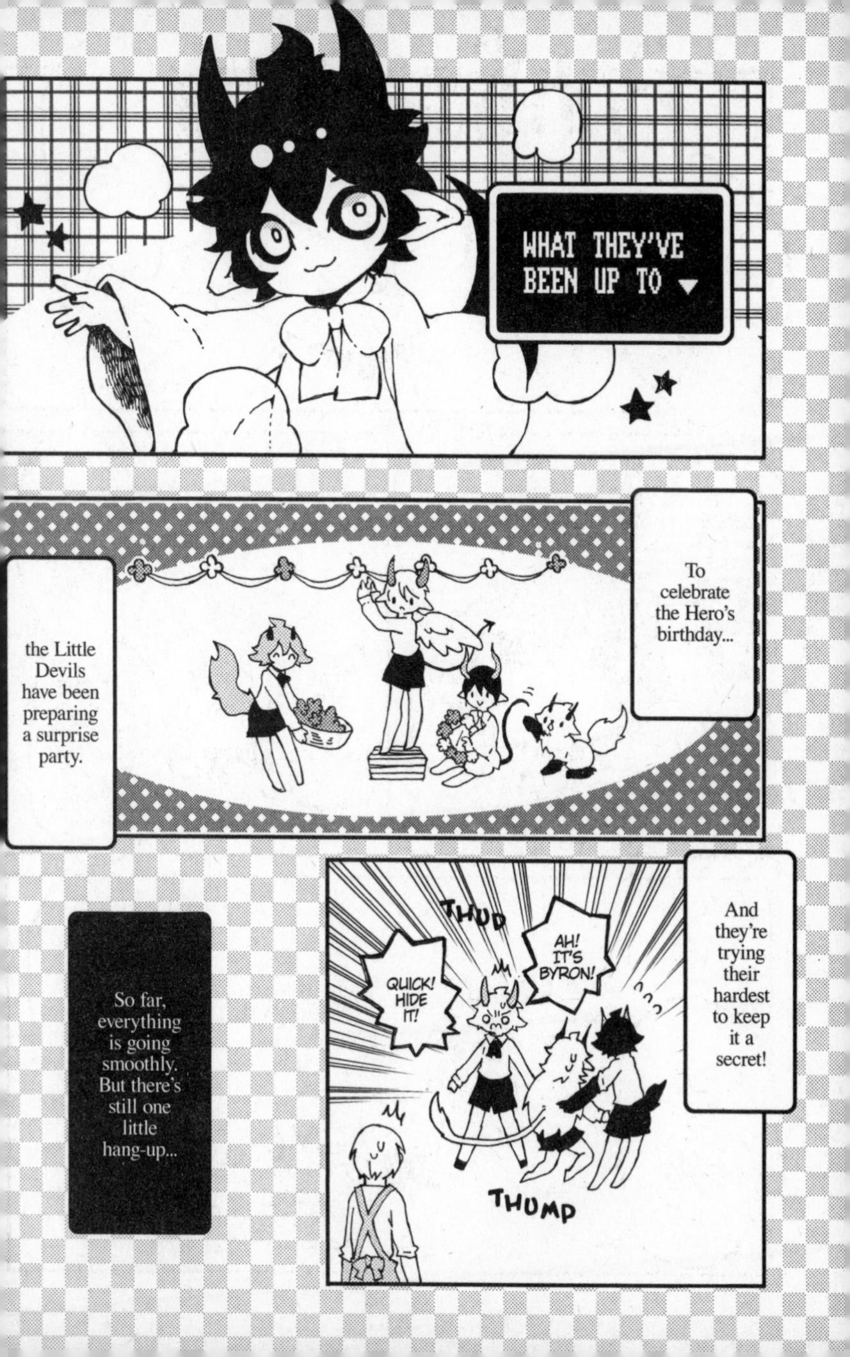
WHAT THEY'VE BEEN UP TO
To celebrate the Hero's birthday...
the Little Devils have been preparing a surprise party.
And they're trying their hardest to keep it a secret!
THUD
AH! IT'S BYRON!
QUICK! HIDE IT!
THUMP
So far, everything is going smoothly. But there's still one little hang-up...

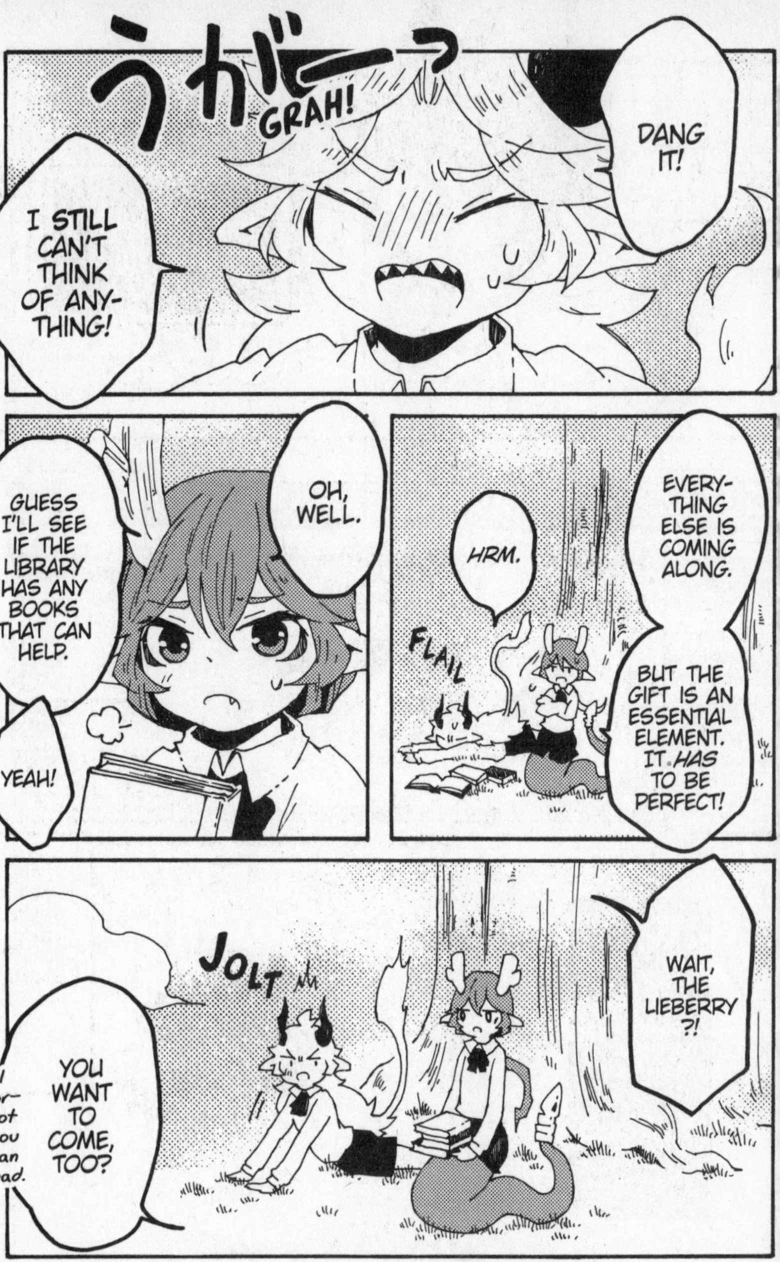
DANG IT!
うがーっ
GRAH!
I STILL CAN'T THINK OF ANY-THING!
EVERY-THING ELSE IS COMING ALONG.
HRM.
FLAIL
BUT THE GIFT IS AN ESSENTIAL ELEMENT. IT *HAS* TO BE PERFECT!
OH, WELL.
GUESS I'LL SEE IF THE LIBRARY HAS ANY BOOKS THAT CAN HELP.
YEAH!
WAIT, THE LIEBERRY?!
JOLT
YOU WANT TO COME, TOO?
I for-got you can read.

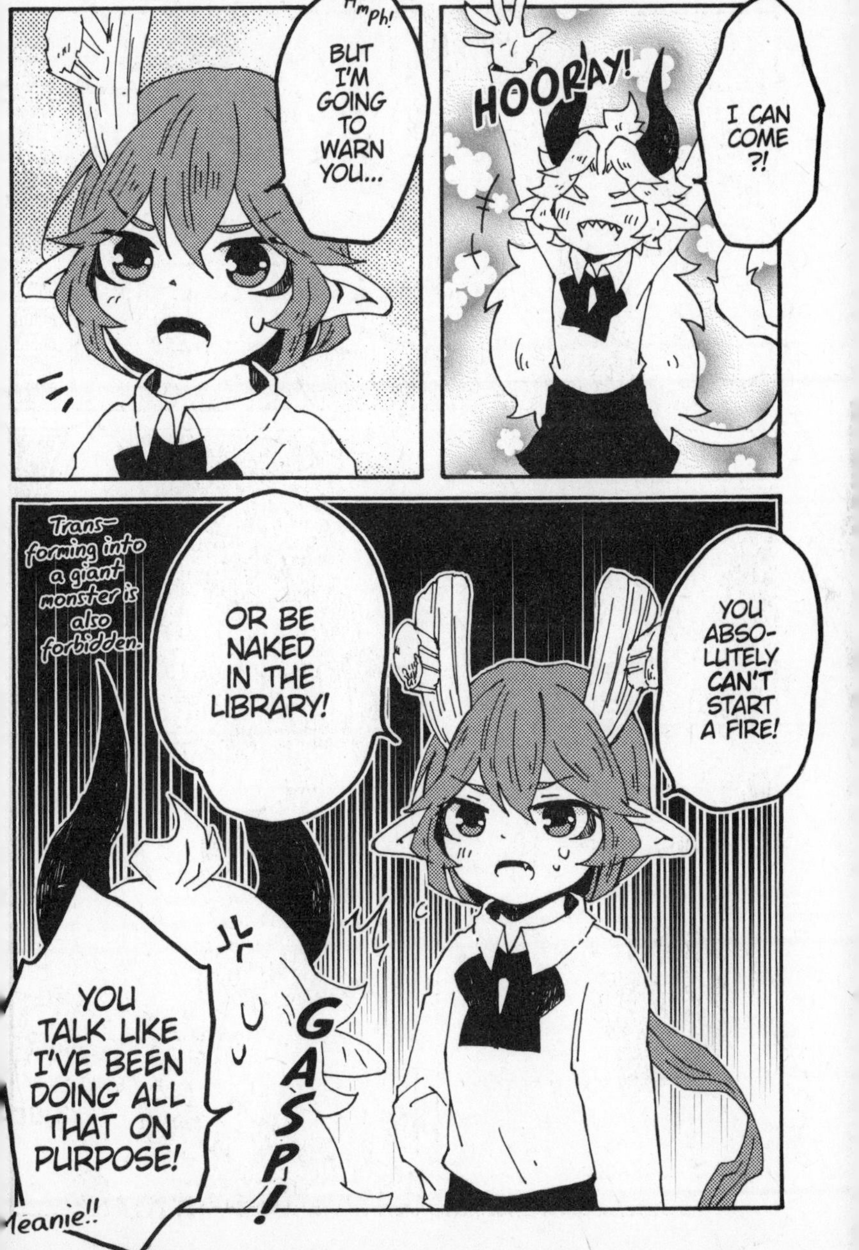

I CAN COME ?!
HOORAY!
Hmph!
BUT I'M GOING TO WARN YOU...
YOU ABSOLUTELY CAN'T START A FIRE!
OR BE NAKED IN THE LIBRARY!
Transforming into a giant monster is also forbidden.
GASP!
YOU TALK LIKE I'VE BEEN DOING ALL THAT ON PURPOSE!
Meanie!!

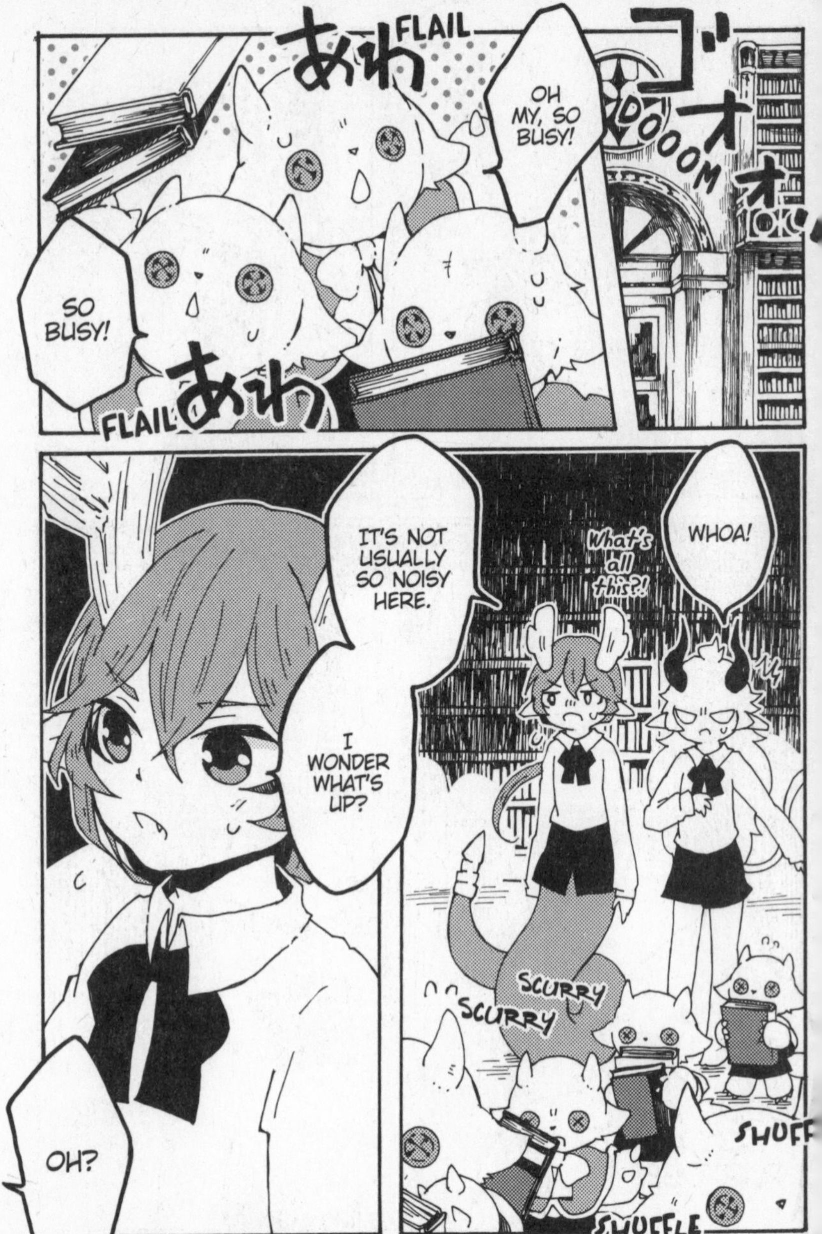
ゴオオ
DOOOOM
OH MY, SO BUSY!
あわ
FLAIL
SO BUSY!
あわ
FLAIL
WHOA!
What's all this?!
SCURRY
SCURRY
SHUFF
SHUFFLE
IT'S NOT USUALLY SO NOISY HERE.
I WONDER WHAT'S UP?
OH?

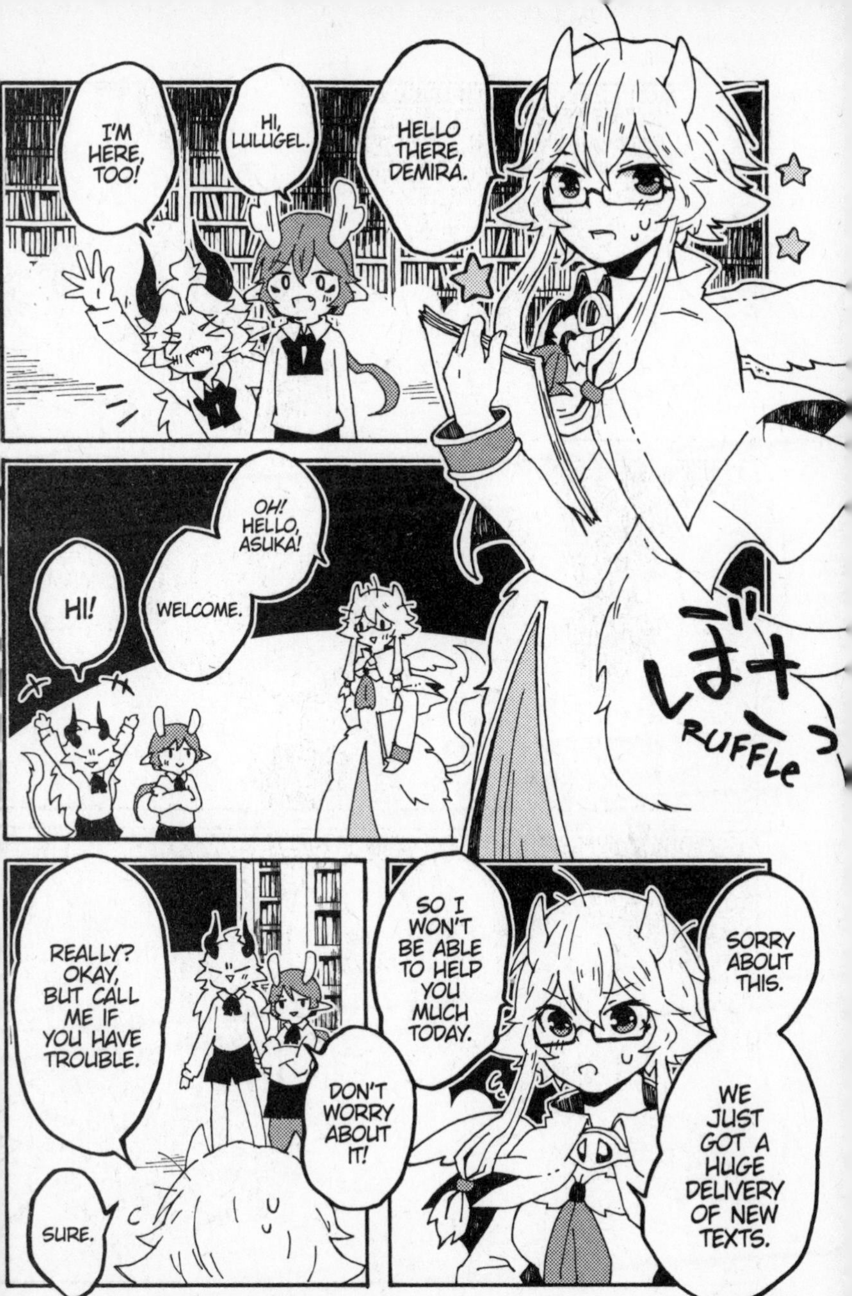
HELLO THERE, DEMIRA.
HI, LULUGEL.
I'M HERE, TOO!
RUFFLE
OH! HELLO, ASUKA!
WELCOME.
HI!
SORRY ABOUT THIS.
WE JUST GOT A HUGE DELIVERY OF NEW TEXTS.
SO I WON'T BE ABLE TO HELP YOU MUCH TODAY.
DON'T WORRY ABOUT IT!
REALLY? OKAY, BUT CALL ME IF YOU HAVE TROUBLE.
SURE.

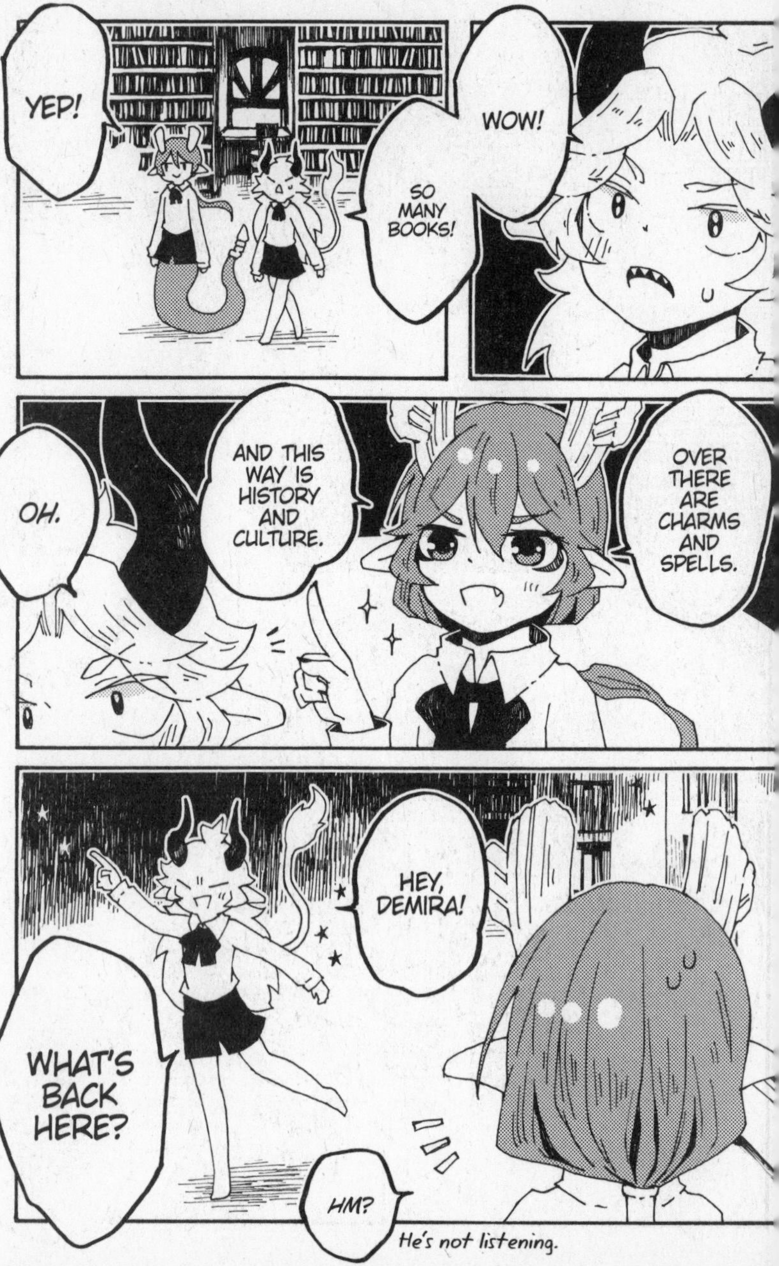
WOW!
SO MANY BOOKS!
YEP!
OVER THERE ARE CHARMS AND SPELLS.
AND THIS WAY IS HISTORY AND CULTURE.
OH.
HEY, DEMIRA!
WHAT'S BACK HERE?
HM?

He's not listening.

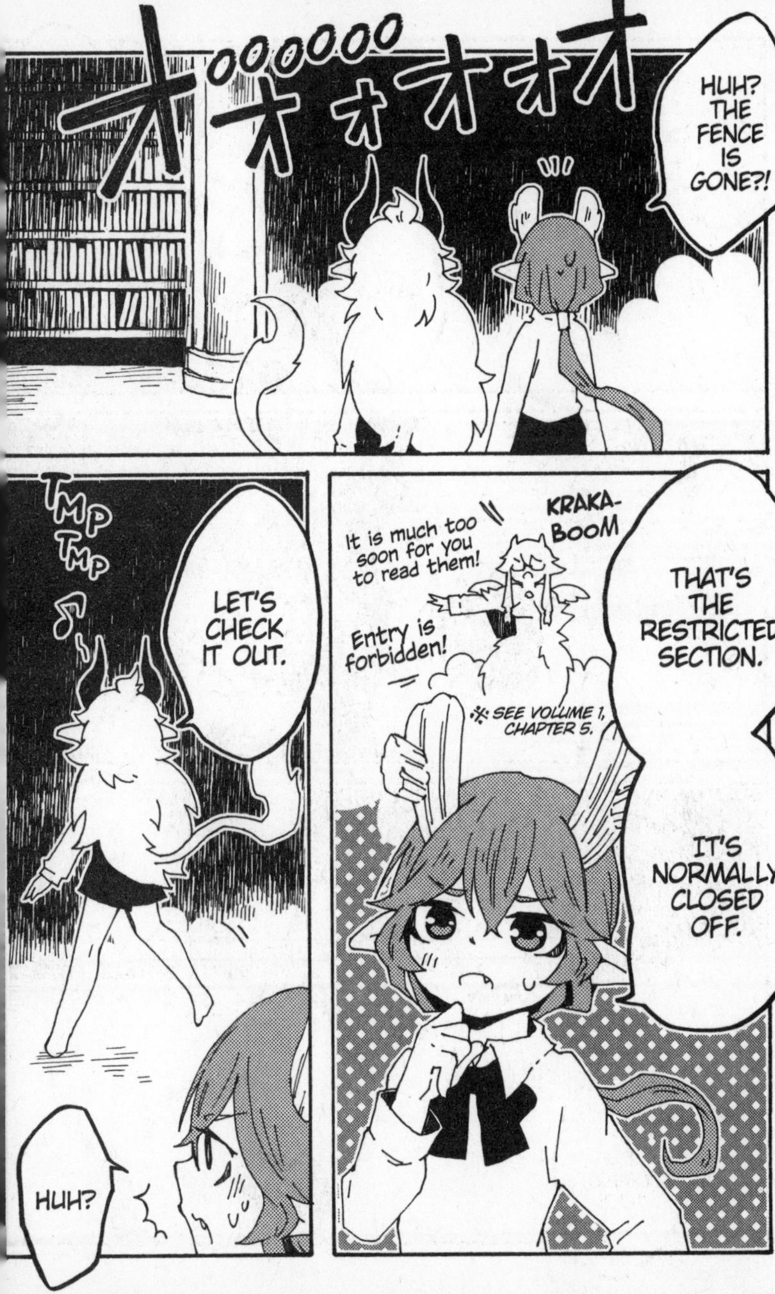
Oooooo
HUH? THE FENCE IS GONE?!
THAT'S THE RESTRICTED SECTION.
KRAKA-BOOM
It is much too soon for you to read them!
Entry is forbidden!
※SEE VOLUME 1, CHAPTER 5.
IT'S NORMALLY CLOSED OFF.
TMP TMP
LET'S CHECK IT OUT.
HUH?

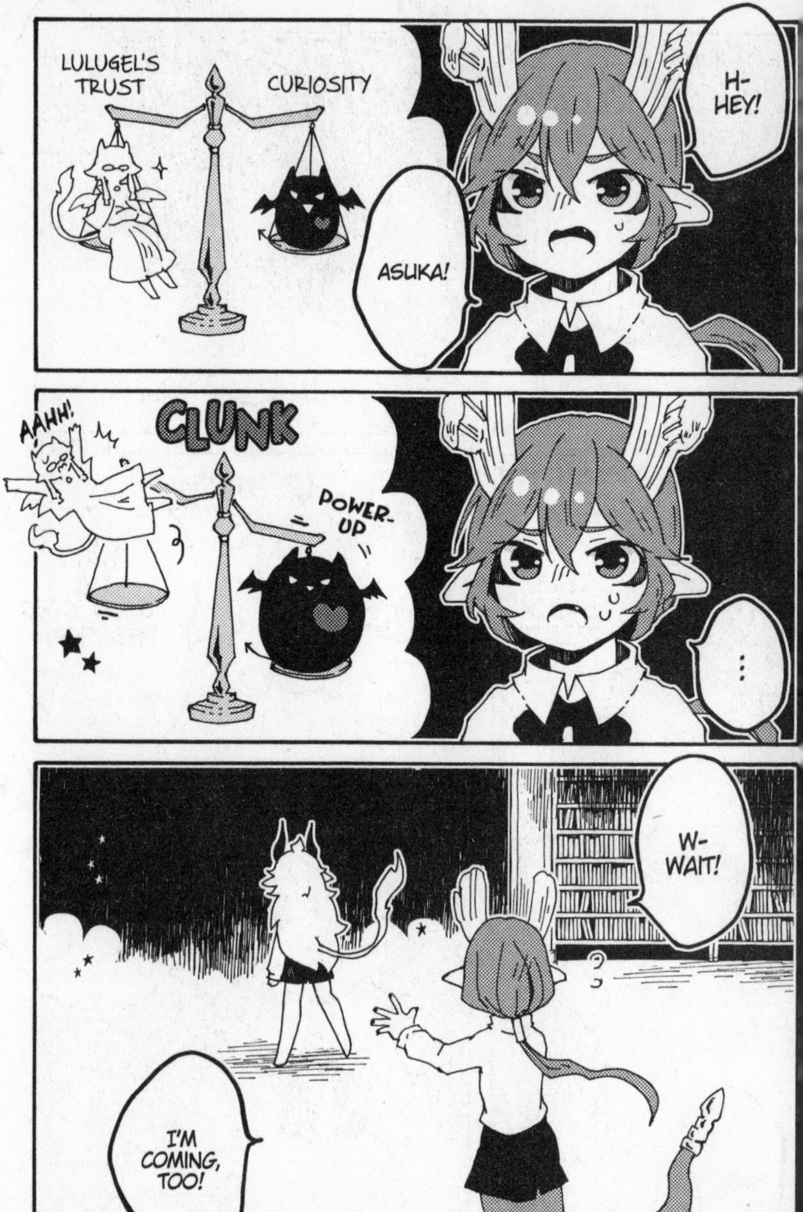
H-HEY!
ASUKA!
CURIOSITY
LULUGEL'S TRUST
...
POWER-UP
CLUNK
AAHH!
W-WAIT!
I'M COMING, TOO!

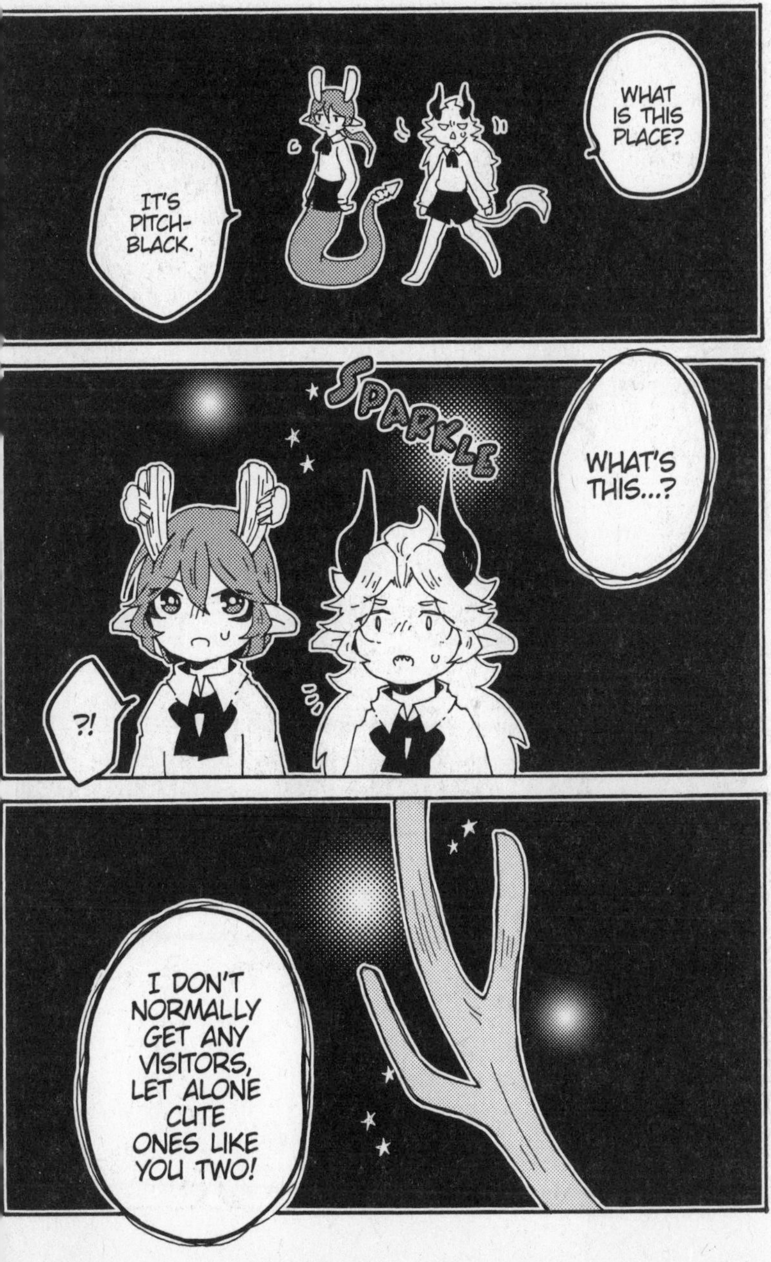
WHAT IS THIS PLACE?
IT'S PITCH-BLACK.
SPARKLE
WHAT'S THIS...?
?!
I DON'T NORMALLY GET ANY VISITORS, LET ALONE CUTE ONES LIKE YOU TWO!

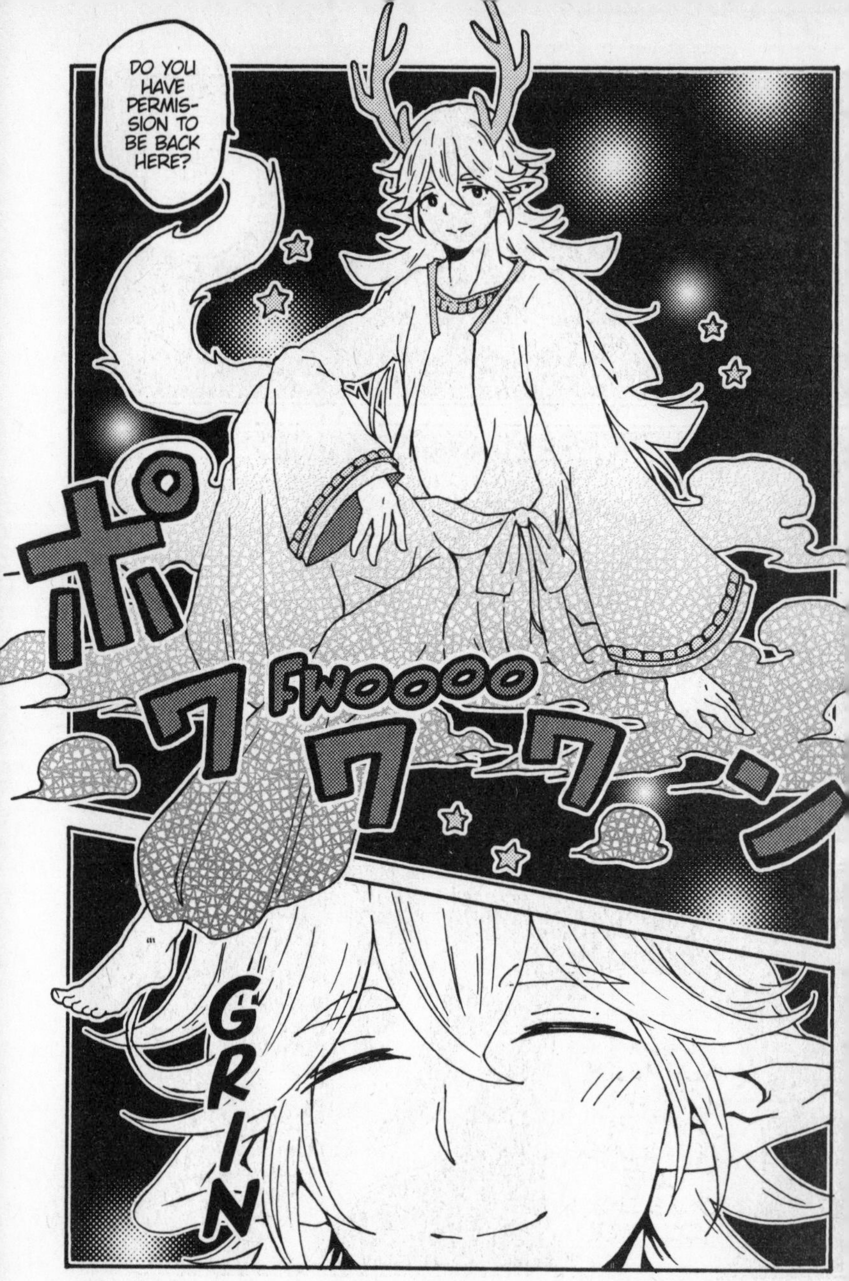
DO YOU HAVE PERMIS- SION TO BE BACK HERE?
ポワワワーン
FWOOOO
GRIN

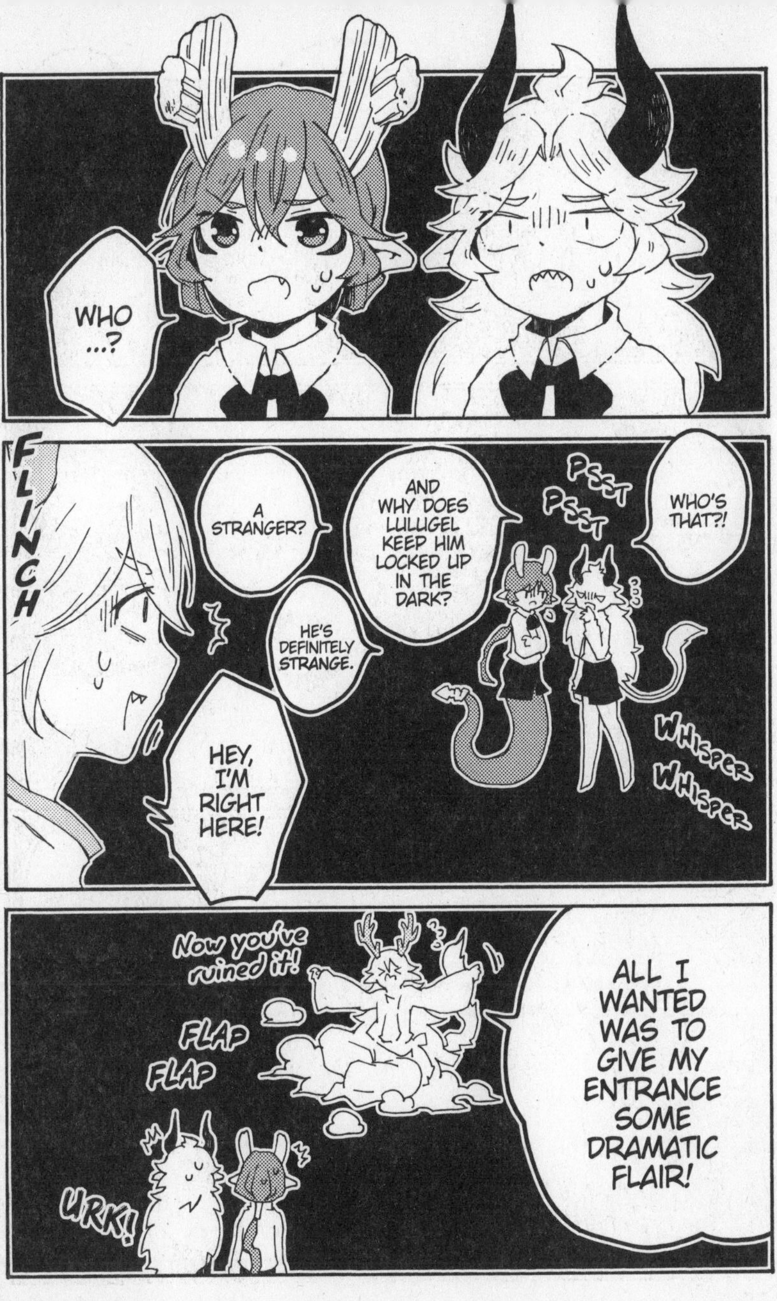
WHO ...?
WHO'S THAT?!
PSSST PSSST
AND WHY DOES LULUGEL KEEP HIM LOCKED UP IN THE DARK?
A STRANGER?
HE'S DEFINITELY STRANGE.
WHISPER WHISPER
FLINCH
HEY, I'M RIGHT HERE!
ALL I WANTED WAS TO GIVE MY ENTRANCE SOME DRAMATIC FLAIR!
Now you've ruined it!
FLAP FLAP
URK!

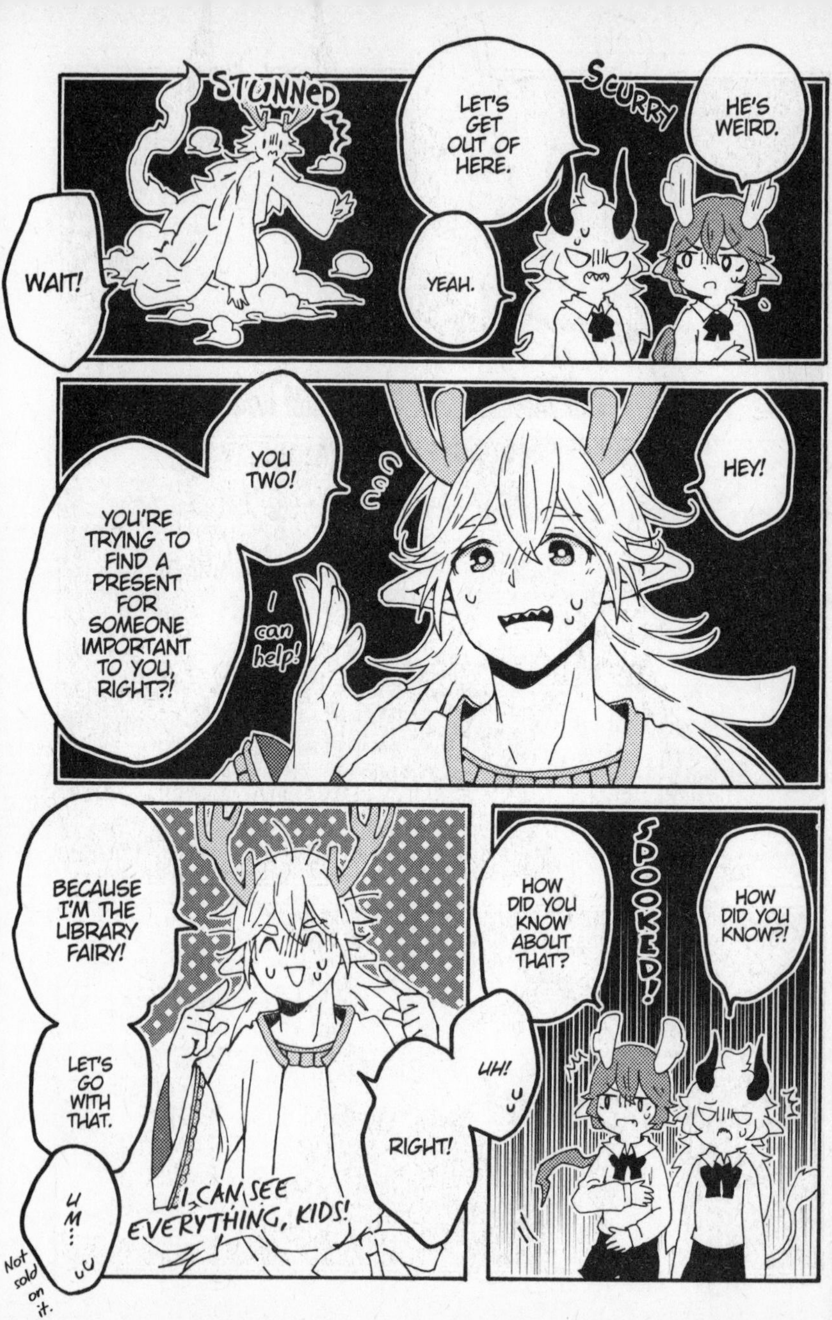
HE'S WEIRD.
SCURRY
LET'S GET OUT OF HERE.
YEAH.
STUNNED
WAIT!
HEY!
YOU TWO!
YOU'RE TRYING TO FIND A PRESENT FOR SOMEONE IMPORTANT TO YOU, RIGHT?!
I can help!
HOW DID YOU KNOW?!
SPOOKED!
HOW DID YOU KNOW ABOUT THAT?
BECAUSE I'M THE LIBRARY FAIRY!
UH! RIGHT!
LET'S GO WITH THAT.
I CAN SEE EVERYTHING, KIDS!
UM...
Not sold on it.

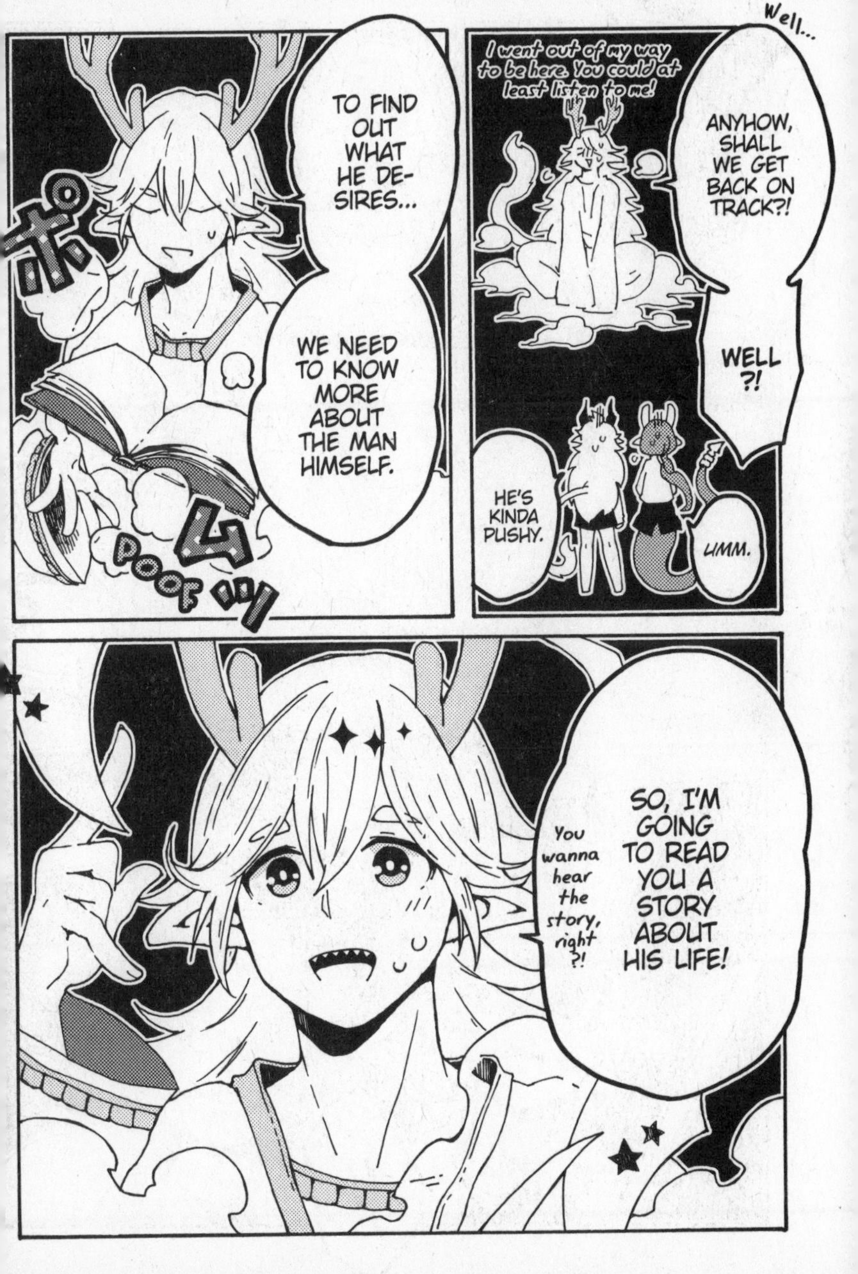
Well...
I went out of my way to be here. You could at least listen to me!
ANYHOW, SHALL WE GET BACK ON TRACK?!
WELL ?!
UMM.
HE'S KINDA PUSHY.
TO FIND OUT WHAT HE DE-SIRES...
WE NEED TO KNOW MORE ABOUT THE MAN HIMSELF.
ポ
POOF
SO, I'M GOING TO READ YOU A STORY ABOUT HIS LIFE!
You wanna hear the story, right?!

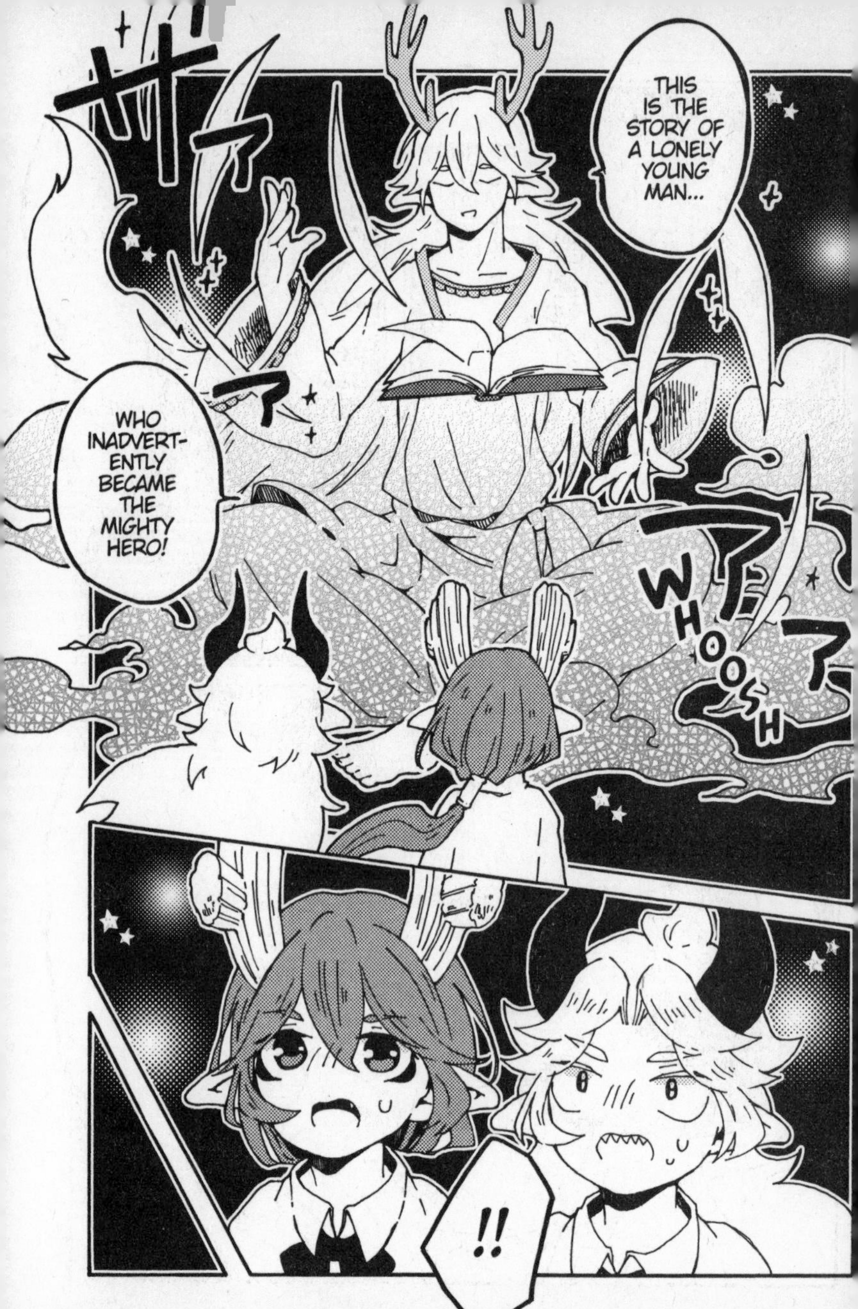
THIS IS THE STORY OF A LONELY YOUNG MAN...
WHO INADVERT-ENTLY BECAME THE MIGHTY HERO!
WHOOSH
!!

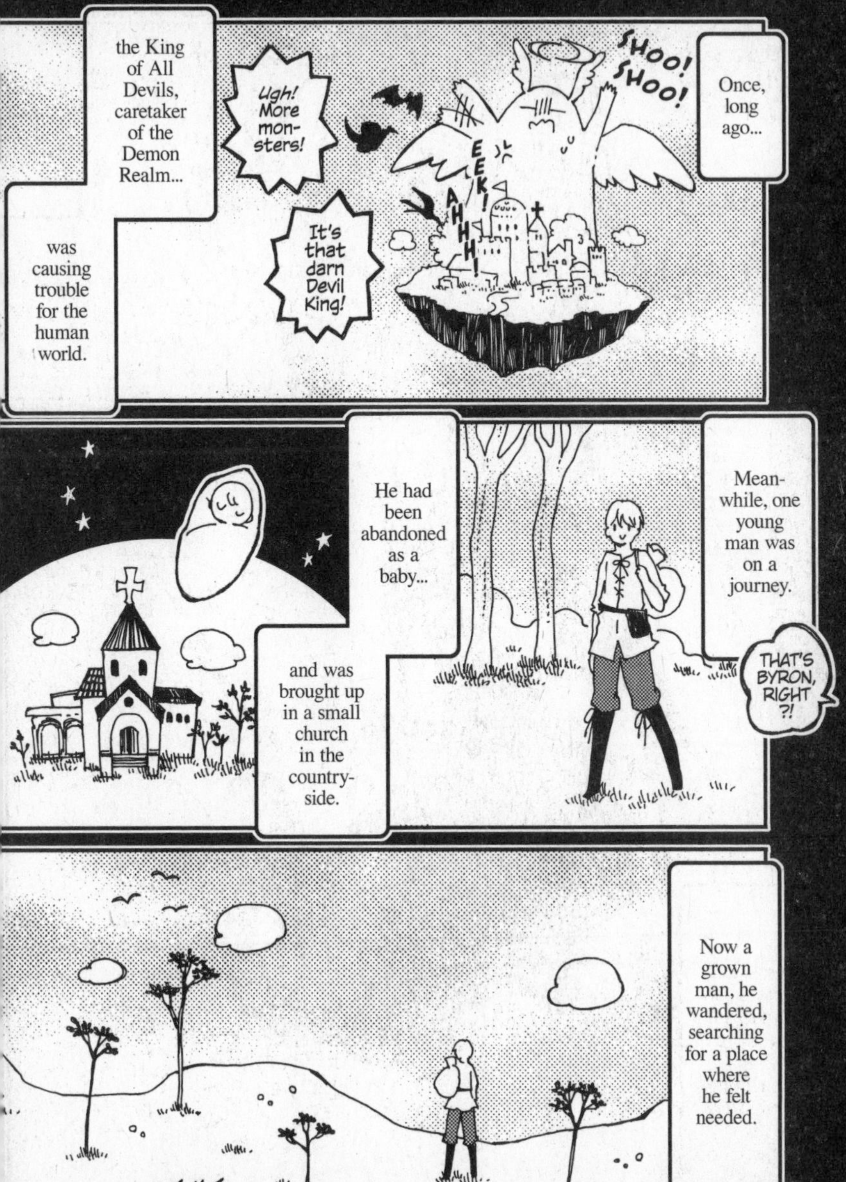
Once, long ago...
SHOO! SHOO!
EEK!
AHHHH!
Ugh! More monsters!
It's that darn Devil King!
the King of All Devils, caretaker of the Demon Realm...
was causing trouble for the human world.
Meanwhile, one young man was on a journey.
THAT'S BYRON, RIGHT?!
He had been abandoned as a baby...
and was brought up in a small church in the countryside.
Now a grown man, he wandered, searching for a place where he felt needed.

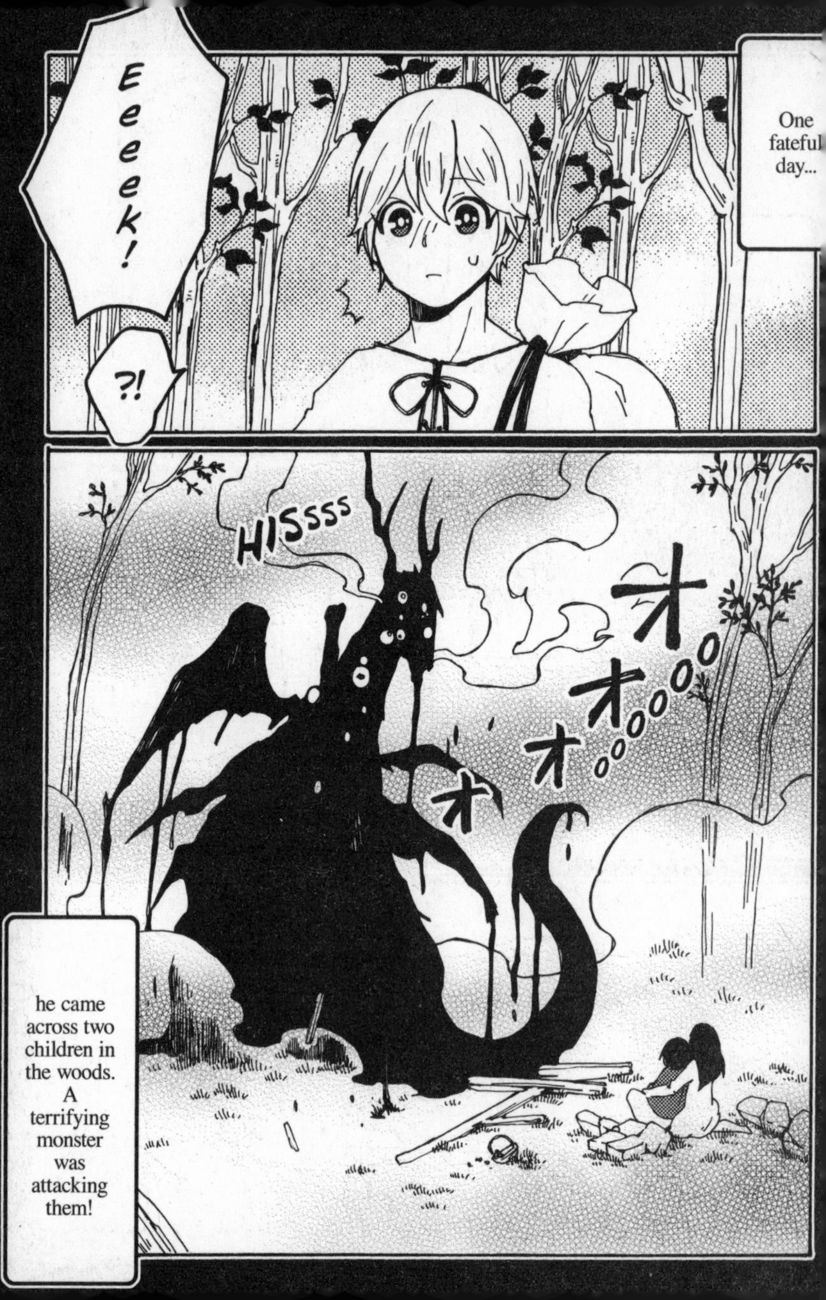
One fateful day...
Eeeek!
?!
HISSSS
オオオオooooooo
he came across two children in the woods. A terrifying monster was attacking them!

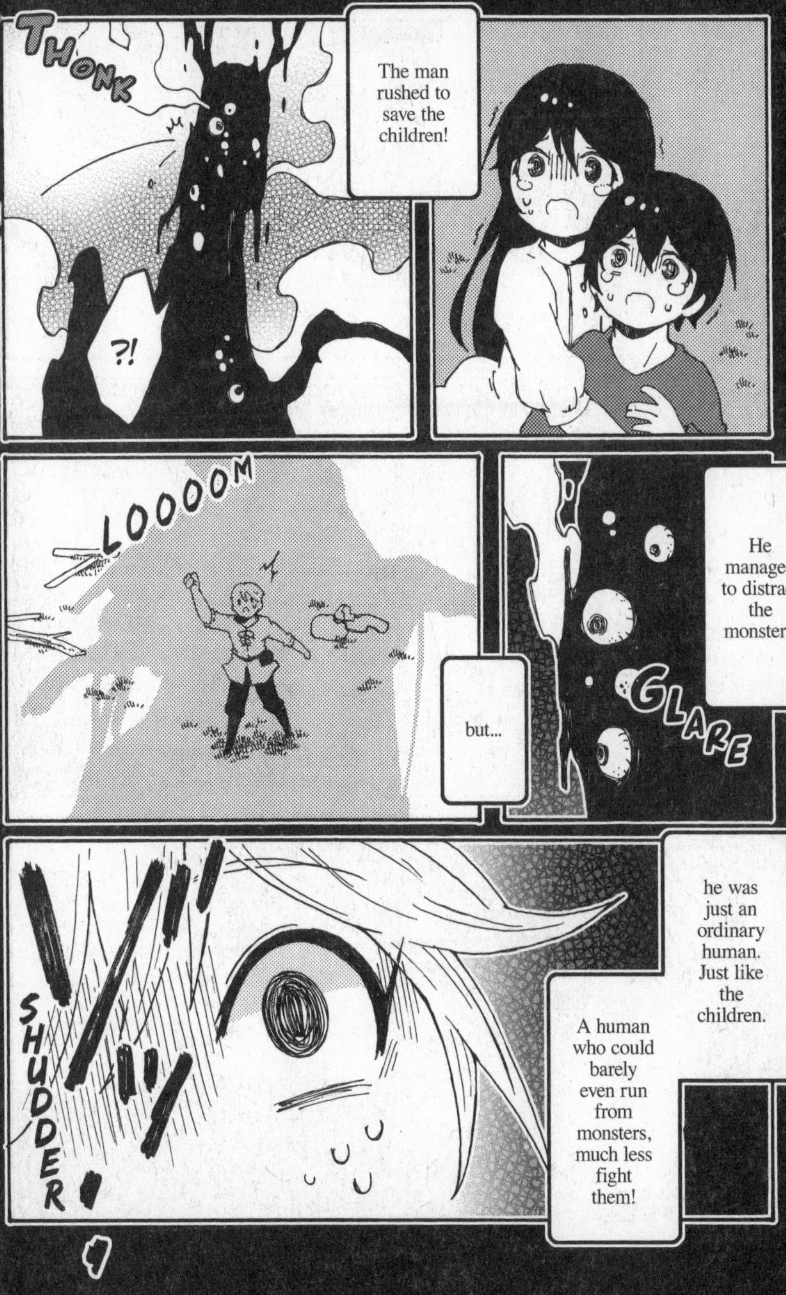
The man rushed to save the children!
THONK
?!
He managed to distract the monster...
GLARE
but...
LOOOOM
he was just an ordinary human. Just like the children.
A human who could barely even run from monsters, much less fight them!
SHUDDER

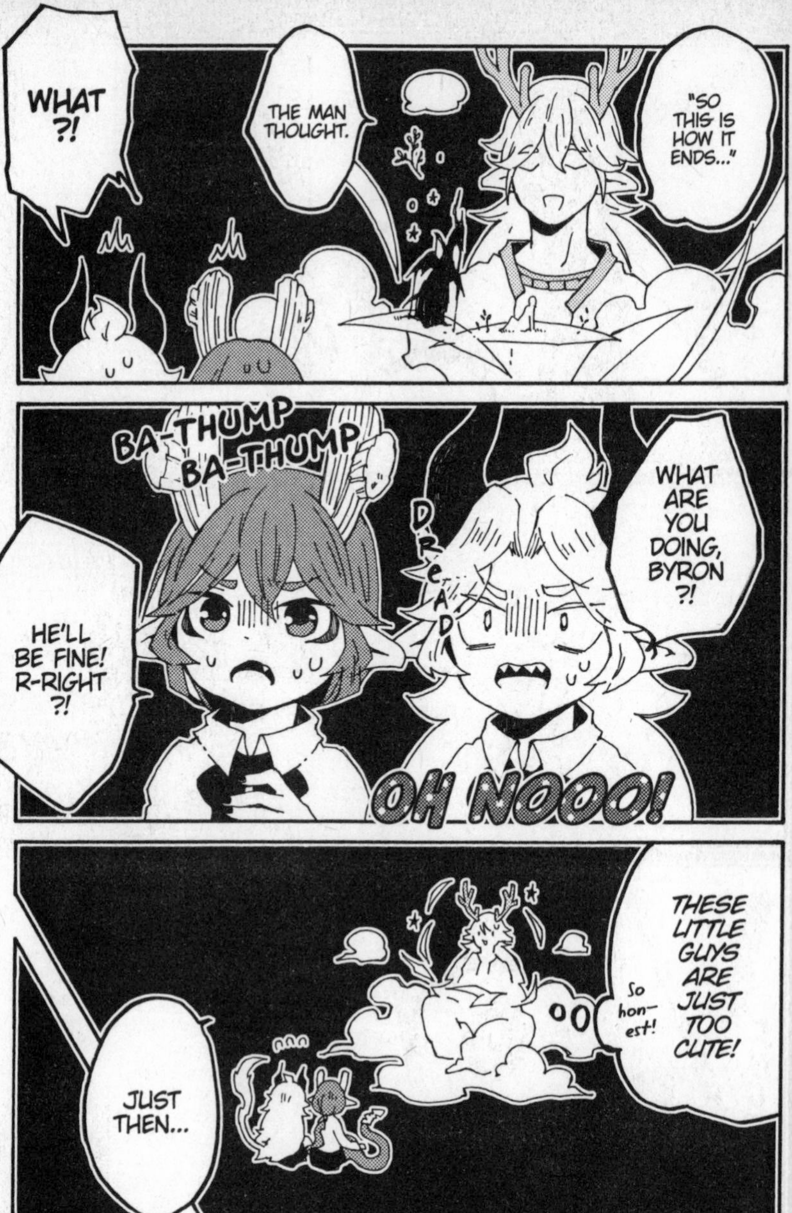
"SO THIS IS HOW IT ENDS..."
THE MAN THOUGHT.
WHAT ?!
WHAT ARE YOU DOING, BYRON ?!
DREAD
BA-THUMP BA-THUMP
HE'LL BE FINE! R-RIGHT ?!
OH NOOO!
THESE LITTLE GUYS ARE JUST TOO CUTE!
So hon-est!
JUST THEN...

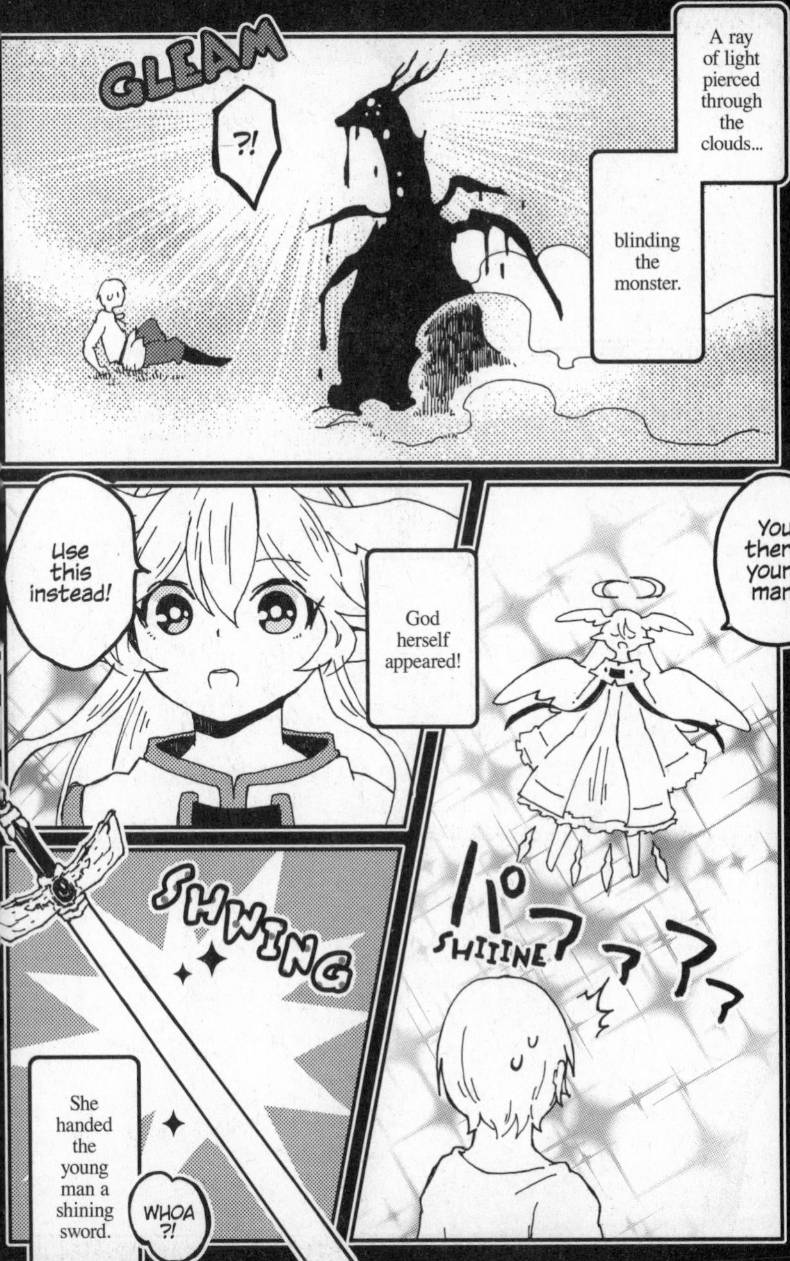
A ray of light pierced through the clouds...
blinding the monster.
GLEAM
?!
You there, young man!
パアアア
SHIIINE
God herself appeared!
Use this instead!
SHWING
She handed the young man a shining sword.
WHOA ?!

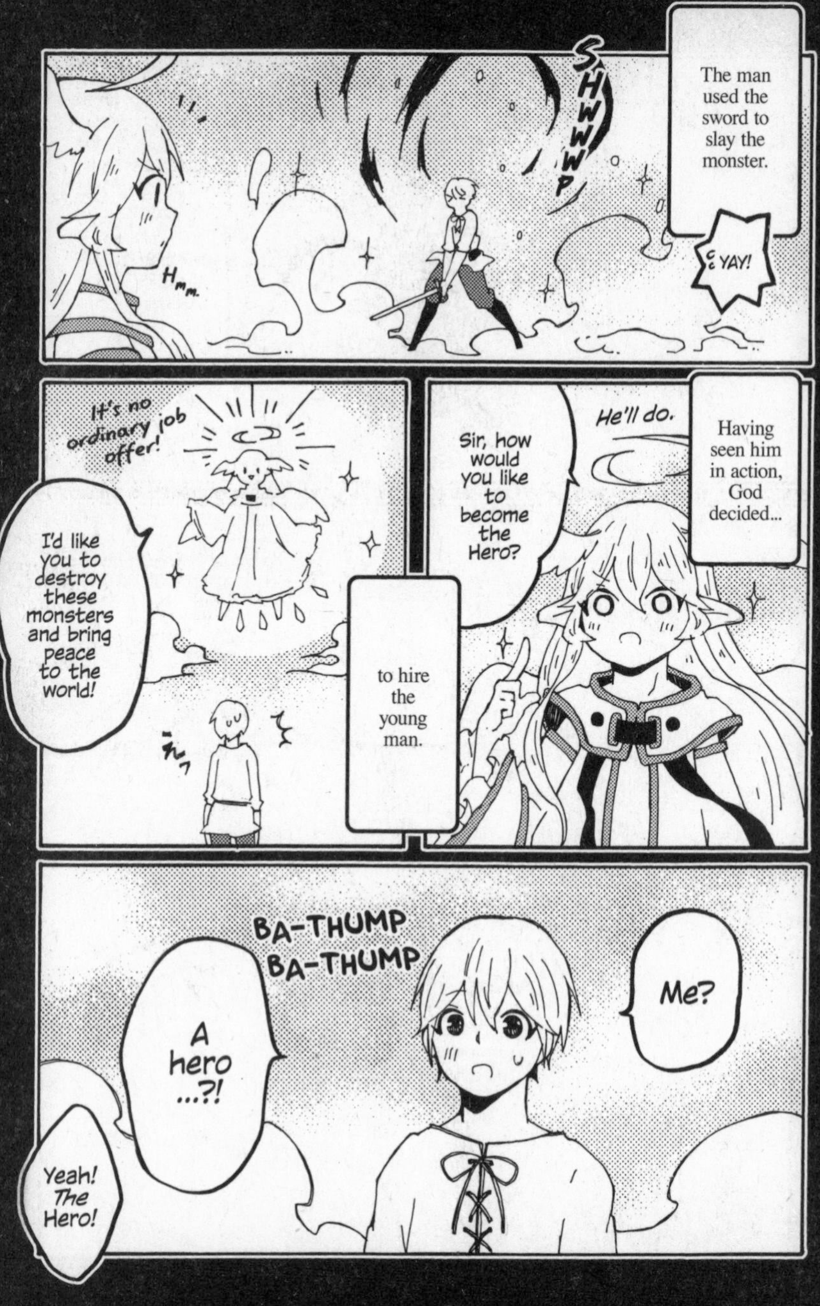
The man used the sword to slay the monster.
SHWWWWP
YAY!
Hmm.
Having seen him in action, God decided...
He'll do.
Sir, how would you like to become the Hero?
to hire the young man.
It's no ordinary job offer!
I'd like you to destroy these monsters and bring peace to the world!
Me?
BA-THUMP BA-THUMP
A hero ...?!
Yeah! The Hero!

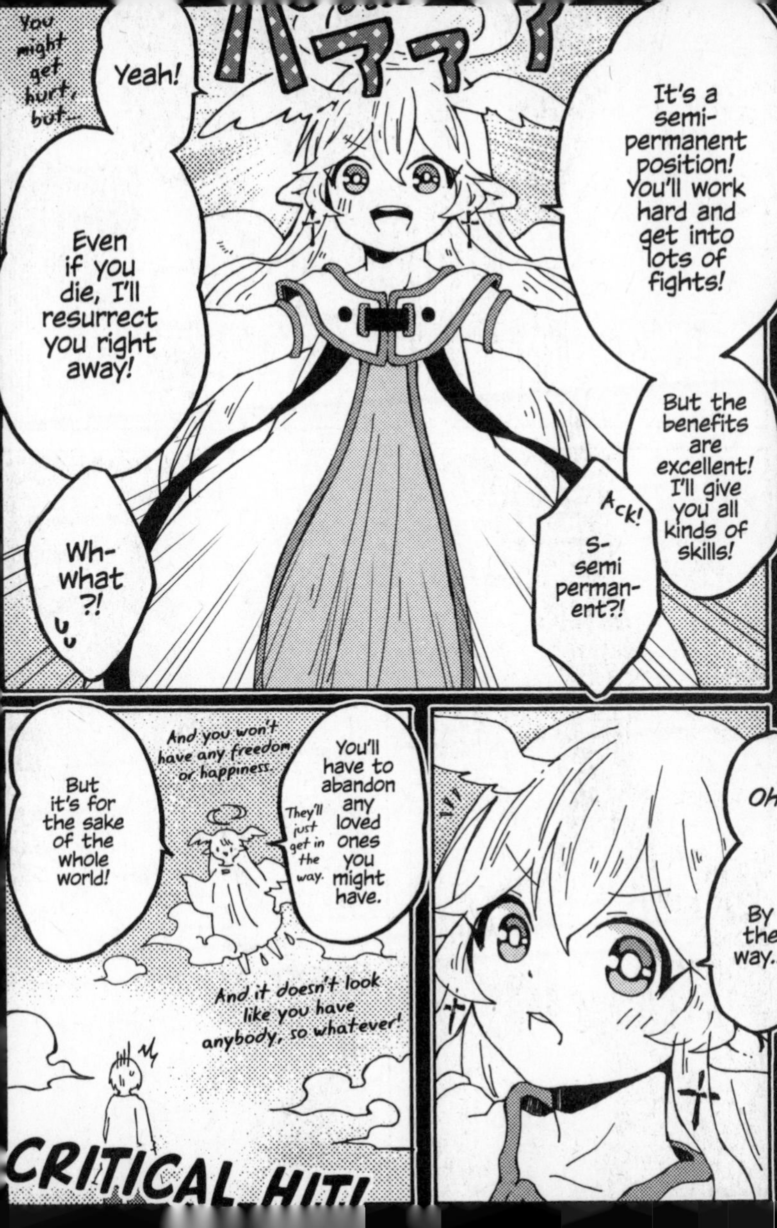
It's a semi-permanent position! You'll work hard and get into lots of fights!
But the benefits are excellent! I'll give you all kinds of skills!
Ack!
S-semi permanent?!
Yeah!
You might get hurt, but...
Even if you die, I'll resurrect you right away!
Wh-what?!
Oh!
By the way...
You'll have to abandon any loved ones you might have.
They'll just get in the way.
And you won't have any freedom or happiness.
But it's for the sake of the whole world!
And it doesn't look like you have anybody, so whatever!
CRITICAL HIT!

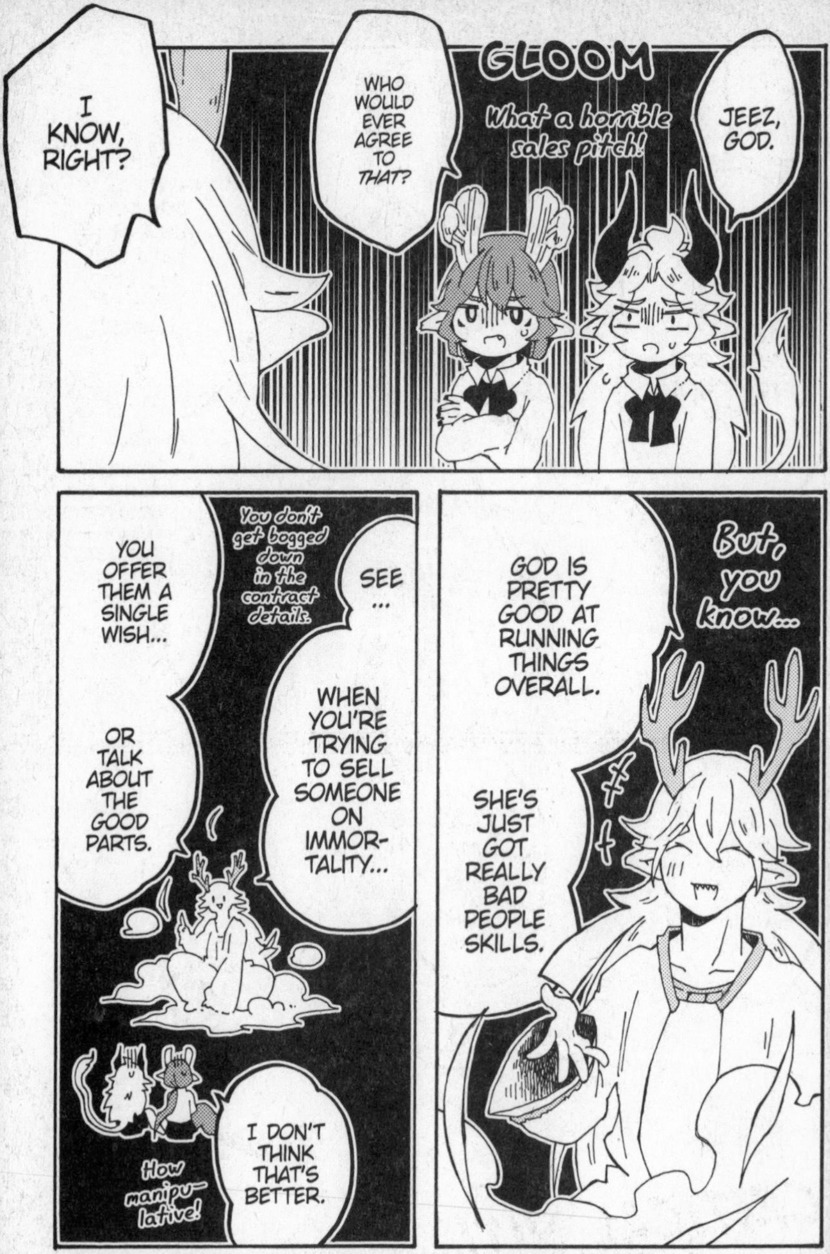
GLOOM
JEEZ, GOD.
What a horrible sales pitch!
WHO WOULD EVER AGREE TO THAT?
I KNOW, RIGHT?
But, you know...
GOD IS PRETTY GOOD AT RUNNING THINGS OVERALL.
SHE'S JUST GOT REALLY BAD PEOPLE SKILLS.
SEE...
WHEN YOU'RE TRYING TO SELL SOMEONE ON IMMORTALITY...
You don't get bogged down in the contract details.
YOU OFFER THEM A SINGLE WISH...
OR TALK ABOUT THE GOOD PARTS.
I DON'T THINK THAT'S BETTER.
How manipu-lative!

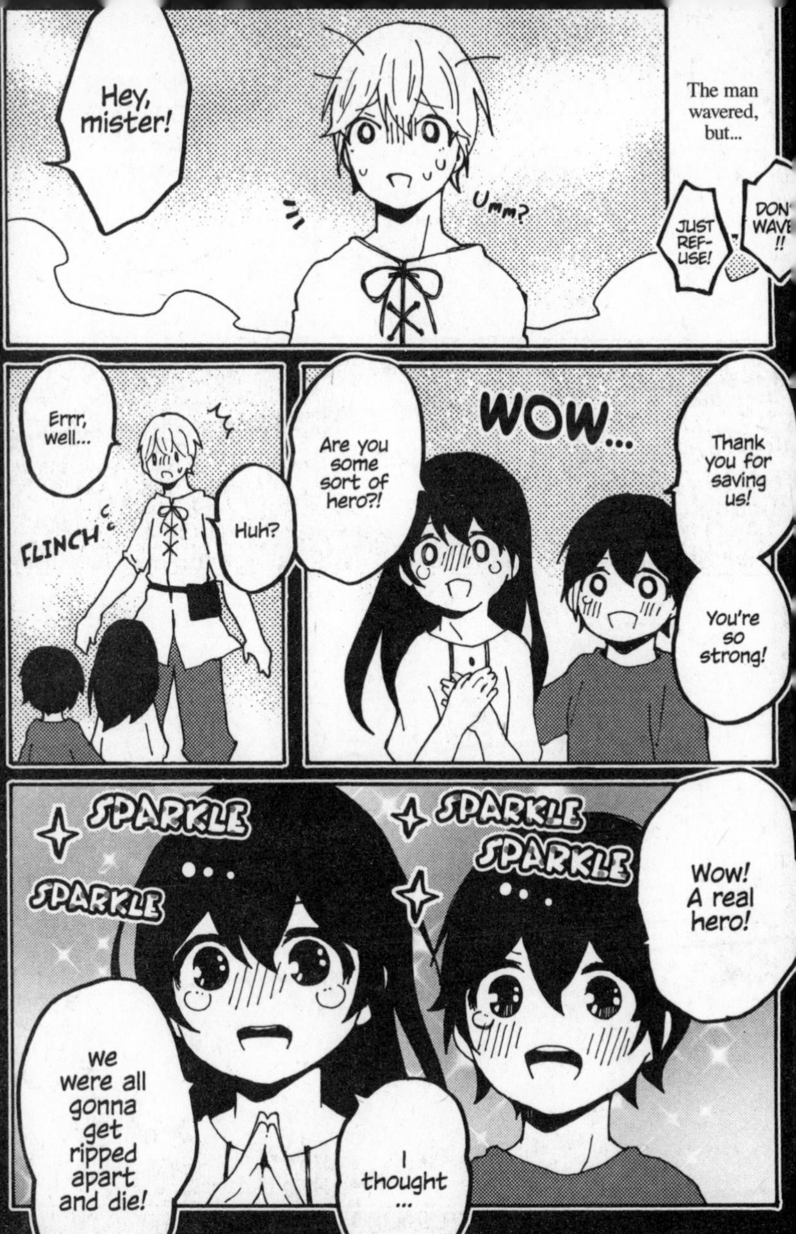
The man wavered, but...
DON' WAVE !!
JUST REF-USE!
Umm?
Hey, mister!
Thank you for saving us!
WOW...
You're so strong!
Are you some sort of hero?!
Huh?
Errr, well...
FLINCH
Wow! A real hero!
SPARKLE SPARKLE
SPARKLE
SPARKLE
I thought...
we were all gonna get ripped apart and die!

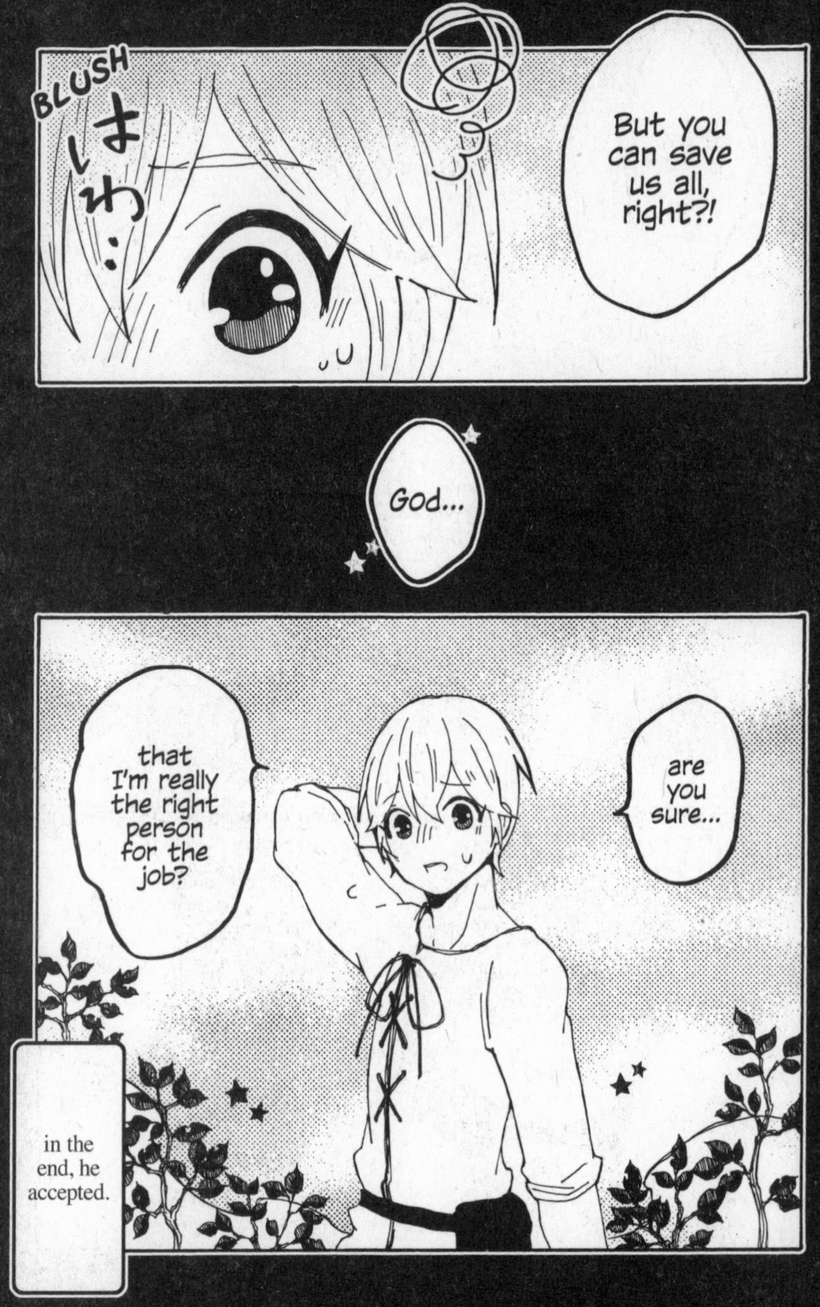
But you can save us all, right?!
BLUSH
はわ…
God...
are you sure...
that I'm really the right person for the job?
in the end, he accepted.

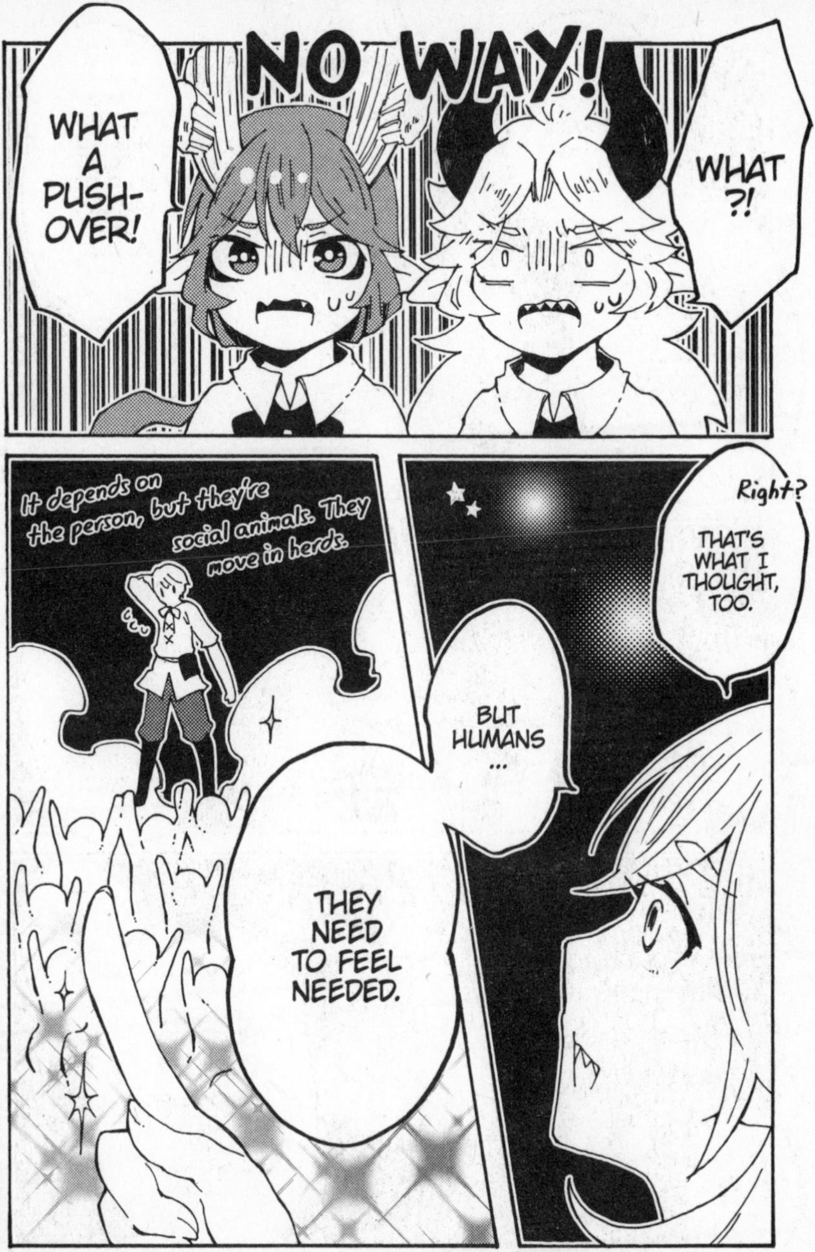
NO WAY!
WHAT ?!
WHAT A PUSH-OVER!
Right?
THAT'S WHAT I THOUGHT, TOO.
BUT HUMANS...
THEY NEED TO FEEL NEEDED.
It depends on the person, but they're social animals. They move in herds.

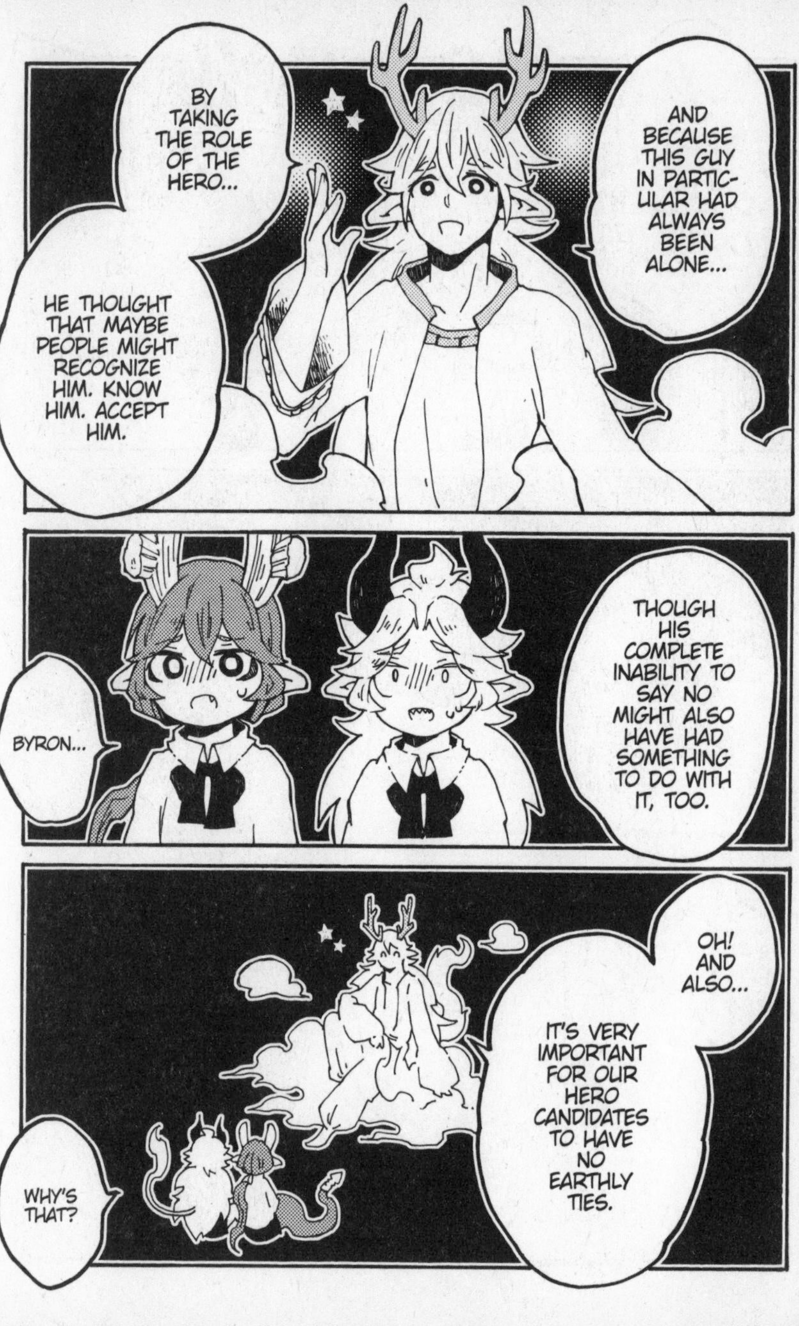
AND BECAUSE THIS GUY IN PARTICULAR HAD ALWAYS BEEN ALONE...
BY TAKING THE ROLE OF THE HERO...
HE THOUGHT THAT MAYBE PEOPLE MIGHT RECOGNIZE HIM. KNOW HIM. ACCEPT HIM.
THOUGH HIS COMPLETE INABILITY TO SAY NO MIGHT ALSO HAVE HAD SOMETHING TO DO WITH IT, TOO.
BYRON...
OH! AND ALSO...
IT'S VERY IMPORTANT FOR OUR HERO CANDIDATES TO HAVE NO EARTHLY TIES.
WHY'S THAT?

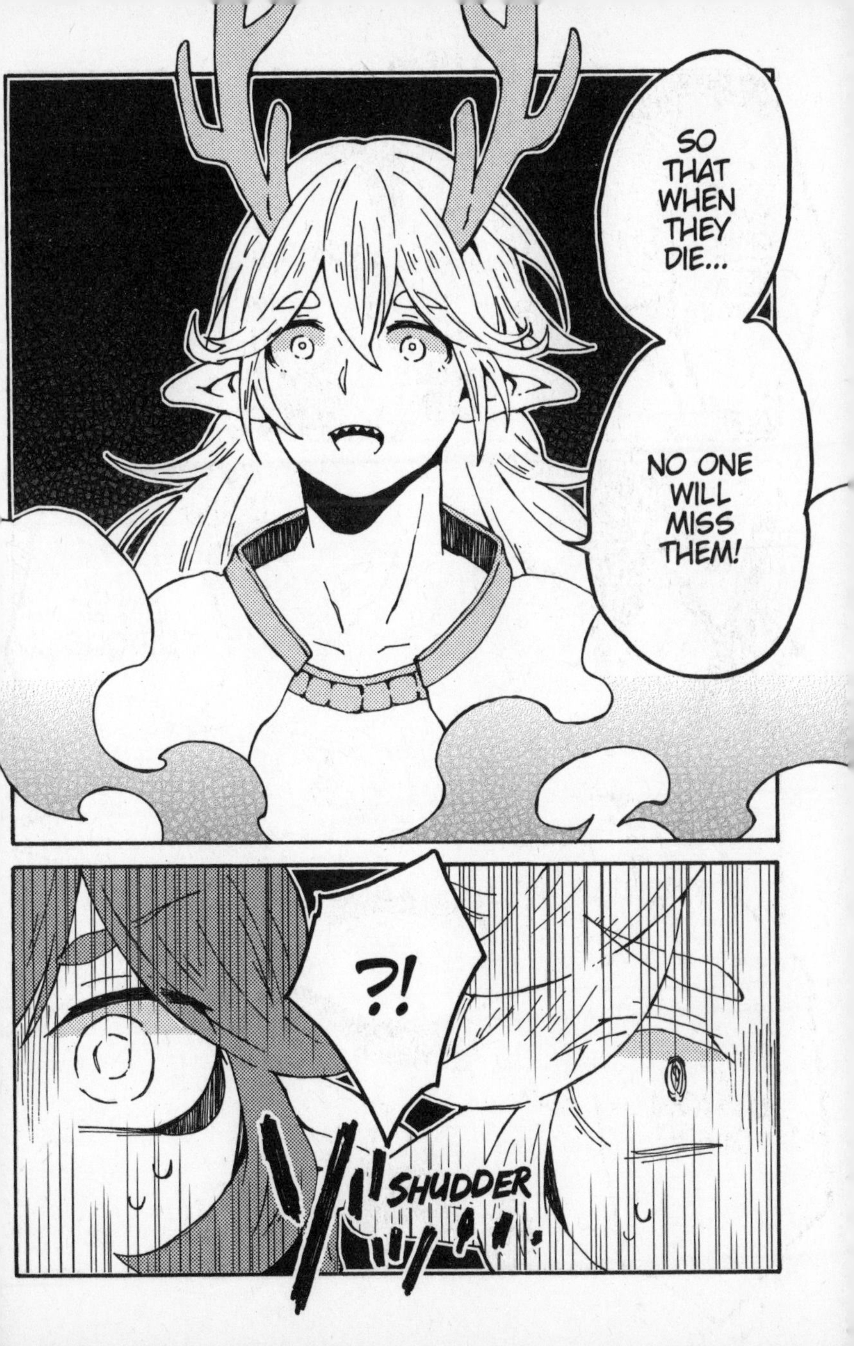
SO THAT WHEN THEY DIE...
NO ONE WILL MISS THEM!
?!
SHUDDER

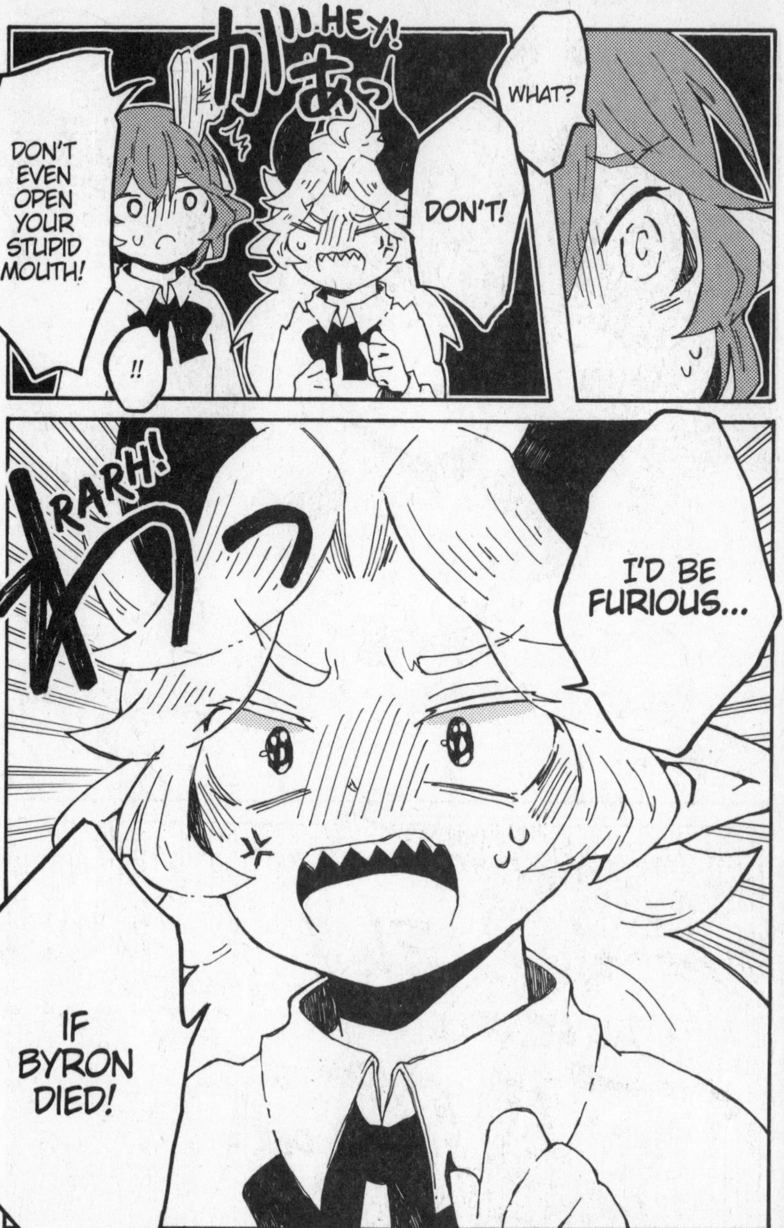
WHAT?
かぁっ
HEY!
DON'T!
DON'T EVEN OPEN YOUR STUPID MOUTH!
!!
I'D BE FURIOUS...
RARH!
IF BYRON DIED!

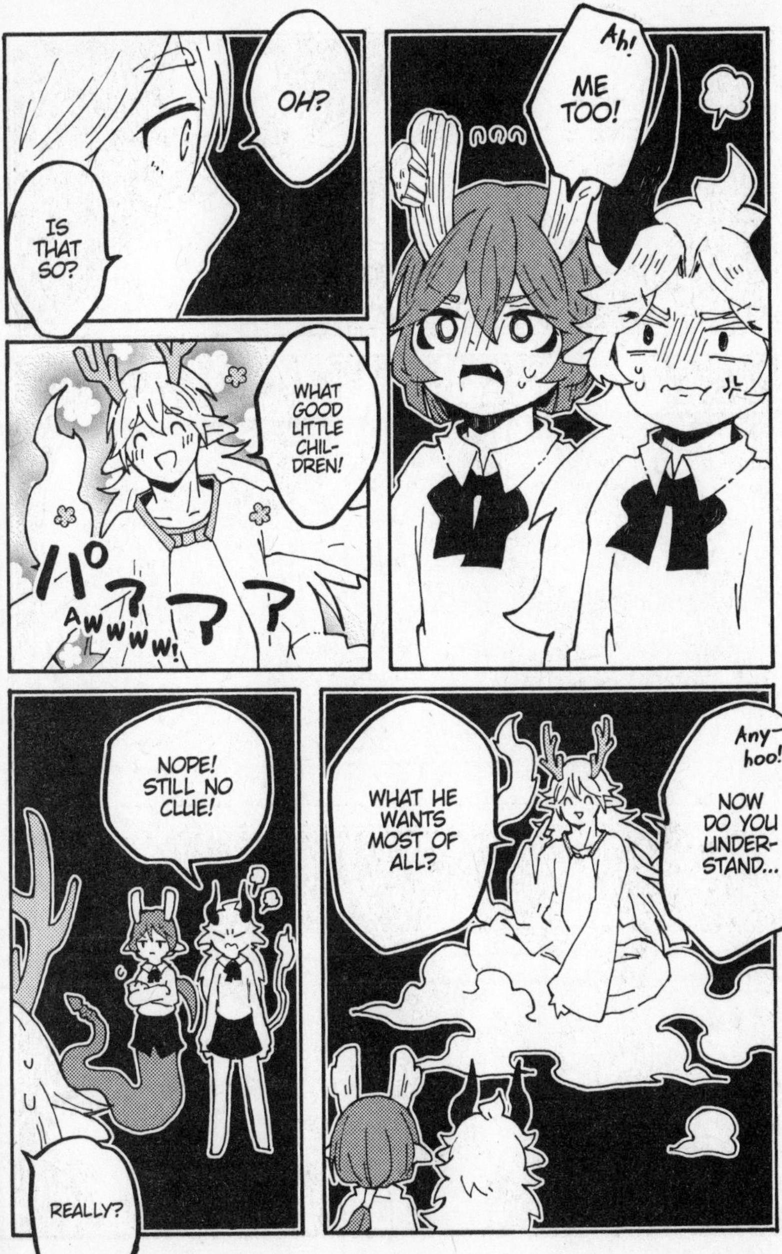
Ah! ME TOO!
OH?
IS THAT SO?
WHAT GOOD LITTLE CHIL-DREN!
パァァァ
AWWWWW!
Any-hoo! NOW DO YOU UNDER-STAND...
WHAT HE WANTS MOST OF ALL?
NOPE! STILL NO CLUE!
REALLY?

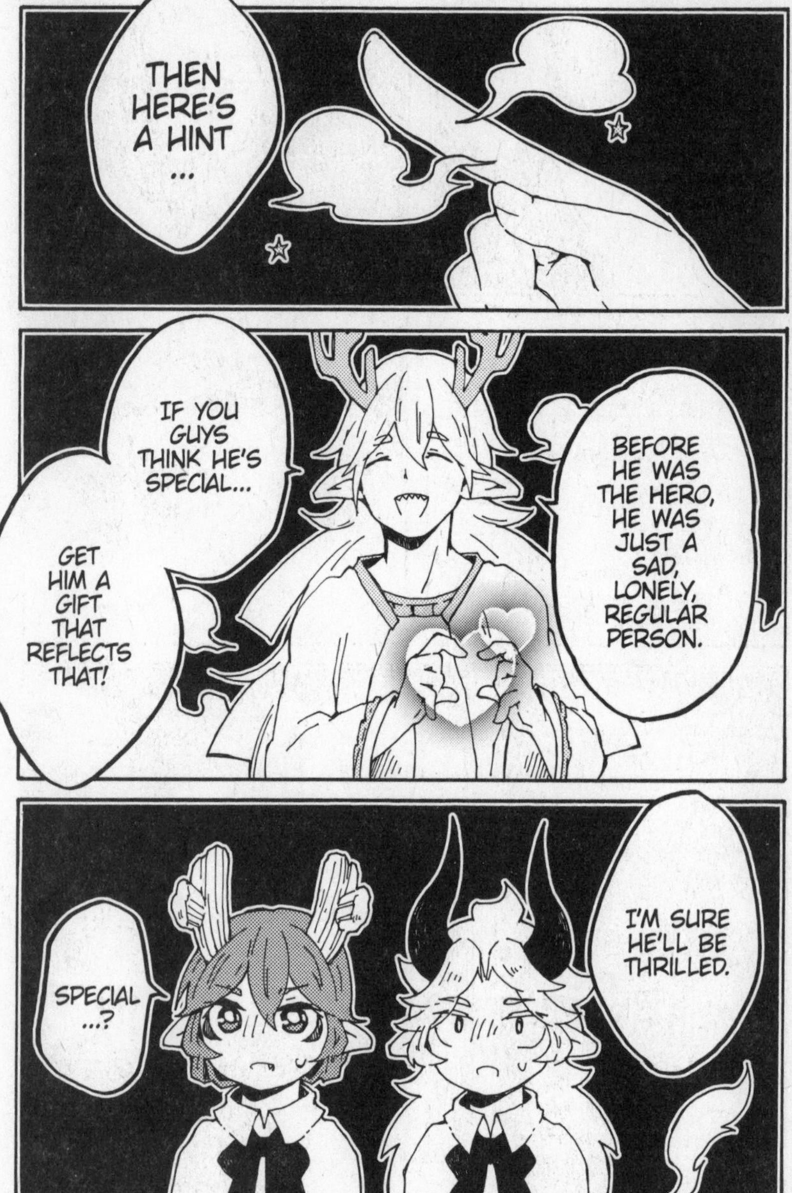
THEN HERE'S A HINT ...
BEFORE HE WAS THE HERO, HE WAS JUST A SAD, LONELY, REGULAR PERSON.
IF YOU GUYS THINK HE'S SPECIAL...
GET HIM A GIFT THAT REFLECTS THAT!
I'M SURE HE'LL BE THRILLED.
SPECIAL ...?

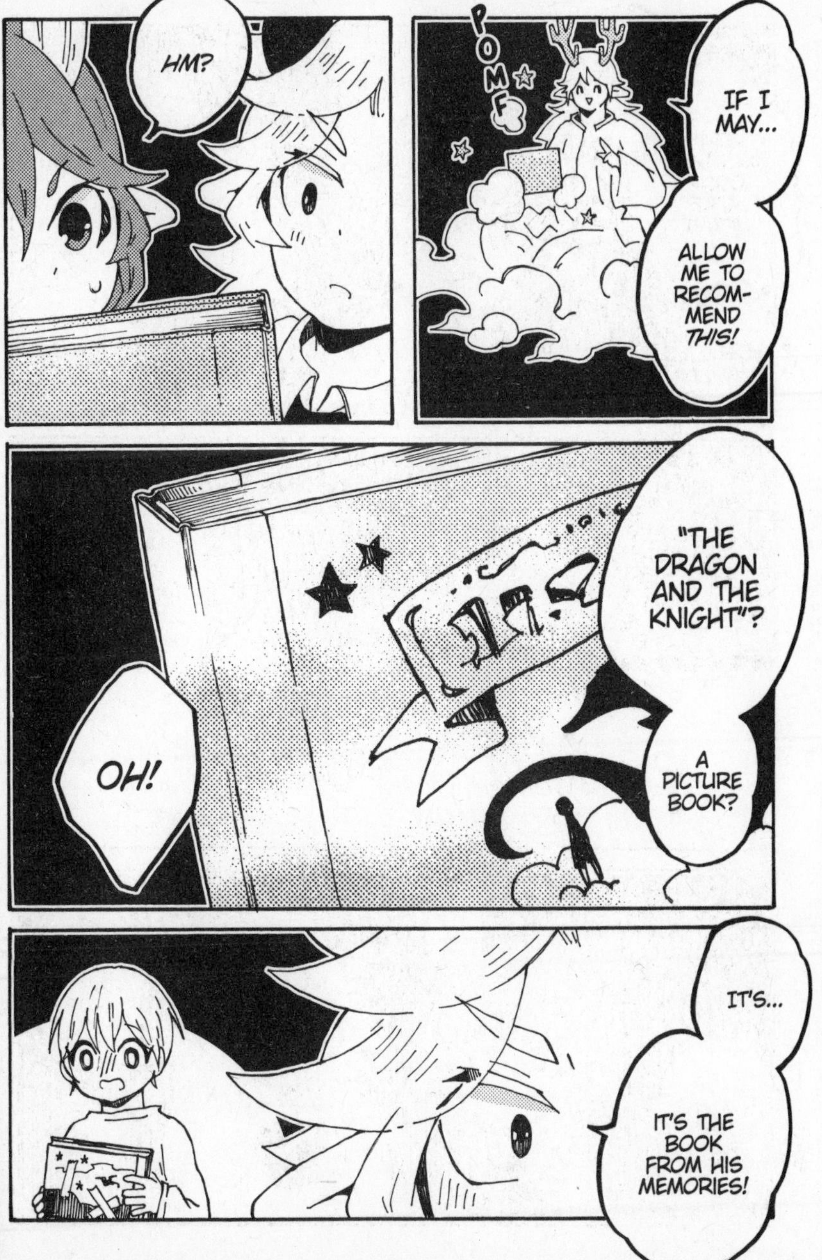
POMF
IF I MAY...
ALLOW ME TO RECOMMEND THIS!
HM?
"THE DRAGON AND THE KNIGHT"?
A PICTURE BOOK?
OH!
IT'S...
IT'S THE BOOK FROM HIS MEMORIES!

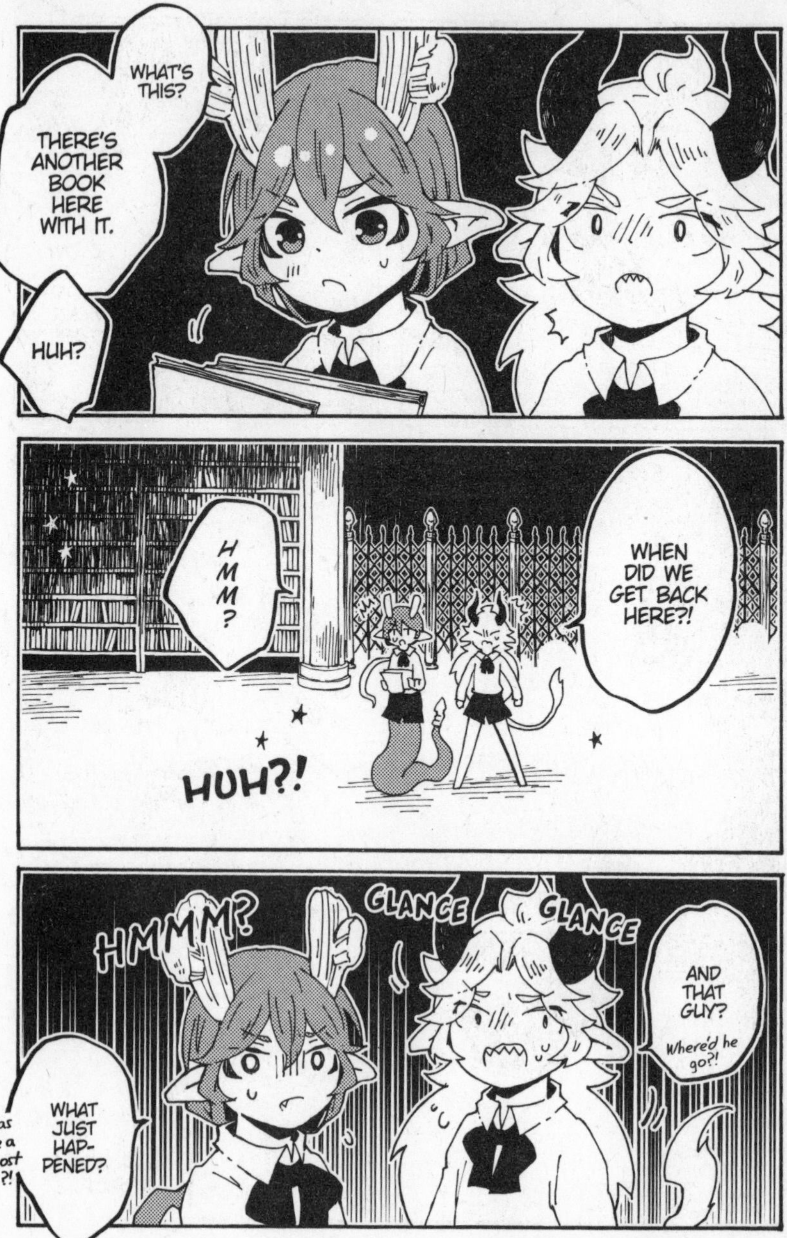
WHAT'S THIS?
THERE'S ANOTHER BOOK HERE WITH IT.
HUH?
WHEN DID WE GET BACK HERE?!
HMMM?
HUH?!
AND THAT GUY?
Where'd he go?!
GLANCE GLANCE
HMMM?
WHAT JUST HAP-PENED?
Was he a ghost?!

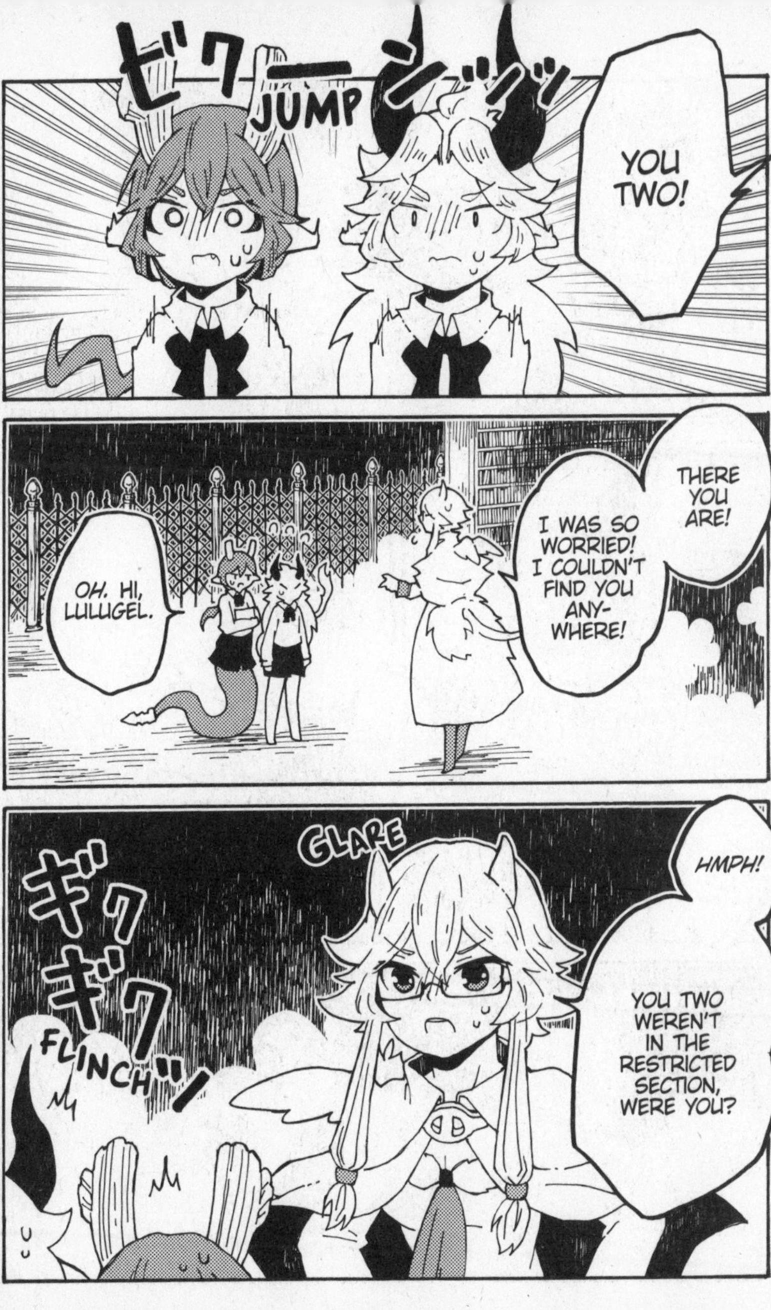
YOU TWO!
JUMP
THERE YOU ARE!
I WAS SO WORRIED! I COULDN'T FIND YOU ANY- WHERE!
OH. HI, LULUGEL.
HMPH!
YOU TWO WEREN'T IN THE RESTRICTED SECTION, WERE YOU?
GLARE
ギクギク
FLINCH

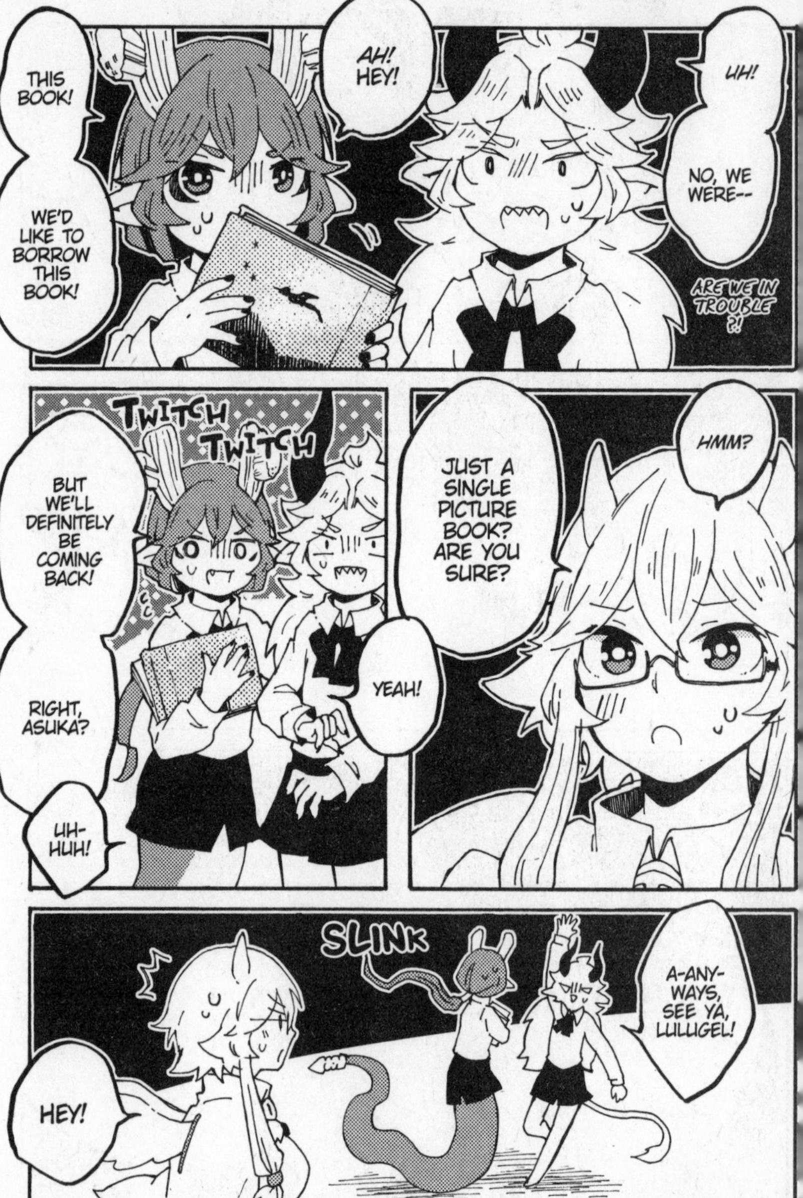
UH!
NO, WE WERE--
ARE WE IN TROUBLE?!
AH! HEY!
THIS BOOK!
WE'D LIKE TO BORROW THIS BOOK!
HMM?
JUST A SINGLE PICTURE BOOK? ARE YOU SURE?
TWITCH TWITCH
YEAH!
BUT WE'LL DEFINITELY BE COMING BACK!
RIGHT, ASUKA?
UH-HUH!
A-ANYWAYS, SEE YA, LULUGEL!
SLINK
HEY!

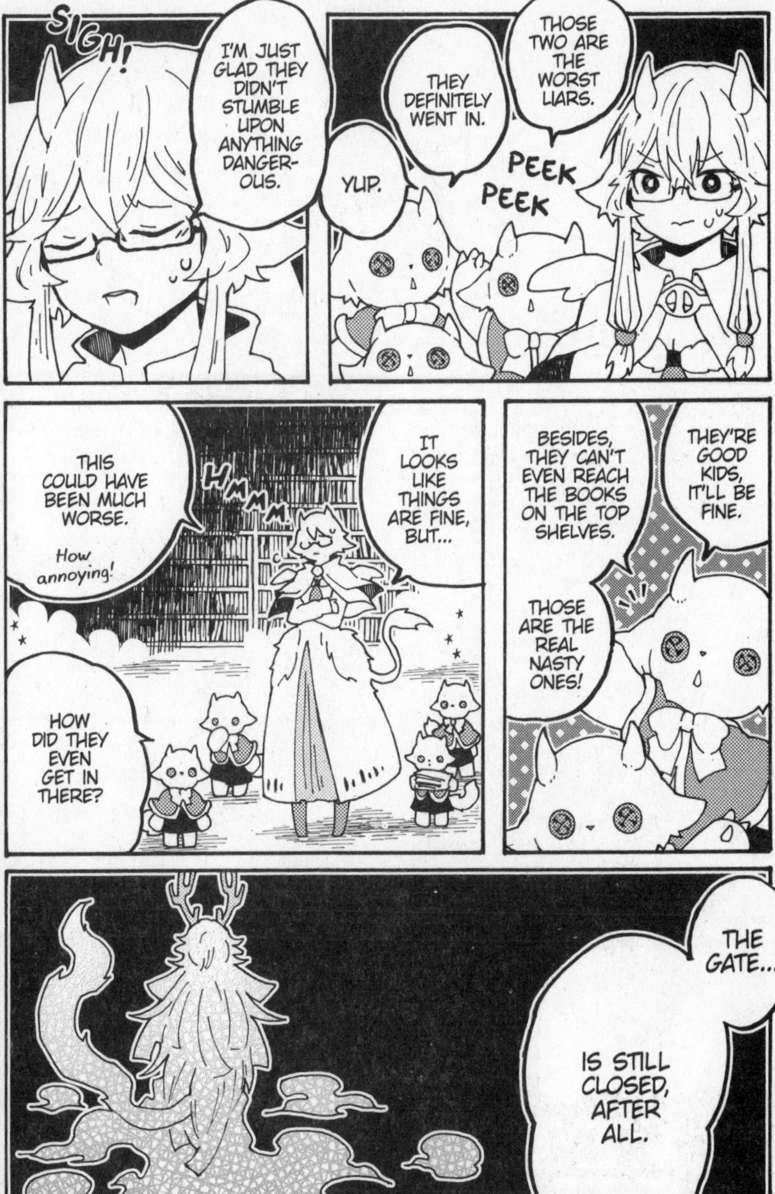
THOSE TWO ARE THE WORST LIARS.
PEEK PEEK
THEY DEFINITELY WENT IN.
YUP.
SIGH!
I'M JUST GLAD THEY DIDN'T STUMBLE UPON ANYTHING DANGER-OUS.
THEY'RE GOOD KIDS, IT'LL BE FINE.
BESIDES, THEY CAN'T EVEN REACH THE BOOKS ON THE TOP SHELVES.
THOSE ARE THE REAL NASTY ONES!
IT LOOKS LIKE THINGS ARE FINE, BUT...
HMMM
THIS COULD HAVE BEEN MUCH WORSE.
How annoying!
HOW DID THEY EVEN GET IN THERE?
THE GATE...
IS STILL CLOSED, AFTER ALL.

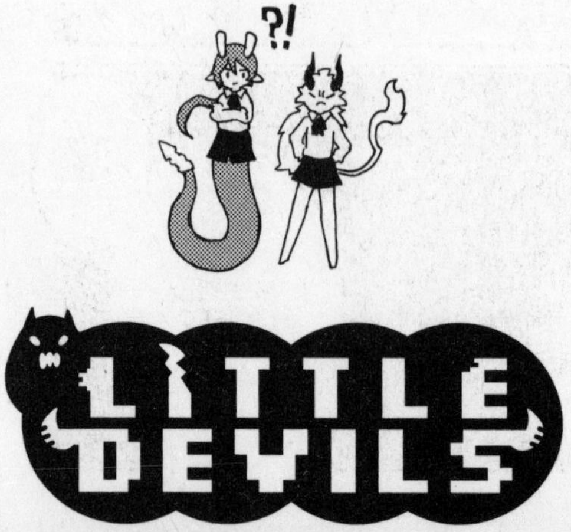
?!

LITTLE DEVILS

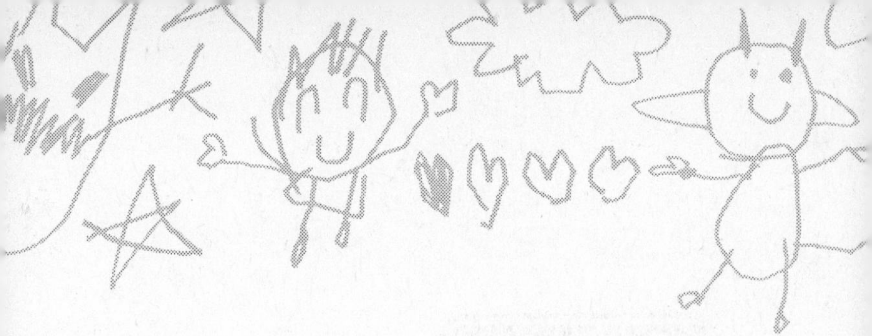
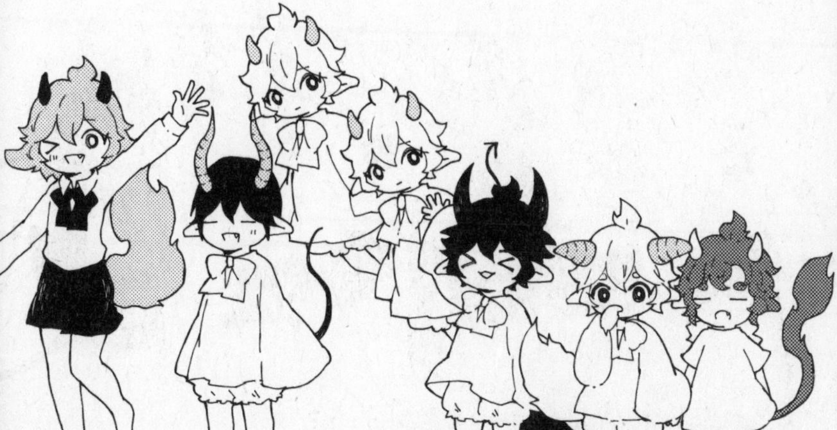

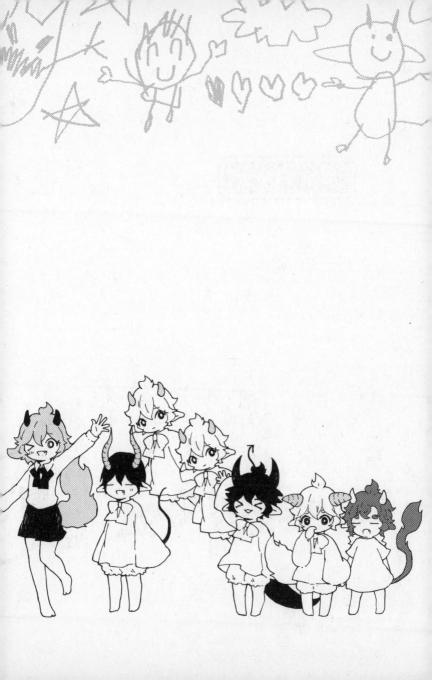

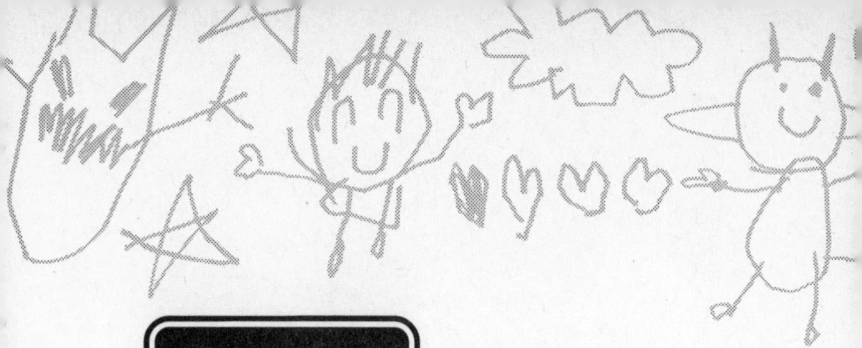

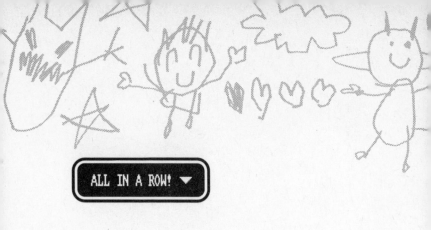

ALL IN A ROW! ▼

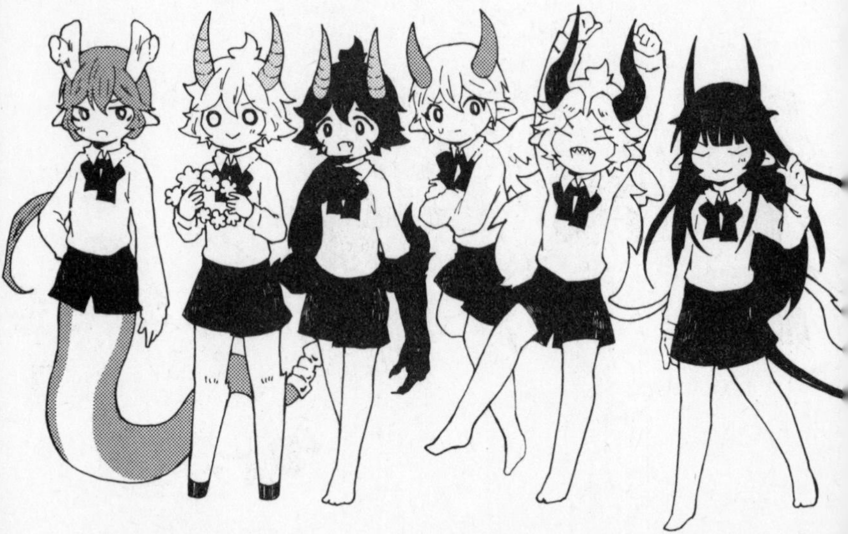

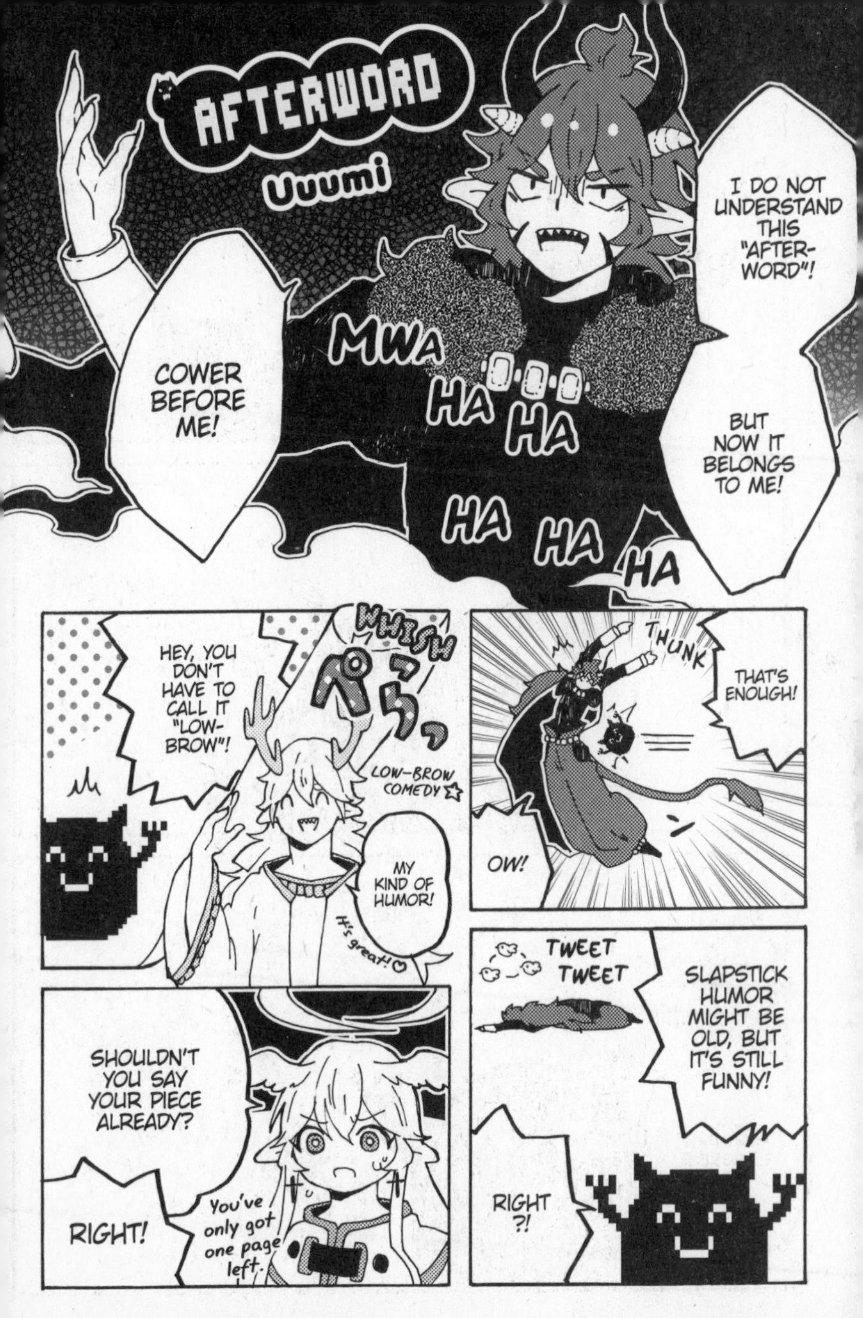
I DO NOT UNDERSTAND THIS "AFTER-WORD"!
AFTERWORD
Uuumi
BUT NOW IT BELONGS TO ME!
MWA HA HA HA HA HA
COWER BEFORE ME!
THUNK
THAT'S ENOUGH!
OW!
WHISH
ぺらっ
HEY, YOU DON'T HAVE TO CALL IT "LOW-BROW"!
LOW-BROW COMEDY☆
MY KIND OF HUMOR!
It's great!♡
TWEET TWEET
SLAPSTICK HUMOR MIGHT BE OLD, BUT IT'S STILL FUNNY!
RIGHT ?!
SHOULDN'T YOU SAY YOUR PIECE ALREADY?
You've only got one page left.
RIGHT!

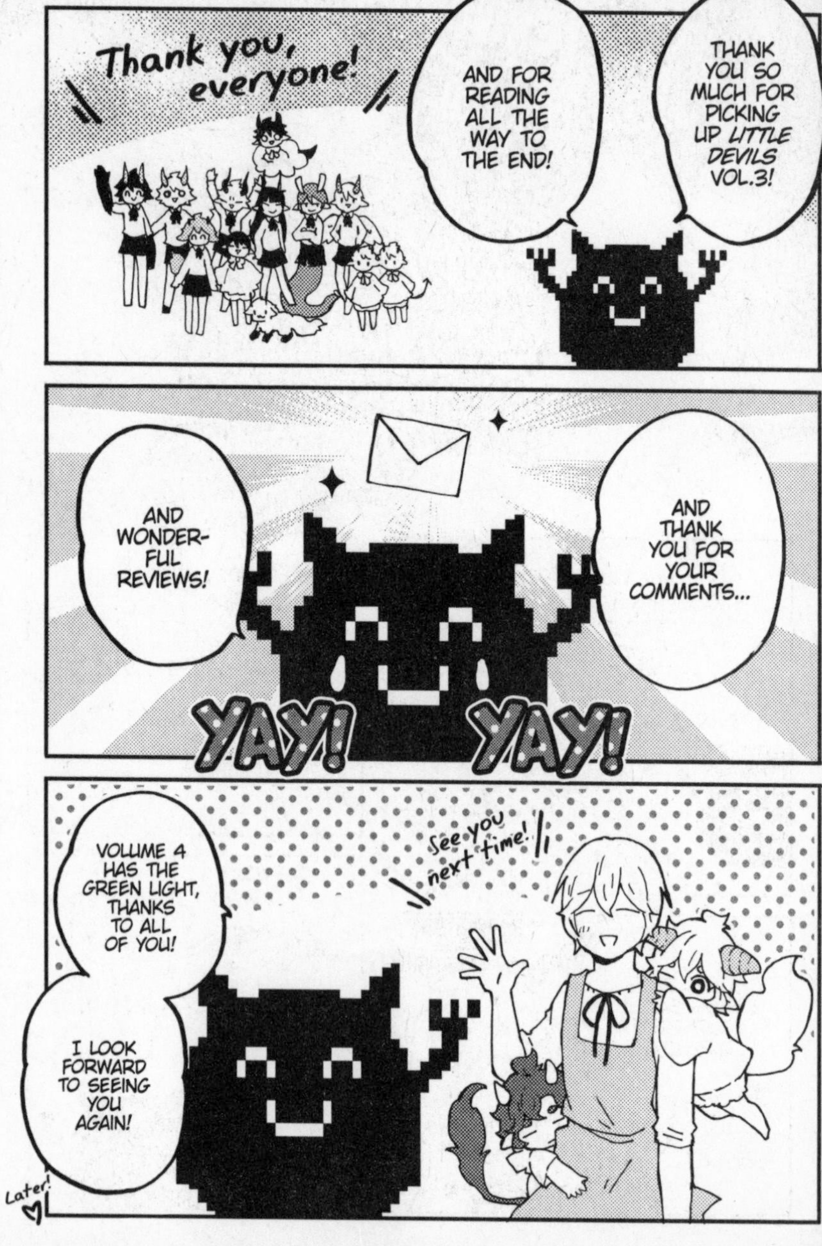
THANK YOU SO MUCH FOR PICKING UP *LITTLE DEVILS* VOL.3!
AND FOR READING ALL THE WAY TO THE END!
Thank you, everyone!
AND THANK YOU FOR YOUR COMMENTS...
AND WONDERFUL REVIEWS!
YAY! YAY!
See you next time!
VOLUME 4 HAS THE GREEN LIGHT, THANKS TO ALL OF YOU!
I LOOK FORWARD TO SEEING YOU AGAIN!
Later!

☆ Special Thanks ☆

I am so grateful to my editor Ikai-san for being there from the start of Little Devils! ♡

Thank you so much!

Uuumi